PORTAL
TO
GOOD
COOKING

PORTAL TO GOOD COOKING

Edited by JEANNE PEARSON

Illustrated by LOU PETERS

Published by
Lake Region • North Region • Lake County Region

WOMEN'S AMERICAN ORT

The editor and publishers wish to express their appreciation to
Miss Priscilla Carr, B.S., for her assistance in the preparation of
this cook book, and Miss Jerrine Leichhardt, B.S., who prepared
the menu chapter. They further wish to thank the members of ORT
who submitted the recipes which made this cook book possible.

INTRODUCTION TO ORT

Women's American Organization for Rehabilitation through Training is a program for the building and re-building of human lives and human dignity through vocational training.

This unique organization of more than 55,000 women has provided vocational training in 475 schools in 20 countries throughout the world. More than 1,000,000 men and women, boys and girls, have received their education at an ORT school learning to be carpenters, laboratory technicians, precision mechanics, refrigeration repairmen, dressmakers and designers, and a multitude of other skilled occupations.

Work to the average person is what creativeness is to the great artist—and work, for the average man, is not only a way of making a living, it is a way of life.

When ORT began over 80 years ago, it had a small program—but it had a history-making idea. The power of the idea and its high ideals took deep root and has spread throughout the world.

The relationship of ORT to those it helps is that of teacher, not of charity . . . teaching a boy or girl to be an independent, economically secure human being, proud of his ability to stand by himself.

ORT believes that self-help is the only lasting aid one can give one's fellow man.

CONTENTS

We believe that every woman in her innermost thoughts wants to be known as a good homemaker and a fabulous hostess. This book is designed to help her achieve this ambition without expending too much time or energy.

Good family dinners and elegant company meals are largely the result of planning and experience in knowing which foods complement each other.

This book will simplify your meal planning and open a whole new vista in how to have fun in the kitchen.

GENERAL HINTS

Read the recipe carefully. Don't start cooking until you read every word.

Set out ingredients and utensils needed. Select pans of proper size, measuring inside from rim to rim. Always have ingredients at room temperature.

Use standard measuring cups and spoons. All measurements are level unless otherwise stated in the recipe.

Sift all flour and confectioners' sugar before measuring unless otherwise directed. Pack brown sugar firmly. NOTE: To keep brown sugar moist and ready for use, store in tightly-covered container with a bread slice or piece of raw apple.

Preheat the oven for 10 to 20 minutes before baking unless recipe directs otherwise. Preheat broiler or follow manufacturer's directions. NOTE: Most broiled foods are cooked at 500°F. (or "Broil")—the distance from top of food to source of heat determines intensity of cooking.

Do not substitute key ingredients such as flour, sugar, liquid or leavening. Except for certain seasonings, best results will be obtained by using the ingredients in the amounts given in the recipes. Seasonings may often be altered to suit particular tastes.

Follow directions exactly as given—don't guess; i.e. stir means *stir*.

The number of servings is given wherever possible. NOTE: A recipe that "Serves 4" is not the same as a recipe that "Makes 4 servings." Servings are average portions unless otherwise stated.

Watch for these symbols: ♟ means the recipe is suitable for Passover.

 indicates a low-calorie recipe. Use your favorite calorie counter to estimate calories per serving.

COOKING TERMS

Baste: To spoon liquid or fat over food while it is cooking.

Beat: To make mixture smooth using electric mixer, egg beater or spoon.

Blend: To combine two or more ingredients well (see *Cream* and *Stir*).

Boil: To cook food in boiling liquid (212°F. at sea level). NOTE: Once liquid boils, reduce heat—slow boiling is as effective as rapid boiling.

Cool: To let stand at room temperature until no longer warm to touch.

Cream: To work soft shortening or shortening and sugar against sides of bowl until mixture is creamy. Your electric mixer does this job readily.

Dissolve: To mix liquid and dry ingredients together until in solution.

Fold: To mix in lighter ingredients such as beaten egg whites with wire whip, rubber spatula or spoon. Pass spatula down side of bowl; turn bowl one quarter, lifting spatula up through center of mixture. Turn spatula over and repeat.

Grease: To rub pan or paper lightly with butter, shortening or salad oil.

Marinate: To let food stand in liquid mixture, usually oil and vinegar, for specific length of time.

Mix: (See *Stir.*)

Pound Meat: To tenderize meat by pounding with meat hammer or edge of heavy saucer or plate.

Purée: To press food through a fine sieve or food mill.

Sauté: To cook food in a small amount of hot fat or salad oil in a skillet.

Scald: To heat liquid to just under the boiling point (usually milk—tiny bubbles will appear around edges).

Sift: To put dry ingredients through flour sifter or fine sieve.

Simmer: To cook just below the boiling point (about 185°F. at sea level).

Stir: To mix with spoon using a circular motion until all ingredients are well blended.

Whip: To beat rapidly with electric mixer or egg beater to increase volume of ingredients such as eggs or cream.

SPECIAL HINTS

To sour milk: Add 1½ to 2 tablespoons vinegar or lemon juice per cup of milk; let stand 5 minutes.

To make double-strength coffee: Make coffee by desired method, doubling amount of ground or instant coffee to usual amount of water.

To blanch almonds: Pour boiling water over almonds, simmer for 2 to 3 minutes, then drain and slip skins off with fingers. Dry on absorbent paper.

To soften brown sugar: Place in covered container in 300° oven for about 15 minutes. Use immediately.

To make quick broth or stock: Dissolve 1 bouillon cube in 1 cup hot water.

To thicken liquid mixtures: Add 1½ tablespoons flour mixed with 3 tablespoons water for each cupful of liquid. Cook, stirring, until thickened.

To cut dates and marshmallows: Dip scissors frequently into hot water.

To chop candied fruits or raisins: Coat fruits with 1 tablespoon of dry ingredients, or grease sharp knife.

To melt unsweetened chocolate: Place squares in small bowl, custard cup or saucepan; set in larger pan containing hot water. Heat, stirring occasionally, until melted.

To melt semi-sweet chocolate pieces: Place in top of double boiler over hot, *not boiling,* water.

To make clear ice cubes: Boil water; cool slightly, pour into ice-cube trays and freeze as usual. For party ice cubes, pour boiled water into trays until about half full; freeze. Place berry, cherry, lemon or orange slice, mint sprig, grape, etc., on each cube. Fill trays with water and freeze.

To flute edge of pastry: Press index finger on edge of pastry; pinch with index finger and thumb of other hand. Repeat around entire edge.

To flake fish: With a fork, separate cooked fish into thin, layer-like pieces.

Other hints are scattered throughout the book. Watch for them— they may save you time, give you ideas for brightening your meals, and may be interesting to try just for fun!

MEASUREMENTS AND EQUIVALENTS

3 teaspoons = 1 tablespoon

2 tablespoons = ⅛ cup

4 tablespoons = ¼ cup

5 tablespoons plus 1 teaspoon = ⅓ cup

16 tablespoons = 1 cup

2 cups = 1 pint

4 cups = 1 quart

4 ounces = ¼ pound = ½ cup

8 ounces = ½ pound = 1 cup

16 ounces = 1 pound = 2 cups

1 fluid ounce = 2 tablespoons

3 tablespoons = 1 jigger

Butter or margarine.................¼-pound bar = ½ cup, 1 pound = 2 cups

Cheese, Cheddar........................½ pound = 2 cups grated or shredded

Cheese, cottage...........................½ pound = 1 cup

Cheese, cream............................3-ounce package = 6 tablespoons

8-ounce package = 1 cup

Chocolate, unsweetened.............1 ounce = 1 square

Cocoa ....¼ cup plus 2 teaspoons shortening = 1 square chocolate

Cornstarch ....1 tablespoon = 2 tablespoons flour

Cream, heavy..............................½ pint = 2 cups whipped

Cream, sour..................................½ pint = 1 cup

Egg whites....................................8 to 11 whites = 1 cup

Egg yolks......................................12 to 14 yolks = 1 cup

Flour, all-purpose.......................1 pound = 4 cups sifted

Flour, cake ....1 pound = 4¾ to 5 cups sifted

Lemon juice..................................1 medium lemon = 3 tablespoons juice

Lemon rind..................................1 medium lemon = 1 tablespoon grated rind

Milk, evaporated ....15-oz. can = 1⅔ cups

Milk, condensed ....15½-oz. can = 1⅓ cups

Nuts, chopped.............................¼ pound = 1 cup

Orange juice................................1 medium orange = ⅓ cup juice

Orange rind.................................1 medium orange = 2 tablespoons grated rind

Sugar, brown..............................1 pound = 2¼ to 2½ cups firmly packed

Sugar, confectioners'.................1 pound = 4 cups sifted

Sugar, granulated ....1 pound = 2¼ cups

APPETIZERS AND COCKTAILS

The best part of
every meal is
its first part.

Irish Proverb

DIPS

GREEN CREAM DIP

1 medium clove garlic

½ teaspoon salt

1 cup mayonnaise or salad dressing

½ cup sour cream

¼ cup finely chopped parsley

3 tablespoons finely chopped chives

2 tablespoons finely chopped anchovies
(or 1½ tablespoons anchovy paste)

1 tablespoon lemon juice

1 tablespoon tarragon vinegar

Coarsely ground black pepper

Crush garlic clove with salt to make a paste. Blend with remaining ingredients. Cover tightly; chill in refrigerator until ready to serve. Makes about 1¾ cups.   *Jean Russell*

LOW-CAL CHEESE DIP

1 cup cottage cheese

3 tablespoons grated onion

3 tablespoons chopped pimiento

½ teaspoon salt

Dash cayenne pepper

Pinch salad herbs

Mix all ingredients together until very smooth. Chill for several hours before serving. Spread on crisp rye squares or round scalloped crackers.

BLUE CHEESE DIP

½ pound Blue cheese

1½ cups creamed cottage cheese

¼ cup sour cream

¼ cup chopped chives

Salt and pepper

Crumble Blue cheese into small pieces. Gently mix with remaining ingredients. Chill in refrigerator until ready to serve. Place in bowl surrounded by assorted crackers and bread sticks. Serves 8 to 10.

Sandy Isenstein

ANCHOVY CHEESE DIP

1 cup cottage cheese

3 anchovies

3 tablespoons chopped parsley

1 tablespoon chopped chives

1 teaspoon poppy seeds

Salt

Freshly ground black pepper

Combine all ingredients in blender container. Blend for several seconds. Turn into serving dish; serve with low-calorie crackers or melba toast.

Marian D. Horwitz

AVOCADO DIP

1 small onion, finely chopped

1 tomato, peeled and finely chopped

2 avocados, pared and pitted

2 teaspoons vinegar

2 teaspoons chili powder

1 teaspoon salt

Mix together onion and tomato. Mash avocados with wooden spoon. Add to tomato mixture. Add vinegar, chili powder and salt. Mix lightly until well blended. Turn into bowl; serve as dip with crackers, potato chips or corn chips. Or serve in lettuce cups as salad. Serves 6.   *Sandra Kaufman*

SURPRISE DIP

2 cups cottage cheese

½ cup soft butter

1 teaspoon cardamom seeds, crushed

Salt and pepper

Combine all ingredients in blender container. Blend until well mixed. Chill in refrigerator for at least 1 hour before serving.   *Joan Florence*

BEST-EVER ROQUEFORT DIP

2 cups thick sour cream

⅛ teaspoon garlic salt

6 drops Worcestershire sauce

1 3-oz. package Roquefort cheese

Blend sour cream thoroughly with garlic salt and Worcestershire. Rub Roquefort against side of bowl to break up, but do not mash. Mix into sour cream with fork. Serve as dip with potato chips, carrot or celery sticks, etc., or as salad dressing.   *Mrs. Maurice Klotz*

CRAB MEAT DIP

white

1 7-oz. can crab meat, shredded or minced

2 hard-cooked eggs, cut into small pieces

¼ cup minced green onions

1 tablespoon horse-radish

½ teaspoon salt

1 cup sour cream

1 3-oz. package soft cream cheese

Blend all ingredients together in order listed. Serve as dip with chips, round scalloped crackers or melba toast.   *Shirley Goldberg*

LOBSTER DIP

1 pound cooked or canned lobster

Juice of 1 lemon

2 3-oz. packages soft cream cheese

¼ cup mayonnaise

¼ cup catchup

1 teaspoon Worcestershire sauce

Grated onion

Sprinkle lobster with lemon juice; break up large pieces with fork. Add cream cheese, mayonnaise, catchup, Worcestershire and grated onion to taste. Mix together until smooth. Serve as dip with crackers or chips.
                                 Perle Jacobs

ANCHOVY DIP

½ tube anchovy paste

2 cups sour cream or soured half-and-half

Combine anchovy paste and sour cream into a smooth paste. Pour into a bowl and serve with celery and carrot sticks or crackers.   *Charlotte Scotch*

DIPS 15

CLAM DIP

1 7-oz. can minced clams

1 clove garlic

2 3-oz. packages soft cream cheese

1 teaspoon lemon juice

1 teaspoon Worcestershire sauce

½ teaspoon salt

Dash pepper

Drain clams, reserving liquid. Rub mixing bowl with garlic. Blend together cream cheese, lemon juice, Worcestershire sauce, salt, pepper, clams and 1 or 2 tablespoons reserved clam liquid. Serve with crackers or potato chips. Serves 12.   *Marge Sandberg*

SHRIMP DIP

1 pound cleaned cooked shrimp

¾ cup mayonnaise

1 tablespoon minced onion

1 teaspoon minced celery

1 teaspoon minced green pepper

½ teaspoon grated lemon rind

2 teaspoons lemon juice

4 to 5 drops Tabasco sauce

¼ teaspoon salt

Dash pepper

Cut shrimp into very fine pieces. Mix together with remaining ingredients. Serve as dip with chips or crackers, or spread on cocktail rye rounds.

Delphine Daniels

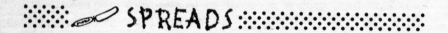 SPREADS

APPETIZER CHEESE CARROTS

1 3-oz. package soft cream cheese

⅓ cup grated carrot

1 tablespoon minced chives or green onion

¼ teaspoon Worcestershire sauce

¼ teaspoon salt

Dash pepper

Parsley

Mix together cream cheese, carrot, chives, Worcestershire sauce, salt and pepper. Shape to resemble small carrots. Place small sprig of parsley in larger end of each. Chill in refrigerator for several hours. Serve as spread with crackers or cocktail rounds. Makes about 1 dozen.   *Maryon Goldware*

PARTY CHEESE BALL

1 8-oz. package soft cream cheese

1½ oz. Roquefort or Blue cheese

1 5-oz. jar smoked or sharp process cheese spread

1 teaspoon Worcestershire sauce

1 tablespoon minced onion

1 tablespoon chopped stuffed green olives

2 tablespoons minced parsley

½ cup chopped nuts

Blend cheeses together; add Worcestershire sauce, onion and olives. Mix thoroughly; cover and chill in refrigerator overnight. Shape into a ball; roll in parsley and nuts. Serve on tray with crackers or cocktail rounds.

Shirley Sokolsky

SMOKY CHEESE BALL

½ pound Cheddar cheese, grated

5 tablespoons cream

¼ cup salad dressing

1 tablespoon vinegar

1 teaspoon Worcestershire sauce

¼ teaspoon liquid smoke

Few drops Tabasco sauce

¾ teaspoon salt

½ teaspoon dry mustard

½ teaspoon garlic powder

½ cup chopped pecans

¼ cup chopped parsley

Combine cheese, cream, salad dressing, vinegar, Worcestershire, liquid smoke, Tabasco, salt, mustard and garlic powder. Mix thoroughly and chill in refrigerator. Shape into a ball; roll in pecans; garnish with parsley. Place on serving tray with crackers or cocktail rounds.   *Sylvia J. Rosenstein*

EVER-READY CHEESE LOG

½ pound sharp process Cheddar cheese, grated

½ cup fine cracker crumbs

¼ cup mayonnaise

1 hard-cooked egg, chopped

3 tablespoons minced green pepper

2 tablespoons chopped pickles

1 to 2 tablespoons minced onion

1 tablespoon chopped pimiento

3 stuffed green olives, chopped

½ teaspoon salt

Combine all ingredients until well blended. Shape into long roll; wrap in waxed paper. Chill in refrigerator until firm. Slice, serve with crackers and garnish with stuffed green olives.   *Marian Peterman*

APPETIZER EGG MOLD

20 hard-cooked eggs, cooled

½ green pepper, grated

1 small onion, grated

½ 2-oz. jar pimiento

3 tablespoons mayonnaise

2 to 3 tablespoons chili sauce

Salt and pepper

Grind eggs; or force through sieve. Add green pepper, onion and finely chopped pimiento. Mix together mayonnaise, chili sauce, salt and pepper. Add to egg mixture; blend well. Pack mixture into ring mold and chill in refrigerator for several hours. Turn out onto serving platter. Surround with olives, radishes or other vegetable garnish. Serve as spread with crackers or melba toast.   *Sydelle Prebish*

Be different! Serve spreads in a hollowed-out pineapple, brandy snifter, green-pepper halves or lobster shells.

CHOPPED HERRING

1 12-oz. jar herring fillets in wine sauce

2 hard-cooked eggs

1 large apple, pared and cored

2 slices day-old bread

1 teaspoon lemon juice

Sugar

Drain herring, reserving wine sauce. Grind together herring, eggs, apple and bread. Place in bowl; add lemon juice and enough reserved wine sauce to make a smooth paste. Add sugar to taste. Serve on crackers or as dip.

Lillian Minkus

CHOPPED EGGPLANT

1 medium eggplant

1 small onion, finely chopped

2 slices white bread

2 tablespoons hot water

1 teaspoon vinegar

Salad oil

Salt

Cook eggplant in boiling water to cover for about 20 minutes. Cut off stem end; pare eggplant and place in chopping bowl. Chop until fine. Chop in

onion. Soak bread slices in hot water and vinegar; drain. Chop into eggplant mixture. Add salad oil, chopping constantly, until mixture is of spreading consistency. Season with salt. Serve as spread with crackers or melba rounds.
Florence Mash

CHOPPED LIVER

2 tablespoons chicken fat	3 large Bermuda onions, finely chopped
1 pound beef liver, cut into pieces	Salt and pepper
1 pound chicken livers	8 hard-cooked eggs

Melt chicken fat in heavy skillet. Sauté livers and onions until done. Season with salt and pepper. Cool; grind or force through sieve with some of fat from pan. Grind eggs. Add more seasoning if necessary. Blend eggs and liver mixture until smooth and of spreading consistency. Spread on crackers or cocktail rye rounds.
Zelda Sklar

CAVIAR DELIGHT

2 8-oz. packages soft cream cheese	Grated onion
2 tablespoons sour cream	1 2-oz. jar black caviar

Blend cheese with sour cream and onion. Shape into oval mound. Spread with caviar. Place sprigs of parsley around mound. Decorate with stuffed green olives, if desired.
Eloise Zweig

TUNA-CHEESE ROLL

1 8-oz. package soft cream cheese	1 7-oz. can tuna, drained and flaked
¼ cup finely chopped parsley	¼ teaspoon Tabasco sauce
1 small onion, minced	Salt and pepper
¼ cup chopped Brazil nuts	

Combine cream cheese, 2 tablespoons parsley, onion, nuts, tuna, Tabasco sauce, salt and pepper. Shape into a roll about 1½ inches in diameter. Sprinkle remaining parsley on sheet of waxed paper; roll cheese roll in parsley; wrap in waxed paper and chill in refrigerator until ready to serve. Place on long tray and serve with assorted crackers and cocktail rounds. Serves 6 to 10.
Cele Malvin

GEFILTE FISH

2 pounds whitefish (or pike, buffalo, sucker or combination)

2 pounds trout

1 large onion

1 large carrot

4 egg yolks, beaten

4 egg whites

4 teaspoons salt

¼ teaspoon saffron

Dash pepper

Celery leaves

2 tablespoons chopped parsley

12 peppercorns

1 carrot, sliced

Clean fish, reserving skin and bones. Grind together fish, onion and carrot. Add egg yolks and mix well. Beat egg whites with salt, saffron and pepper until stiff; fold into fish mixture. Shape into balls about 1 inch in diameter. Cover bottom of Dutch oven with fish skin and bones, celery leaves and parsley; add peppercorns. Place fish balls in Dutch oven; cover with boiling salted water; add sliced carrot. Simmer, covered, for about 2 hours. Cool in cooking water. Drain fish balls and chill in refrigerator until ready to serve. Makes 3½ to 4 dozen. *Judy Goldberg*

EGG SALAD CUPS

12 thin slices bread

Soft butter

5 hard-cooked eggs, grated

¼ cup minced green pepper

1 teaspoon grated onion

¼ cup mayonnaise

1 tablespoon vinegar

1 tablespoon Worcestershire sauce

Drop Tabasco sauce

½ teaspoon salt

½ teaspoon dry mustard

Dash cayenne pepper

Cut bread slices into 2-inch rounds. Spread both sides lightly with butter. Press into small muffin cups. Bake at 375° until edges are lightly browned, (about 8 to 10 minutes). Meanwhile, mix together remaining ingredients. Fill toasted bread cups. Garnish with bits of parsley, pimiento or sliced stuffed olives. Or serve mixture as spread with melba toast or crackers. Makes 1 dozen. *Ruth Rose*

DEVILED EGGS

Hard-cooked eggs

Buttermilk, skim milk or lemon juice

Vinegar

Salt and white or cayenne pepper

Shell eggs while still slightly warm. Cut into halves, lengthwise; remove yolks. Mash yolks with buttermilk; season with vinegar, salt and pepper. Mix well. Fill egg whites with yolk mixture. Garnish with dash of paprika. Chill in refrigerator.

ANCHOVY EGGS: Add anchovy paste and a bit of fresh dill with vinegar. Omit salt. Top with chopped radish.

CAPER EGGS: Substitute brine from capers for vinegar. Add a little dry mustard and top with a few capers.

CAVIAR EGGS: Omit salt. Press finely chopped onions or chives into yolks. Top with ¼ teaspoon caviar. *Dee Stein*

SHRIMP-CHEESE PUFFS

Pastry for Eclairs, page 264, or ½ package cream puff mix (follow directions on package)

½ cup canned shrimp, cut into small pieces

¼ cup grated sharp Cheddar cheese

3 tablespoons mayonnaise

1 tablespoon lemon juice

1 tablespoon chopped pimiento

Salt and pepper

Drop pastry by teaspoonfuls onto baking sheet. Bake as directed. Cool; cut off tops. Mix together shrimp, cheese, mayonnaise, lemon juice, pimiento, salt and pepper. Fill miniature cream puffs with shrimp mixture. Replace tops. Makes 3 to 3½ dozen. *Cele Malvin*

SHRIMP HORS D'OEUVRES

1 pound fresh shrimp

1 bay leaf

1 teaspoon salt

Dash cayenne pepper

½ cup low-calorie mayonnaise

1 tablespoon tomato paste

1½ teaspoons horse-radish

1 teaspoon Worcestershire sauce

Place shrimp in cold water to cover; add bay leaf, salt and pepper. Bring to boiling; cook until shrimp turn bright pink. Cool in cooking water. Shell; de-vein and insert wooden picks. Mix together mayonnaise, tomato paste, horse-radish and Worcestershire. Serve as dip for shrimp.

CHEESE-SARDINE BALLS

1 can sardines	1 teaspoon grated onion
2 3-oz. packages soft cream cheese	¼ teaspoon salt
1½ teaspoons prepared mustard	Dash cayenne pepper
1 teaspoon lemon juice	¾ cup finely chopped nuts

Drain sardines and mash. Add cheese and mix until smooth. Add mustard, lemon juice, onion, salt and pepper. Mix well. Chill in refrigerator overnight. Shape into small balls; roll in chopped nuts. Chill until ready to serve. Have wooden picks handy. Makes about 5 dozen.   *Poppy Brooks*

TUNA APPETIZER BALLS

2 7-oz. cans tuna	4 eggs, beaten
2 small onions, grated	8 cups water
2 carrots, grated	2 onions, sliced
1¼ cups bread crumbs	2 carrots
1½ teaspoons salt	1 tablespoon sugar
1 teaspoon sugar	1 teaspoon salt
½ teaspoon paprika	Dash pepper and paprika

Flake tuna; combine with grated onions, grated carrots, crumbs, 1½ teaspoons salt, 1 teaspoon sugar and ½ teaspoon paprika. Add eggs and mix thoroughly. Shape into small balls. Combine in large kettle water, sliced onions, carrots, 1 tablespoon sugar, 1 teaspoon salt, pepper and dash paprika. Drop in tuna balls and bring water to boiling. Cook, covered, over medium heat for 1 hour; uncover and cook for 30 minutes longer. Cool; chill in refrigerator for 1 hour before serving. Have wooden picks handy. Makes 4 dozen.
Mrs. Saul Lubar

STUFFED RIPE OLIVES

1 3-oz. package soft cream cheese	2 9-oz. cans pitted ripe olives
1 3-oz. package Roquefort cheese	

Mix together cream cheese and Roquefort until completely blended and smooth. Stuff olives carefully. (If olives become smeared, wipe with dampened absorbent paper.) Decorate with tinted cream cheese rosebuds made with a pastry tube. Chill until ready to serve.   *Mignon Kaplan*

HOT APPETIZERS

PETITE CABBAGE ROLLS

1 medium head cabbage	Salt and pepper
Boiling water	SYRUP:
FILLING:	½ cup light corn syrup
1½ pounds ground beef	1 7-oz. bottle catchup
1 egg	1 teaspoon lemon juice
¼ cup bread crumbs	

Separate cabbage leaves; place in boiling water to soften. Drain on absorbent paper. Combine beef, egg, crumbs, salt and pepper. Shape into small meat balls. Using smaller cabbage leaves, place meat ball in center of each leaf and roll up. Combine corn syrup and catchup; mix until smooth. Pack cabbage rolls tightly into heavy saucepan. Pour syrup mixture over top; cook, covered, over low heat for 30 minutes. Add lemon juice and continue to cook for 1 hour longer, or until cabbage is glazed. Add water as necessary. Serve in chafing dish. Makes 15 to 25 rolls. *Sondra Homer*

CREAM CHEESE PUFFS

1 3-oz. package soft cream cheese	Paprika
Cream or half-and-half	Chopped green onions
1 egg yolk, beaten	Bread rounds
Salt and pepper	

Combine cream cheese with enough cream to soften. Mix in egg yolk, salt, pepper and paprika; add chopped green onions to taste. Place bread rounds on ungreased baking sheets and place under broiler until lightly browned on one side. Spread cream cheese mixture on untoasted sides. Broil 5 to 8 minutes, or until cheese puffs and is golden brown. Serve hot. Makes 50 to 60 hors d'oeuvres. *Helen Comm*

MUSHROOM CHEESE PUFFS

½ pound fresh mushrooms

2 3-oz. packages soft cream cheese

1 egg yolk, beaten

⅛ teaspoon minced onion

Bread rounds

Sauté mushroom caps in small amount of butter. Blend cream cheese, egg yolk and onion together. Toast bread rounds (as many as there are mushroom caps) under broiler on one side. Place dab of cheese mixture on untoasted sides. Top with mushroom caps, round-side down. Cover with cheese mixture. Broil until puffy and slightly brown.   *Ruth Rose*

OATMEAL PUFFS

1 cup hot water

½ cup shortening

½ teaspoon salt

½ cup quick-cooking rolled oats

½ cup sifted flour

3 eggs

1 5-oz. jar soft cheese spread

Combine water, shortening and salt in heavy saucepan; heat to boiling. Quickly stir in rolled oats and flour. Stir vigorously over low heat for 1½ to 2 minutes, or until mixture clings together in a ball. Turn into bowl and add eggs, one at a time, beating vigorously after each. Beat for 1 minute longer. Drop by teaspoonfuls onto ungreased baking sheet about 1 inch apart. Bake at 450° for 5 minutes. Reduce oven temperature to 350° and bake for 10 minutes longer, or until brown. Cut off tops; fill with cheese spread. Heat at 350° for about 10 minutes, or until cheese is melted. Garnish with bits of pimiento. Serve hot. Makes 1½ to 2 dozen.
Lee Bateman

TANGY CHEESE BAKES

2 cups grated sharp Cheddar cheese

1 egg, beaten

1 teaspoon Worcestershire sauce

10 drops Tabasco sauce

¼ teaspoon salt

2 small loaves unsliced bread

Soft butter

Mix cheese with egg, Worcestershire sauce, Tabasco sauce and salt. Trim crusts from bread; cut into 1-inch cubes. Spread butter on each; top with spoonful of cheese mixture. Bake at 450° until brown, or place under broiler. Serve immediately. Makes about 6 dozen.   *Joyce Hazelkorn*

POPPY SEED CHEESE STRIPS

6 slices day-old bread

2 tablespoons poppy seeds

6 tablespoons sharp cheese spread

Trim crusts from bread slices. Spread slices with cheese; sprinkle with poppy seeds. Cut each slice into 3 or 4 strips. Place on greased baking sheet, 1 inch apart. Bake at 450° for about 3 minutes, or until cheese is bubbly and bread toasts. Makes 18 to 24 strips.   *Jean Russell*

LIVER SAUSAGE CANAPÉS

Bread rounds

Soft butter

Prepared mustard

Liver sausage

Grated onion

Worcestershire sauce

Sliced stuffed green olives

Toast bread rounds on one side under broiler. Spread butter on untoasted sides, then spread with mustard. Mash liver sausage with grated onion to taste; add a few drops Worcestershire sauce; mix well. Heap generously on toasted rounds. Broil at 400° until liver is hot and puffy. Garnish with olive slices. Serve hot.   *Edith Lirtzman*

CHAFING DISH MEAT BALLS

1 pound ground beef

½ cup fresh bread crumbs

1 package onion soup mix

¼ cup minced celery

½ teaspoon salt

1 tablespoon minced parsley

2 eggs, slightly beaten

SAUCE:

½ cup tarragon vinegar

½ cup water

½ cup catchup or chili sauce

1 tablespoon granulated sugar

⅓ cup raisins (optional)

Mix together beef, crumbs, ½ package soup mix, celery, salt, parsley and eggs. Shape into balls about 1 inch in diameter or smaller. Mix together in heavy saucepan vinegar, water, catchup, remaining soup mix, sugar and raisins. Stir to mix; bring to boiling over medium heat. Drop meat balls into sauce; cook over low heat for 1 hour. Serve in chafing dish. Makes 60 to 65.   *Maryon Goldware*

SARDINE CANAPÉS

1 15-oz. can sardines with tomato sauce

2 tablespoons mayonnaise

2 tablespoons chili sauce

½ teaspoon Worcestershire sauce

Catchup

Bone sardines and mash thoroughly. Combine with mayonnaise, chili sauce and Worcestershire sauce. Spread on cocktail rye bread. Top each with dab of catchup. Broil at 350° for about 5 minutes. Makes 2 dozen.

Mrs. Jack Frost

SARDINE ROLLS

2 cans sardines, drained

4 teaspoons lemon juice

¾ teaspoon horse-radish

8 thin bread slices

Melted butter or margarine

Mash sardines; mix well with lemon juice and horse-radish. Trim crusts from bread slices. Spread sardine mixture on slices. Roll as for jelly roll. Brush with melted butter. Place under broiler until brown. Serves 8.

Sara Slutsky

COCKTAIL FRANK DIP

½ cup firmly packed brown sugar

½ cup soy sauce

½ cup brandy

Cocktail franks

Simmer all ingredients until well blended and piping hot. Add cocktail frankfurters; pour into a chafing dish. Have wooden picks handy.

Glady Carman

CHICKEN LIVER HORS D'OEUVRES

1 tablespoon minced onion

1 tablespoon butter

½ cup chicken livers

¼ cup chopped mushrooms

⅛ teaspoon salt

1 egg, slightly beaten

Grated Parmesan cheese

Sauté onion in butter for several minutes. Add livers; cook over low heat for 10 minutes, turning livers often. Add mushrooms and salt; cook for several minutes longer. Stir in beaten egg and cook only until mixture begins to thicken. Spread on toasted bread rounds; sprinkle with grated cheese. Place under broiler until bubbly. Makes 2 dozen.

STUFFED MUSHROOMS

1 pound fresh mushrooms	2 tablespoons grated onion
1 teaspoon salt	1 tablespoon grated Parmesan cheese
½ teaspoon paprika	1 pimiento, chopped
⅛ teaspoon pepper	½ teaspoon salad oil

Wash and drain mushrooms. Remove stems; chop fine, reserving whole caps. Add salt, paprika, pepper, onion, cheese and pimiento to chopped mushrooms. Mix well; stuff mushroom caps. Brush baking sheet with oil; place mushrooms on sheet. Bake at 375° for 10 minutes. Serves 4.

HOT SALMON BALLS

1 8-oz. can salmon	1 egg, slightly beaten
1 cup mashed potatoes	¼ teaspoon salt
1 tablespoon grated onion	⅓ cup bread crumbs
¼ cup minced celery	Salad oil

Flake and bone salmon. Drain well. Combine with potatoes, onion, celery, egg and salt. Shape teaspoonfuls of mixture into balls. Roll balls in bread crumbs until coated. Sauté in hot oil until golden brown on all sides. Or place in greased pan and bake at 375° for 15 minutes. Makes 2½ dozen.

Gladys Sabath

CHEESE APPETIZER BALLS

½ cup soft butter	¼ teaspoon dry mustard
2 cups shredded sharp Cheddar cheese	¼ teaspoon paprika
1 cup sifted flour	⅛ teaspoon salt

Cream butter; blend in cheese. Add flour, mustard, paprika and salt. Mix well. Shape into balls about ¾ inch in diameter. (If dough is too sticky to handle, chill in refrigerator for several hours.) Place balls on greased baking sheet, about 2 inches apart. Bake at 350° for 10 minutes. Remove from sheet while still warm. Makes 3 dozen.

Mrs. Richard Blair

SHRIMP VESUVIO

2 pounds cooked jumbo shrimp

Juice of 2 lemons

1 clove garlic

¼ cup butter

½ cup Thousand Island dressing

2 tablespoons bread crumbs

Paprika

Marinate shrimp in lemon juice for at least 1 hour. Drain, reserving juice; sauté shrimp with garlic in hot butter until lightly browned. Remove from pan and coat each shrimp with dressing. Arrange in flat bake-and-serve dish. Brown bread crumbs in butter in which shrimp was sautéed. Sprinkle over shrimp. Pour in reserved lemon juice. Sprinkle lightly with paprika. Place under broiler until brown. Serve hot on wooden picks. Serves 12.

Eleanor Gabel

HOT LOBSTER CANAPÉS

1 6½-oz. can lobster

2 tablespoons minced green pepper

1 tablespoon minced onion

2 tablespoons butter

¼ cup cream

2 eggs yolks, slightly beaten

½ teaspoon salt

½ teaspoon paprika

4 bread slices

Sauté lobster, green pepper and onion in butter for 5 minutes. Mix cream, egg yolks, salt and paprika. Stir into lobster mixture and cook over low heat for 3 minutes. Trim crusts from bread slices; cut each slice into 4 squares. Toast on one side under broiler. Pile lobster mixture on untoasted sides; broil until bubbly. Serve hot. Makes 16 canapés. *Alice B. Weitzenfeld*

FRUIT COCKTAILS

BAKED OR BROILED ORANGE

1 very large orange

2 large berries or pitted cherries

2 teaspoons unsweetened Bing or sour red cherry juice

¼ teaspoon ground ginger

Halve the orange. Separate sections with sharp knife. Press indention in center of each half. Place 1 berry in each indention. Combine juice with ginger. Sprinkle over orange halves. Bake at 450° for 20 minutes, or broil for 10 minutes, or until golden brown. Serves 2.

FRUIT SOUP

1 pound mixed fresh fruit (sour cherries, peaches, apricots and pears)	1 quart water
	Juice of 2 lemons
4 or 5 cloves	Pinch salt

Wash fruit. Pit cherries, peaches and apricots. Pare and core pears. Cut up apricots and peaches. Stick cloves into pears. Bring water to boiling in saucepan; add fruit, lemon juice and salt. Cook 5 to 7 minutes. Cool and chill in refrigerator. Serve cold, garnished with sprig of fresh mint, or spoon 1 tablespoon buttermilk over each serving. Serves 4.

HONEYDEW MELON COCKTAIL

½ cup granulated sugar	2 tablespoons orange juice
⅓ cup boiling water	2 tablespoons lime juice
2 tablespoons lemon juice	1 honeydew melon, chilled

Combine sugar and water and boil gently for several minutes. Cool. Add lemon, orange and lime juices. Chill in refrigerator. Cut balls from melon, using melon-ball cutter or measuring spoon (half teaspoon). Chill. When ready to serve, place melon balls in chilled cocktail glasses. Pour chilled syrup over balls. Garnish with sprigs of fresh mint, if desired. Serves 8.

Cele Malvin

FROSTY FRUIT COCKTAIL

6 large oranges, sectioned	½ cup dry white wine
1 large grapefruit, sectioned	Fresh or thawed frozen strawberries
¼ cup granulated sugar	

Set temperature control of refrigerator at coldest point. Drain juice from orange and grapefruit sections; add sugar and wine. Let stand for 1 hour. About 45 minutes before serving, turn into ice-cube tray; place in lower section of freezing compartment. Chill until ½ inch of crystals form along sides of tray. Arrange in frosted sherbet glasses; garnish with strawberries. Makes 8 servings.

Alma E. Perlish

HOT SHRIMP COCKTAIL

2 pounds cleaned shrimp

Garlic powder

Salt

½ cup finely chopped green pepper

½ cup finely chopped celery

½ cup finely chopped onion

3 or 4 sweet pickles, chopped

6 stuffed green olives, thinly sliced

2 tablespoons butter

1 can cream of tomato soup

½ cup consommé

2 tablespoons butter

Cook shrimp with garlic powder and salt to taste in boiling water. Cool in cooking water and drain. Sauté green pepper, celery, onion, pickles and olives in 2 tablespoons hot butter in large skillet. Combine tomato soup and consommé in saucepan; heat thoroughly. Sauté cooked shrimp in 2 tablespoons hot butter over high heat for 2 minutes. Add sauce and shrimp to mixture in skillet. Heat thoroughly. Serve hot in cocktail glasses. Makes 8 to 10 servings.   *Mrs. Robert Kaufman*

SHRIMP ARNAUD

3 tablespoons olive oil

1 tablespoon tarragon or basil vinegar

1 tablespoon prepared hot mustard

¾ teaspoon salt

½ teaspoon pepper

8 green onions, chopped

1 tablespoon prepared hot mustard

1 teaspoon horse-radish

1 teaspoon monosodium glutamate

¼ teaspoon garlic salt

¼ teaspoon paprika

2 pounds cleaned cooked shrimp

Combine oil, vinegar, 1 tablespoon mustard, salt and pepper. Set aside. Blend together onions, 1 tablespoon mustard, horse-radish, monosodium glutamate, garlic salt and paprika. Mix well with vinegar mixture. Pour over shrimp. Chill in refrigerator for several hours. Serve in cocktail glasses or on shells. Serves 8 to 10.   *Marian D. Horwitz*

SHRIMP CONTINENTAL

1 clove garlic

Salt and pepper

Sugar

1 cup salad oil

¼ cup vinegar

3 tablespoons mayonnaise

Cooked shrimp

Mash garlic with salt, pepper and sugar to taste. Add oil, vinegar and mayonnaise; mix well. Pour over cooked shrimp; marinate in refrigerator for 4 or 5 hours. Place shrimp on lettuce in cocktail glasses; pour remaining marinade over top. *Ruth Ellyne*

CRAB MEAT APPETIZER

1 cup bread crumbs

Butter

2 6-oz. packages thawed frozen crab meat

2 hard-cooked eggs, chopped

1 cup mayonnaise

1 teaspoon chopped onion

1 teaspoon Worcestershire sauce

1 teaspoon minced parsley

1 teaspoon prepared mustard

1 teaspoon lemon juice

½ teaspoon salt

¼ cup sherry

Brown bread crumbs in hot butter. Set aside. Flake crab meat; add remaining ingredients in order listed. Mix gently. Turn into individual shells or ramekins; top with buttered bread crumbs. Bake at 400° for 15 to 20 minutes. May also be baked in large casserole for 25 to 30 minutes. Makes 8 servings. *Helen Reiff*

SWEET HERRING

6 herring (milkers)

1 quart vinegar

2 tablespoons granulated sugar

1 tablespoon white raisins

1 tablespoon mixed pickling spices

6 large onions, thinly sliced

Soak herring overnight, changing water twice. Clean herring; cut into 6 slices leaving bones in. Combine vinegar, sugar, raisins, and spices in saucepan; add onion slices and cook for 20 minutes. Add herring and cook for 1 minute longer. Cool; pour into jar with tight-fitting cover. Place in refrigerator and let stand at least 1 week. Serve as cocktail. *Evelyn Yavitz*

SOUPS AND SOUP GARNISHES

Beautiful soup! Who cares for fish
Game, or any other dish?

Lewis Carroll

CLEAR SOUPS

POT-AU-FEU (Pot-on-the-Fire)

1 pound lean beef, cut into 1-inch pieces

2 cups cold water

½ teaspoon salt

1 leek

¼ medium onion

1 clove

½ carrot, quartered lengthwise

Sprig fresh thyme (or ¼ teaspoon dried)

Sprig fresh parsley (or ¼ teaspoon dried)

1 bayleaf

5 peppercorns

Cook beef in water over medium heat for 30 minutes. *Do not boil.* Skim constantly. Increase heat; add salt. Remove scum brought to surface by salt. Slit leek; stick clove into onion. Add to meat with carrot, thyme, parsley, bay leaf and peppercorns. Bring mixture to boiling; skim again. Cover tightly and cook over low, *even* heat just at boiling until carrot is soft. Do not add water to pot while cooking. Strain off liquid; serve as soup. Meat may be served as main dish. Makes 3 servings.

FRENCH ONION SOUP

6 medium onions, sliced	Salt and pepper
½ cup butter or margarine	1 cup sherry
5 cups bouillon or beef broth	½ cup grated Parmesan cheese
3 slices white bread	

Sauté onions in ½ cup hot butter until golden brown. Add hot bouillon and simmer for 20 minutes. Meanwhile, toast bread slices; spread with butter and cut into quarters. Season soup to taste with salt and pepper. Add sherry. Pour into individual casseroles or one large casserole; float toast squares on top and sprinkle generously with cheese. Place casseroles in oven at 425° for about 10 minutes, or until cheese is lightly browned. Serves 4 to 6.

Cele Malvin

ONION SOUP

4 cups thinly sliced onions	¼ teaspoon pepper
¼ cup butter	3 slices buttered white bread, toasted and cubed
4½ cups chicken consommé	¾ cup grated Parmesan cheese
1 teaspoon salt	

Sauté onion slices in hot butter until glazed and golden. Add consommé, salt and pepper; bring to boiling and simmer, covered, for 30 minutes. Pour soup into bowls; float toast cubes on top; sprinkle generously with cheese. Makes 4 to 6 servings.

Perle Jacobs

Soup boiled is soup spoiled! Cook soup gently and evenly.

SOUP GARNI À LA NEW ORLEANS

2 eggs	Slivered almonds
4 cups chicken or beef broth	2 limes, quartered

Beat eggs until frothy. Turn into hot, buttered skillet and cook as for omelet, until firm but not browned. Cool; cut into small pieces. Drop into hot broth with slivered almonds. Serve with lime as garnish. Makes 6 to 8 servings.

Evelyn Lipschultz

VEGETABLE SOUPS

VEGETABLE SOUP

1½ pounds shortribs

3 quarts water

1 onion

1 No. 2 can tomatoes

¼ pound fresh peas

¼ pound green string beans

4 large carrots, diced

4 or 5 stalks celery, diced

¼ cup large lima beans

1 small rutabaga, cut up

1 medium sweet potato, cut up

¼ cup cooked rice

Parsley

Monosodium glutamate

Salt and pepper

1 tablespoon granulated sugar
(optional)

Place meat in water; add onion and bring to boiling. Add tomatoes, peas, green beans, carrots, celery, lima beans, rutabaga and potato in order listed. Simmer, covered, for 2 hours. Add rice, parsley, monosodium glutamate, salt and pepper to taste, and sugar, if desired. Serves 8 to 10.   *Evelyn Harris*

SWEET-AND-SOUR CABBAGE SOUP

2 pounds chuck or 2 to 3 pounds
shortribs (with most of fat removed)

Soup bones

1 onion, sliced

2 quarts water

3 pounds cabbage, shredded

2 No. 303 cans tomatoes

Juice of 1½ lemons

½ cup granulated sugar

1 teaspoon salt

¼ teaspoon pepper

½ teaspoon ground ginger

Place meat, bones and onion in large saucepot or kettle; add water and bring to boiling. Simmer for 1½ hours, skimming as necessary. Add cabbage, tomatoes, lemon juice, sugar, salt and pepper. Continue cooking for 1 hour longer, adding more sugar and lemon juice, if desired. Just before serving, add ginger. Makes 10 servings. *Gilda Fisher*

BARLEY, BEAN AND MUSHROOM SOUP

2 or 3 soup bones or 1½ pounds shortribs

3 tablespoons chicken fat

1 onion

3 quarts water

½ cup large barley

½ cup dried mushrooms

½ cup large lima beans

½ cup quick-cooking rolled oats

Carrots

Celery

Parsley

Salt and pepper

Monosodium glutamate

Place bones, chicken fat and onion in saucepot or kettle. Add water; cover and simmer for about 1½ to 2 hours. Skim as necessary. Soak mushrooms in hot water; drain. Add with remaining ingredients to pot and continue cooking until vegetables are tender (about 30 minutes). Makes 8 to 12 servings. *Mrs. Irwin Harris*

MINESTRONE

1 cup diced celery

½ cup diced onion

½ cup diced green pepper

1 clove garlic

¼ cup butter or salad oil

1½ cups canned tomatoes

1 cup diced carrots

1 cup fresh or frozen green beans or peas

¼ cup snipped parsley

2 quarts boiling water

4 bouillon cubes

2 or 3 teaspoons salt

½ teaspoon pepper

¼ teaspoon marjoram

1 bay leaf

1 cup diced potatoes

Grated Parmesan cheese

In large saucepot or kettle, sauté celery, onions, green pepper and garlic in hot butter. Add tomatoes, carrots, beans, parsley, boiling water, bouillon cubes, salt, pepper, marjoram and bay leaf. Simmer for 45 minutes. Add potatoes and continue cooking for 30 minutes longer. Serve sprinkled with cheese. Makes 6 to 8 servings. *Mina Siegel*

VEGETABLE-BEEF SOUP

1 medium onion, coarsely chopped

3 tablespoons butter or salad oil

1½ pounds ground beef

1½ cups canned tomatoes

3 cans consommé

2 soup cans water

4 carrots, quartered

4 celery tops

6 sprigs parsley

1 bay leaf

1 tablespoon salt

½ teaspoon thyme

10 peppercorns

In large saucepot or kettle, sauté onion in hot butter, until soft, but not browned. Add beef and brown lightly. Add tomatoes, consommé and water. Add remaining ingredients. Bring to boiling; cover and simmer for about 1 hour. Serve with toasted bread rounds sprinkled with grated cheese. Serves 6 to 8.   *Jeanne Berkowitz*

VEGETARIAN VEGETABLE SOUP

1 cup dried lima beans

6 cups water

1 No. 2 can tomatoes

1 cup diced carrots

1 cup diced potatoes

1 cup diced onions

2 tablespoons butter

1½ teaspoons salt

¼ teaspoon pepper

Cook beans in water until tender, about 3 hours. Add remaining ingredients; bring to boiling and simmer for 1 hour longer. Makes 8 servings.
                                                        Raye Korshak

CABBAGE SOUP

1½ pounds shortribs

2 quarts water

1 small head cabbage (about 1 lb.), shredded

1½ cups canned tomatoes

2 carrots, diced

1 large onion, cut up

1 apple, cored and pared

¼ pound raisins

Lemon juice

Sugar

Cook meat in 2 quarts water for 1 hour, skimming as necessary. Pour boiling water over cabbage; let stand for several minutes; drain. Add to meat with tomatoes, carrots, onion, apple, raisins, lemon juice and sugar to taste. Continue cooking until meat is tender, about 1 hour. Makes 6 to 8 servings.

Bessie Reimer

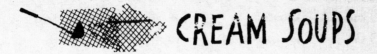 # CREAM SOUPS

CREME DE POTAGE CRESSONNIERE

2 leeks, chopped	4 cups water
2 onions, diced	1 teaspoon salt
3 medium bunches water cress	Freshly ground black pepper
¼ cup unsalted butter	2 egg yolks
3 potatoes, sliced	¼ cup sour cream

Sauté leeks, onions and water cress in hot unsalted butter for 5 minutes. Add potatoes, water, salt and pepper; simmer, covered, for 1 hour. Force mixture through grinder and return to saucepan; keep hot. When ready to serve, beat egg yolks with sour cream. Add a little hot mixture to egg yolks, than add yolks to potage. Heat almost to boiling; drop in generous chunk butter. Serve with croutons. Makes 6 servings.

CREAM OF CHICKEN SOUP WITH VEGETABLES

1½ quarts chicken broth or bouillon	¼ cup celery strips
3 tablespoons uncooked rice	⅓ cup carrot strips
1 teaspoon salt	¼ cup butter or chicken fat
⅛ teaspoon pepper	5 tablespoons flour
¼ cup chopped onion	⅓ cup cream

Bring chicken broth to boiling; add rice, salt and pepper and simmer for about 10 minutes. Add onion, celery and carrots; cook for about 15 minutes, or until rice and vegetables are tender. Melt butter in small saucepan; stir in flour. Remove from heat; slowly add a little of chicken broth, stirring until well blended. Stir into hot soup. Bring to boiling and boil for 2 minutes, stirring constantly. Just before serving, add cream. Serves 6. *Lee Bateman*

GOLDEN CHEESE SOUP

⅓ cup grated carrots	¼ cup flour
⅓ cup chopped celery	2 cups milk
1 cup boiling water	2 cups chicken bouillon
2 tablespoons chopped onion	1¼ cups grated Cheddar cheese
3 tablespoons butter or margarine	

Cook carrots and celery in boiling water until tender; do not drain. Sauté onion in hot butter until golden but not browned; stir in flour. Add milk gradually; cook, stirring constantly, until thick. Add bouillon, cheese, carrots and celery, including cooking water. Stir over low heat until cheese melts. Cover and cook for 20 minutes longer. Makes 6 servings.   *Edith Lirtzman*

NEW ENGLAND CORN CHOWDER

1 large onion, diced	2 cups half-and-half
¼ cup butter	2 cups milk
2 or 3 cups diced potatoes	Salt and pepper
1 No. 303 can cream-style corn	

Sauté onion in hot butter until lightly browned. Place potatoes in large saucepot or kettle with enough water to cover; cook until soft but not mushy. Add corn and onion; mix well. Add half-and-half, milk, salt and pepper to taste. Simmer until thoroughly heated. Do not boil. Makes 6 generous servings.

PHILADELPHIA PEPPER POT

¼ cup diced onion	5 cups white or brown stock
¼ cup diced green pepper	2 teaspoons salt
¼ cup diced celery	¾ teaspoon pepper
1½ cups diced potatoes	1 tablespoon butter
3 tablespoons butter	½ cup cream
3½ tablespoons flour	⅓ cup cooked rice

Sauté onion, green pepper, celery and potatoes in 3 tablespoons hot butter for 15 minutes, stirring frequently to prevent scorching. Add flour; stir until well mixed. Add stock, salt and pepper; simmer for about 1 hour, or until vegetables are tender. Add 1 tablespoon butter, cream and rice. Serve very hot. Makes 6 servings.   *Mrs. Alex Friedman*

THICK SOUPS

SPLIT PEA SOUP

½ to 1 pound chuck or other soup meat

1 large soup bone

4 quarts water

½ pound green or yellow split peas

¼ cup large barley

Salt and pepper

3 small onions

3 medium carrots

3 stalks celery

2 tomatoes

Place meat and soup bone in 8-qt. kettle; add water and bring to boiling. Simmer for about 1 hour. Rinse split peas; add to soup pot with barley. Add salt and pepper to taste. Cook until peas begin to soften, then add onions, carrots and celery. Continue cooking, partially covered, for about 2 hours, or until peas are soft and soup is smooth. Add tomatoes for last 5 minutes of cooking period. Keeps well in refrigerator, or may be frozen; reheat and serve. Serves 8 to 10.   *Mary Tavalin*

LIMA BEAN SOUP WITH MEAT

2 cups dried lima beans

2 pounds lean shortribs

4 onions, cut into small pieces

1 cup diced celery

1 cup canned tomatoes

1 clove garlic

1 tablespoon Worcestershire sauce

1 teaspoon salt

Dash pepper

Cover beans with cold water and soak overnight. Drain beans, reserving liquid. Make purée by forcing beans through sieve or grinder. Place meat in large saucepot or kettle with reserved bean liquid; if necessary, add water to cover. Add remaining ingredients and beans; simmer for about 2 hours, or until meat is tender. Makes 6 to 8 servings.   *Tillie Shafer*

LEEK AND POTATO SOUP

4 leeks, finely chopped	3 cups water
3 tablespoons butter	½ teaspoon salt
4 large potatoes, thinly sliced	⅛ teaspoon pepper

Sauté leeks in hot butter for 5 minutes. Add potatoes and cook for 5 minutes longer. Add water, salt and pepper; simmer for 40 minutes, or until potatoes are very soft and mixture may be stirred smooth. Makes 4 servings.

Edith Lirtzman

QUICK PEA SOUP

Leftover cooked peas	1 onion, diced
1 or 2 frankfurters, or salami slices	Salt and pepper

Place peas, frankfurters, onion, salt and pepper in blender container; add enough water to bring to desired consistency. Blend until smooth. Heat.

Judy Goldberg

HOT BORSHT

1 can consommé	1 teaspoon salt
2 jars chopped beets (baby food)	½ teaspoon garlic powder
1½ cups water	¼ teaspoon pepper
3 tablespoon grated onion	⅛ teaspoon cayenne pepper
2 tablespoons tarragon vinegar	2 tablespoons sour cream

Pour consommé into saucepan. Add beets, water, onion, vinegar, salt, garlic powder and peppers. Heat to piping hot. Top with sour cream. Serves 6.

Isabelle Dinitz

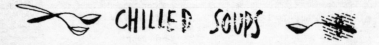 CHILLED SOUPS

JELLIED SHRIMP BOUILLON

1 7-oz. can shrimp	4 cups boiling water
2 envelopes unflavored gelatine	Dash pepper
4 bouillon cubes	Sliced stuffed green olives

Drain shrimp, reserving liquid. Add enough cold water to reserved liquid to make ½ cup; add gelatine. Dissolve bouillon cubes in boiling water; add gelatine and pepper; stir until gelatine is dissolved. Pour small amount of bouillon mixture into each of 6 bouillon cups. Place a few shrimp in each cup; chill in refrigerator until firm. Pour remaining bouillon into cups; float olive slices and any remaining shrimp on top. Chill until ready to serve. Makes 6 servings. *Mrs. Merrill Swartz*

BORSHT

1 No. 303 can shoestring beets	Pinch salt
2 cups water	2 eggs
Juice of 1 lemon	1 cup sour cream
2 tablespoons granulated sugar	

Combine beets and water in saucepan; bring to boiling. Add lemon juice, sugar and salt. Beat eggs with sour cream; blend into beet mixture. Chill in refrigerator until ready to serve. Serve with hot boiled potato in each soup plate, or top with sour cream. Serves 6. *Mrs. William Schero*

SPINACH BORSHT

1 package frozen chopped spinach	2½ teaspoons salt
5 cups water	¼ teaspoon citric acid crystals
Juice of 1 lemon	

Combine all ingredients in saucepan; bring to boiling. Simmer until spinach is completely thawed. Cool and chill. Serve garnished with diced hard-cooked egg and sour cream. Makes 6 servings. *Florence M. Mayron*

NEW TWIST SPINACH BORSHT

1 pound fresh rhubarb	2 packages frozen chopped spinach
2 quarts water	Sugar and salt

Cut rhubarb into 1-inch pieces. Place in saucepan with water and bring to boiling. Add spinach, sugar and salt to taste. Simmer until spinach is completely thawed and rhubarb is mushy. Cool and chill in refrigerator. Makes 6 servings. *Madeline Spark*

SOUP GARNISHES

CROUTONS ALA TRACU VIC

4 slices white bread

Butter

Chopped parsley

Grated Parmesan cheese

Trim crusts from bread slices; cut bread into ¼-inch cubes. Sauté bread cubes in hot butter until well browned. Drain on absorbent paper. Place parsley and cheese in paper or plastic bag; add bread cubes and shake until well coated. Store in tightly covered container. *Ceil Luke*

POTATO DUMPLINGS

5 or 6 Idaho potatoes, grated

1 egg

½ teaspoon salt

Dash pepper

¼ cup matzo meal

⅛ cup flour

Place grated potatoes on absorbent paper or towel and squeeze to remove liquid. Place in bowl and add remaining ingredients in order listed, beating well. Shape into walnut-size balls. Drop into boiling salted water. Cook for 45 minutes. Serve in soup, or add to gravy from roast meat or poultry. Serves 6 to 8. *Rose Gontovnick*

MATZO BALLS

2 eggs

½ cup matzo meal

½ teaspoon baking powder

½ teaspoon salt

Dash pepper

Beat eggs; mix in remaining ingredients. Place in refrigerator for at least 10 minutes. Shape into walnut-size balls. Drop into boiling salted water. Balls are done when they float to the top. Makes 1 dozen. *Bess Talman*

BREADS

Why has our poetry eschewed
The rapture and response of food?
What hymns are sung, what praises
said
For home-made miracles of bread?

Louis Untermeyer

QUICK BREADS

ORANGE PUFFS

2 cups sifted flour

¼ cup granulated sugar

3 teaspoons baking powder

1 teaspoon salt

3 to 4 teaspoons grated orange rind

¾ cup milk

¼ cup salad oil

1 egg

Sift together flour, sugar, baking powder, salt and orange rind. Add milk, oil and egg. Stir with fork until thoroughly mixed. Drop by teaspoonfuls into hot deep fat (375°). Fry, only a few at a time about 3 minutes, or until golden brown. Drain on absorbent paper. While warm, roll in cinnamon-sugar or confectioners' sugar. Makes about 2 dozen.   *Gus Dobrofsky*

POPOVERS

1½ cups water

2 tablespoons butter or shortening

1 teaspoon salt

1 cup matzo meal

4 eggs

Combine water, butter and salt in saucepan; bring to boiling; add matzo meal and stir until dissolved. Cool. Add eggs, one at a time, beating well after each. Fill greased muffin cups half full. Bake at 375° for about 1 hour. Makes about 8 muffins.   *Shirley Goldberg*

RAISIN BANANA MUFFINS

1 egg, beaten	2 cups sifted flour
½ cup mashed banana	⅓ cup granulated sugar
½ cup buttermilk	3 teaspoons baking powder
¼ cup melted shortening	1 teaspoon salt
1 cup raisins	¼ teaspoon baking soda

Combine egg, banana, buttermilk, shortening and raisins. Sift together flour, sugar, baking powder, salt and soda. Add to banana mixture all at once, stirring only until dry ingredients are moistened. Fill greased muffin cups two-thirds full. Bake at 400° for 20 to 25 minutes. Makes 1 dozen.

Florence Fine

ORANGE MUFFINS

2 tablespoons soft shortening	1 cup sifted flour
½ cup granulated sugar	2½ teaspoons baking powder
1 egg	½ teaspoon salt
1 cup corn flakes	2 tablespoons grated orange rind
⅔ cup orange juice	

Cream shortening and sugar. Add egg and beat well. Stir in corn flakes and orange juice. Sift together flour, baking powder and salt. Add to creamed mixture. Add grated rind. Stir only until dry ingredients are moistened. Fill greased muffin cups two-thirds full. Bake at 400° for 30 minutes. Makes about 1 dozen.

Hattie Atkins

CORN CAKES

½ cup soft butter	½ teaspoon cinnamon
½ cup granulated sugar	¼ teaspoon nutmeg
¾ cup sifted flour	2 eggs
½ cup corn meal	½ cup milk
2 teaspoons baking powder	

Cream butter until smooth. Add sugar, beating until light and fluffy. Sift together flour, corn meal, baking powder, cinnamon and nutmeg. Add to creamed mixture, beating well. Add eggs and milk; mix thoroughly. Pour into greased muffin cups. Bake at 350° for 20 minutes. Serve hot or cold, as sweet bread with dinner or as a dessert. Makes ½ dozen.   *Sandra Kaufman*

BAKING POWDER BISCUITS

2 cups sifted flour	¼ teaspoon cream of tartar
4 teaspoons baking powder	½ cup shortening
2 tablespoons granulated sugar	⅔ cup milk
½ teaspoon salt	

Sift together flour, sugar, baking powder, salt and cream of tartar. Add shortening; cut in with pastry blender or 2 knives until mixture resembles coarse meal. Add milk; mix until dough clings together. Knead gently on lightly floured surface. Roll out to about ½-inch thickness. Cut with biscuit cutter. Bake at 450° for 12 to 15 minutes. Makes 1½ to 2 dozen.

Shirley Brosilow

An important reminder—the quicker the mixing, the better the batter! Never overmix the dough or batter for quick breads.

FRESH PEACH KUCHEN

1½ cups sifted flour	BUTTER STREUSSEL:
2 tablespoons granulated sugar	¾ cup granulated sugar
1 teaspoon baking powder	2 tablespoons flour
½ teaspoon salt	⅛ teaspoon nutmeg
½ cup butter	2 tablespoons butter
1 egg, slightly beaten	1 cup sour cream (optional)
5 large peaches, skinned and pitted	

Sift together 1½ cups flour, 2 tablespoons sugar, baking powder and salt. Cut in ½ cup butter with pastry blender or 2 knives. Add egg; blend well. Spread on bottom and part way up sides of greased 13x9x2-inch pan. Slice peaches; arrange in rows almost overlapping over dough. Blend together ¾ cup sugar, 2 tablespoons flour, nutmeg and 2 tablespoons butter with pastry blender or fork. Sprinkle over peaches. Bake at 400° for 40 minutes, or bake for 35 minutes; cover with sour cream and bake for 5 minutes longer.   *Florence M. Mayron*

COFFEE CAKE RING

½ cup soft butter	1 teaspoon baking soda
1 cup granulated sugar	Pinch salt
2 eggs, beaten slightly	1 teaspoon vanilla
1 cup sour cream	¼ cup granulated sugar
2 cups sifted flour	1 teaspoon cinnamon
1 teaspoon baking powder	¼ cup chopped nuts or coconut

Cream butter and 1 cup sugar. Add eggs; blend well. Stir in sour cream. Sift together flour, baking powder, soda and salt. Blend into sour cream mixture. Stir in vanilla. Pour into well greased 10-inch ring mold. Combine ¼ cup sugar, cinnamon and nuts. Sprinkle over batter. Bake at 350° for 45 to 50 minutes. Cool 10 minutes. Remove from pan. If desired, melt ½ cup semi-sweet chocolate pieces with 2 tablespoons butter in top of double boiler over hot, *not boiling,* water. Drizzle over cooled cake.   *Gerry Freedman*

SYLVIA'S NUT BREAD

3 cups sifted flour	1 egg, well beaten
1 cup granulated sugar	¾ cup coarsely cut nuts
3 teaspoons baking powder	1 cup milk
1 teaspoon salt	

Sift together flour, sugar, baking powder and salt. Add eggs; stir in nuts. Add milk; stir and let stand for 20 minutes. Pour batter into greased 10x5x3-inch pan. Bake at 325° for about 55 minutes.   *Slyvia Abrams*

FILLED COFFEE CAKE

½ cup soft butter	1 teaspoon vanilla
2 cups granulated sugar	FILLING AND TOPPING:
4 eggs, well beaten	2 cups firmly packed brown sugar
3 cups sifted flour	4½ teaspoons melted butter
2 teaspoons baking powder	2 tablespoons flour
½ teaspoon salt	2 teaspoons cinnamon
1 cup milk	1 cup chopped walnuts

Cream soft butter well; add granulated sugar, a little at a time, creaming after each addition. Add eggs, stirring vigorously. Sift together 3 cups flour, baking powder and salt. Add to creamed mixture alternately with milk, beginning and ending with flour. Add vanilla; mix well. Cream brown sugar with melted butter. Add 2 tablespoons flour and cinnamon. Stir in walnuts. Pour half of batter into greased 9x9x2-inch pan. Top with half of nut mixture. Repeat with remaining batter and nut mixture. Bake at 375° for 40 minutes. Cool; cut into squares. Makes 9 to 12 servings.   *Dee Stein*

DUTCH STREUSSEL COFFEE CAKE

3½ cups sifted flour	3 eggs
2 cups granulated sugar	1 15-oz. can evaporated milk
3 teaspoons baking powder	1 teaspoon vanilla
½ cup butter	

Sift together flour, sugar and baking powder. Cut in butter; mix well. Set aside scant cup of flour mixture for Streussel topping. Beat eggs, milk and vanilla together. Add to remaining flour mixture; mix. (This will not be a smooth batter.) Pour into greased 13x9x2-inch pan; sprinkle Streussel topping over top. Sprinkle with cinnamon and chopped nuts, if desired. Bake at 350° for 45 minutes, or until done. Cool; cut into squares. Makes 12 to 16 servings.   *Dora Berkowitz*

DELICIOUS COFFEE CAKE

4 egg whites	3 teaspoons baking powder
½ cup soft shortening	1 cup milk
¼ cup soft butter	FILLING AND TOPPING:
1½ cups granulated sugar	½ cup granulated sugar
4 egg yolks	1 tablespoon cocoa
1½ cups sifted flour	1 teaspoon cinnamon

Beat egg whites until stiff; refrigerate. Cream shortening and butter well; add 1½ cups sugar and egg yolks. Sift together flour and baking powder. Add alternately with milk to egg yolk mixture, beginning and ending with flour. Fold in chilled egg whites. Pour half of batter into greased 9 or 10-inch tube pan. Combine ½ cup sugar, cocoa and cinnamon. Sprinkle with half of filling mixture. Top with remaining batter and sprinkle remaining filling over top. Bake at 350° for 1 hour. Makes 12 to 14 servings.   *Dorothy Salkin*

APPLE KUCHEN

1 cup sifted flour

2 tablespoons granulated sugar

⅛ teaspoon baking powder

½ cup butter

2 tablespoons cream or half-and-half

½ teaspoon vanilla

TOPPING:

½ cup granulated sugar

¼ cup flour

Pared apple slices (Greening or Rome Beauty)

Butter

Cinnamon

Sift together flour, 2 tablespoons sugar and baking powder. Cut in butter with pastry blender. Add cream and vanilla; mix with fork. Bring to sides of bowl using silver knife. Press dough into ungreased 9-inch round or 9x9x2-inch pan. Sift together ½ cup sugar and ¼ cup flour. Arrange apple slices on dough in rows, slightly overlapping. Spoon sugar mixture over top. Dot with butter and sprinkle with cinnamon to taste. Bake at 350° for 1 to 1½ hours. Cut into squares. Makes about 12 servings.   *Caryl Loevy*

REFRIGERATOR ROLLS

1 cup shortening

1 cup hot water

1 cup cold milk

2 cakes compressed yeast

⅓ cup granulated sugar

1 teaspoon salt

2 eggs, beaten

6 cups sifted flour

Melt shortening in hot water. Add cold milk. Pour mixture over yeast and stir until yeast is dissolved. Add sugar and salt to eggs. Add flour to yeast mixture, ½ cup at a time, alternately with egg mixture, beating vigorously after each addition. Place dough in greased bowl. Cover and chill in refrigerator overnight. (Dough will keep for up to 1 week in refrigerator; use as desired.) Roll out dough on lightly floured surface. Shape into cloverleafs, Parker House rolls, snails, fan-tans, etc. Place on greased baking sheets or in muffin cups. Let rise for 30 to 60 minutes, or until doubled in size. Bake at 425° for 15 minutes, or until delicately browned. Makes 3 dozen.

Shirley Sostrin

OAT ROLLS

1 cup scalded milk	2 cups sifted flour
½ cup butter	2 eggs
½ cup firmly packed brown sugar	1 cake compressed yeast
1 tablespoon salt	1½ cups quick-cooking rolled oats
1 cup cold water	3½ to 4 cups sifted flour

Pour scalded milk over butter, sugar and salt. Add cold water and cool to lukewarm. Stir in 2 cups flour. Add eggs and crumbled yeast; beat with rotary beater for 2 minutes. Add rolled oats. Add 3½ to 4 cups flour, or enough to make a soft dough. Turn out onto light floured surface and knead until satiny (about 10 minutes). Shape dough into a ball and place in greased bowl. Cover and let rise in warm place until light (about 1 hour). Punch down; cover and let rest for 10 minutes. Shape into rolls (cloverleafs, Parker House, crescents, snails, etc.) and place on greased baking sheets or in muffin cups. Brush tops lightly with melted shortening. Cover and let rise until doubled in size (about 45 minutes). Bake at 400° for 20 to 25 minutes. Makes 3 dozen.

RAISIN OR DATE ROLLS: Add 1 cup raisins or 1 cup chopped dates with rolled oats. Shape into small balls. Bake in greased muffin cups as directed above. Makes about 3 dozen.

CINNAMON ROLLS: Roll dough into rectangle ¼ inch thick. Brush lightly with 3 tablespoons melted butter. Combine 1 cup sugar, 2 tablespoons cinnamon and ⅔ cup chopped nuts. Sprinkle over dough; roll as for jelly roll. Cut into 1-inch slices; place close together in greased pan. Brush with melted shortening and let rise until doubled in size. Bake as directed above. Makes 3 dozen.

PECAN ROLLS: Grease muffin cups; into each place ½ teaspoon water, 1 teaspoon brown sugar, ½ teaspoon butter and 3 or 4 pecan halves. Roll dough into rectangle ½ inch thick. Brush lightly with 2 tablespoons melted butter. Sprinkle with ⅔ cup brown sugar; roll as for jelly roll. Cut into 1-inch slices. Place in muffin cups; cover and let rise until doubled in size. Bake at 375° for 20 to 25 minutes. Let stand 1 minute before removing from pans. Makes 3 dozen.

Eve Pomrenze

CHOREG (Miniature Egg Bread Twists)

1 package active dry yeast	1 teaspoon salt
½ cup lukewarm water	6 cups unsifted flour
1½ cups melted butter	½ teaspoon ground anise seed
1 cup lukewarm milk	¼ teaspoon ground cardamom seed
3 eggs	1 egg, beaten
3 tablespoons granulated sugar	Sesame seeds (optional)

Dissolve yeast in lukewarm water. Mix together melted butter, milk, eggs, sugar, salt and yeast. Add flour mixed with anise and cardamom seed; stir to form a soft dough. Let stand in warm place until doubled in bulk. Roll out dough on lightly floured surface to about ¾-inch thickness. Cut into diamonds, squares, triangles, etc. Or cut into strips about 3½-inches long and ½-inch thick; braid 3 together. Place on greased baking sheets; brush tops with beaten egg; sprinkle with sesame seeds, if desired. (For browner tops, mix a little cream with beaten egg.) Let rise for 1 to 2 hours, or until doubled in size. Bake at 375° for 15 to 20 minutes, or until browned. Makes 3½ dozen. *Florence Bezazian*

First choice for storing breads—your home freezer.

COFFEE PUFFS

¾ cup scalded milk	2 cups sifted flour
¼ cup shortening	½ cup blanched almonds, finely chopped
3 tablespoons granulated sugar	
1 teaspoon salt	3 tablespoons granulated sugar
1 package active dry yeast	1 teaspoon cinnamon
2 eggs, beaten	

Combine milk, shortening, 3 tablespoons sugar and salt; cool to lukewarm. Dissolve yeast in milk mixture; add eggs, stirring well. Add flour and ¼ cup almonds. Beat until well blended and smooth. Cover and let rise until doubled in bulk (about 1 hour). Mix remaining almonds with 3 tablespoons sugar and cinnamon. Punch down dough. Drop by spoonfuls into greased muffin cups, filling cups about half full. Sprinkle dough with almond mixture. Cover and let rise until doubled in size (about 30 minutes). Bake at 375° for 15 to 20 minutes. Makes 1 dozen. *Sue Weissman*

CRESCENTS

4¼ cups sifted flour	1 cup sour cream
2 packages active dry yeast	FILLING:
2 tablespoons granulated sugar	3 egg whites
½ cup lukewarm water	¾ cup granulated sugar
½ teaspoon salt	1 teaspoon vanilla
3 egg yolks	2 cups chopped nuts
¾ cup melted butter	

Sift flour into large bowl. Dissolve yeast and 2 tablespoons sugar in lukewarm water. Make well in center of flour; add yeast mixture. Add salt, egg yolks, melted butter and sour cream in order listed. Mix well. Beat egg whites until stiff, gradually adding ¾ cup sugar; add vanilla and nuts. Divide dough into 8 parts. Roll out 1 part on lightly floured surface as thin as possible. Cut into 8 wedges. Place nut mixture in center of each wedge and roll up to pointed end. Repeat with remaining dough and filling. Place crescents on ungreased baking sheets. Sprinkle lightly with cinnamon-sugar, if desired. Bake at 350° for 20 minutes. Serve as sweet rolls, as pastry dessert, or as cookies. Makes 64 crescents.   *Eve Gurvey*

COTTAGE CHEESE PINWHEEL ROLLS

1 package active dry yeast	1 egg, beaten
¼ cup lukewarm water	FILLING:
2½ cups sifted flour	¾ cup firmly packed brown sugar
¼ cup granulated sugar	3 tablespoons melted butter
1 teaspoon salt	½ teaspoon vanilla
½ cup butter	½ teaspoon almond extract
1½ cups creamed cottage cheese	⅔ cup chopped nuts

Dissolve yeast in lukewarm water. Sift together flour, granulated sugar and salt. Cut in butter with pastry blender until mixture resembles fine meal. Add cottage cheese, egg and yeast; mix well. If necessary, add more flour to make dough easier to handle. Combine brown sugar, melted butter, vanilla, almond extract and nuts. Roll out dough on lightly floured surface to 14-inch square. Spread nut mixture on dough and roll as for jelly roll. Cut into 18 slices with a sharp knife. Place on greased baking sheet; let rise for about 30 minutes, or until doubled in size. Bake at 375° for 20 to 25 minutes. Makes 1½ dozen.   *Jean Russell*

SCHNECKEN

1 package active dry yeast	2 eggs
1 tablespoon granulated sugar	½ cup soft butter
¼ cup lukewarm water	1 cup chopped pecans
½ cup granulated sugar	1 cup firmly packed brown sugar
1 teaspoon salt	¼ cup currants
1 cup scalded milk	1 teaspoon cinnamon
1 cup sifted flour	⅔ cup melted butter
4 cups sifted flour	1 cup small pecan halves

Dissolve yeast and 1 tablespoon sugar in lukewarm water. Place ½ cup sugar and salt in large bowl; add scalded milk. Cool to lukewarm; stir to dissolve sugar; add 1 cup flour and blend well. Add yeast, mixing well. Add 2 cups flour to yeast mixture and beat until smooth. Add eggs, stirring vigorously. Add soft butter. Beat in remaining flour to make a soft dough. Knead well on lightly floured surface; shape into large ball and place in greased bowl. Cover and let rise until doubled in bulk. Punch down dough and let rise again until doubled. Combine brown sugar, chopped pecans, currants and cinnamon. Place 1 teaspoonful melted butter in each of 24 greased muffin cups. Sprinkle 2 teaspoonfuls currant-nut mixture into each muffin cup. Press 3 or 4 pecan halves into mixture in each cup. Punch down dough and divide into 2 parts. Roll out 1 part on lightly floured surface into 12x8-inch rectangle. Brush with half remaining melted butter; sprinkle with half remaining currant-nut mixture. Roll into tight, long roll. Cut into 12 slices. Repeat with remaining dough and filling. Place slices in muffin cups. Cover and let rise until doubled in size. Bake at 375° for 20 minutes. Invert on wire rack; let stand 5 minutes. Makes 2 dozen.

Sue Weissman

CHALLI

4 cups flour, sifted twice	¼ cup salad oil
1 cake compressed yeast	Scant ½ cup sugar
¼ cup warm water	½ teaspoon salt
2 eggs	1 egg yolk, beaten

Make well in center of flour; add crumbled yeast and warm water. Mix. Let rise for 10 minutes. Add eggs, oil, sugar and salt. Knead. Let rest for 1 hour. Knead again. Shape into loaf. Brush top with egg yolk mixed with a small amount of water. Place on greased baking sheet. Bake at 375° for 40 minutes. Makes 1 loaf.

Stella Ellyne

MERINGUE COFFEE CAKES

1¾ cups sifted flour	3 egg whites
1 cup melted butter	¼ teaspoon salt
3 egg yolks	1 cup granulated sugar
2 tablespoons granulated sugar	Cinnamon
1 cake compressed yeast	1 cup raisins
¼ cup warm milk	1 cup chopped nuts or coconut
1 tablespoon granulated sugar	Confectioners' sugar

Combine flour, butter, egg yolks and 2 tablespoons sugar; cream well. Dissolve yeast in warm milk; add 1 tablespoon sugar. Add to flour mixture; mix well. Chill in refrigerator overnight. Divide dough into 2 parts. Roll out half on lightly floured surface to rectangle about ¼ inch thick. Beat egg whites with salt until stiff; gradually add 1 cup sugar. Spread half of egg white mixture over rolled dough. Sprinkle with cinnamon to taste and half of raisins and nuts. Roll as for jelly roll and place on greased baking sheet. Repeat with remaining dough and filling. Bake at 350° for 30 minutes. When cool, sprinkle with confectioners' sugar; cut into 2-inch slices.

Beck Prince

APRICOT COFFEE CAKES

3 cups sifted flour	FILLING:
2 tablespoons granulated sugar	1 cup dried apricots
1 teaspoon salt	1 cup water
1 cup butter	¾ cup granulated sugar
1 package active dry yeast	2 teaspoons cinnamon
½ cup lukewarm milk	½ cup chopped nuts
2 eggs	

Sift together flour, 1 tablespoon sugar and salt; add butter and cut in with pastry blender. Dissolve yeast in lukewarm milk; add to flour mixture. Add eggs and beat well. Cover; let rise in cool place until doubled in bulk. Mix apricots and water in saucepan; cover and simmer until soft. Mash well with pastry blender; add ¾ cup sugar, cinnamon and nuts. Mix well. Divide dough into 2 parts. Roll out half of dough on well floured surface. Spread with apricot mixture; fold dough over. Place on greased baking sheet; snip one edge at regular intervals with scissors. Repeat with remaining dough and filling. Let rise for 1 hour. Bake at 375° for 30 minutes. Cool; sprinkle with confectioners' sugar.

June Lefkovitz

REFRIGERATOR COFFEE RING

1 cake compressed yeast	3 eggs, beaten
1 cup warm milk	Melted butter
4 cups sifted flour	¼ cup granulated sugar
1 cup soft butter or shortening	1 teaspoon cinnamon
3 tablespoons granulated sugar	Raisins
1 teaspoon salt	Chopped walnuts

Dissolve yeast in warm milk. Sift flour into a bowl; cut in butter with pastry blender. Add 3 tablespoons sugar, salt and eggs to yeast mixture; blend well. Add to flour mixture; beat until smooth. Place in greased bowl. Cover and chill in refrigerator overnight. Roll out dough on lightly floured surface to ½-inch thickness. Brush with melted butter. Combine ¼ cup sugar and cinnamon; sprinkle over dough. Cover with raisins and chopped walnuts. Roll as for jelly roll. Shape into a ring and place on greased baking sheet. Snip outer edge at 1½-inch intervals with scissors. Cover and let rise for 1 hour, or until doubled in size. Bake at 350° for 35 minutes, or until nicely browned. When cool, glaze with confectioners' sugar icing, if desired.

Sylvea Zimmerman

APPLE-RAISIN COFFEE RINGS

1 package active dry yeast	½ cup sour cream
1 teaspoon granulated sugar	½ cup melted butter
¼ cup lukewarm water	FILLING:
4½ cups sifted flour	⅔ cup butter
½ cup granulated sugar	Cinnamon-sugar
½ teaspoon salt	Thin apple slices (or jelly)
2 eggs, beaten	Raisins
1 cup milk	

Dissolve yeast and 1 teaspoon sugar in lukewarm water. Sift together flour, ½ cup sugar and salt. Add yeast, eggs, milk, sour cream and melted butter. Mix well. Chill in refrigerator overnight. Divide dough into 2 parts. Roll out half of dough on lightly floured surface until very thin. Dot with butter; sprinkle with cinnamon-sugar. Cover with apple slices; sprinkle with raisins. Roll as for jelly roll. Place in greased 9-inch tube pan. Repeat with remaining dough and filling. Bake at 325° for about 1 hour. Cool; drizzle confectioners' sugar icing over tops, if desired.

Ruth J. Leavitt

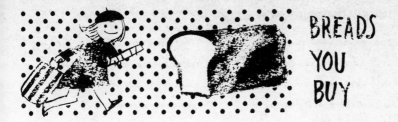

CURRIED TOAST ROLLS

Very thin fine-textured white bread
 slices

Melted butter

Curry powder

Salt

Trim crusts from bread slices. Combine butter with curry powder and salt to taste. Spread on bread slices. Roll each slice and secure with wooden pick; place on baking sheet. Toast on all sides at 200°. Allow to dry in oven.

Mrs. Marshall Paskind

SEA-FOOD PIE

1 2-lb. round loaf rye bread

Soft process cheese spread

1 jar red caviar

1 jar black caviar

2 tins rolled anchovies with capers,
 sliced crosswise

2 cans chopped ripe olives

1 can shrimp

1 can sardines

1 can crab meat

1 jar stuffed green olives

1 jar pickled onions

Cut bread into crosswise slices ¼-inch thick. Use the 3 center slices; reserve remainder for other food preparation. Spread slices with cheese; stack. Place teaspoon caviar in center of top. Make ring of cheese with pastry tube. Then arrange anchovies, ripe olives, shrimp, sardines and crab meat alternately in spokes. Place spoonfuls of caviar between spokes. Garnish with whole olives and pickled onions. Chill in refrigerator until ready to serve. Cut in wedges. Ingredients and garnishes may be varied to suit taste. Makes 8 servings.

Joy Reich

For another "Breads You Buy" recipe, see Tuna Treasure Loaf, page 116.

HOT LUNCHEON SANDWICH LOAF

1 large unsliced white sandwich loaf

1 can cream of mushroom soup

6 hard-cooked eggs, chopped

⅓ cup chopped stuffed green olives

1 7-oz. can tuna, flaked

1½ teaspoons minced onion

2 tablespoons mayonnaise

½ cup melted butter

⅓ cup cream or half-and-half

Trim crusts from sandwich loaf; cut into thirds lengthwise. Combine ¼ cup mushroom soup with eggs and olives. In another bowl, combine tuna, onion and mayonnaise. Spread soup mixture on one slice; cover with second slice. Spread with tuna mixture; top with third slice. Place on baking sheet. Brush top and sides with melted butter. Bake at 400° for about 20 minutes, or until toasted. Meanwhile, combine remaining soup with cream. Heat, stirring until smooth. Serve as sauce with luncheon loaf. Makes 6 to 8 servings.   *Mrs. Milton Smith*

DEVILED BREAD STICKS

1 unsliced white sandwich loaf

½ cup butter

1 clove garlic, crushed

1 teaspoon herb mustard

1 teaspoon bottled meat sauce

1 teaspoon Worcestershire sauce

2 teaspoons poppy seeds

Slice bread into 1-inch slices; then cut slices into 1-inch sticks, about 3 inches long. Melt butter; add garlic and simmer for several minutes. Add mustard, meat sauce and Worcestershire sauce; stir well. Dip sticks in butter mixture, then in poppy seeds, coating well. Place on baking sheet. Bake at 300° until crisp, turning occasionally. Serve hot.   *Mrs. Merrill Swartz*

BREAD-WITH-A-FLAVOR

1 loaf French or Italian bread

Butter

Clove garlic, onion salt, chives or anchovies

Cut bread into ½-inch thick diagonal slices, but do not cut through bottom crust. Combine butter with seasoning; spread generously on all slices. Press loaf firmly back into shape; wrap in very wet towel. Let stand for at least 2 hours. Remove bread from towel; place on greased baking sheet. Bake at 350° for about 20 minutes.   *Dee Stein*

MEAT DISHES

We do not eat for the good of living, but because the meat is savory and the appetite is keen.

Ralph Waldo Emerson

BEEF

BROILED BEEF TENDERLOIN WITH MUSHROOM SAUCE

3 tablespoons butter

1 large clove garlic, slivered

½ pound fresh mushrooms, sliced

2 medium onions, sliced

¼ pound ground beef (or ground beef tenderloin trimmings)

⅔ cup dry red wine

¼ cup beef bouillon

2 tablespoons chili sauce

1 tablespoon bottled meat sauce

¼ teaspoon Worcestershire sauce

4 drops Tabasco sauce

½ teaspoon flour

½ teaspoon salt

Pinch hickory smoked salt

Pinch each of marjoram and thyme

1 5 to 6-pound beef tenderloin

Melt butter in large skillet. Add garlic, mushrooms and onion. Sauté for about 5 minutes, or until onions are tender. Add ground meat, breaking up with fork and stirring constantly. Cook 4 to 5 minutes, then add remaining ingredients except beef tenderloin. Stir mixture well; simmer until ready to use. Have tenderloin at room temperature. Broil about 1 inch from heat for 8 minutes. Turn and broil 7 minutes longer. Remove from broiler; place in roasting pan and pour sauce over top. Bake at 325° for 10 to 15 minutes. Serve tenderloin on heated serving platter with mushroom sauce. Makes 8 to 10 servings. *Lee Bateman*

PEPPER STEAK

2 green peppers, sliced lengthwise

1 box fresh mushrooms

1 teaspoon orégano

1 large clove garlic, crushed

¼ cup salad oil

1 pound beef tenderloin, cut into strips

Salt and pepper

2 tablespoons cooking sherry

2 firm red tomatoes, cut into eighths

Sauté green peppers, mushrooms, orégano and garlic in hot oil for about 10 minutes. Set aside. Sauté meat about 5 minutes on each side. Season to taste with salt and pepper. Cover, cook until tender. Add sherry. Add green pepper mixture and tomatoes. Cook for about 5 minutes until heated through. Makes 3 or 4 servings.   *Beverly Kaluzna*

LONDON BROIL

1 2-pound flank steak

4 tablespoons soy sauce

2 tablespoons garlic dressing

1 tablespoon Russian dressing

1 can mushrooms, drained

Combine soy sauce, garlic and Russian dressings. Pour over steak and chill in refrigerator from 4 to 12 hours. Drain steak, reserving marinade. Broil about 15 minutes on each side for medium. Pour marinade and mushrooms over steak during last 2 minutes. Slice diagonally and serve with sauce. Makes 4 servings.   *Edith Weiser*

ROUND STEAK ROLL-UPS

1 4-oz. can mushrooms

1 small onion, thinly sliced

3 tablespoons bread crumbs

1 tablespoon chopped parsley

¼ teaspoon sage

3 tablespoons shortening

2 1½-pound round steaks

½ cup water or stock

Salt and pepper

Sauté mushrooms, onion, bread crumbs, parsley and sage in hot shortening. Meanwhile, trim steaks and cut into 2x3-inch pieces. Place teaspoonful sautéed mixture on each piece of steak. Roll up and secure with wooden picks. Brown in skillet used for sautéing mixture. Add water; simmer for 1 hour, or until meat is tender. Makes 6 to 8 servings.   *Robin Crystal*

SHISH KEBAB (with beef)

⅓ cup soy sauce

⅓ cup wine (chianti, dry sherry or port)

1 teaspoon granulated sugar

⅛ teaspoon pepper

⅛ teaspoon garlic powder (or 1 clove garlic, mashed)

3 pounds beef tenderloin, cut into large cubes

1 13-oz. can pineapple tidbits, drained

4 green peppers, cut into 1x2-inch pieces

2 8-oz. cans boiled onions, drained (or fresh onions, cut in eighths)

Combine soy sauce, wine, sugar, pepper and garlic powder. Pour over beef. Marinate in refrigerator from 4 to 8 hours. Alternate meat, pineapple, green peppers and onions on long skewers. Broil on charcoal grill for 7 to 10 minutes, turning frequently. Or place under broiler. Serves 8.

Mildred Adler

New idea! Marinate meats in a tightly sealed plastic bag, thus making turning easy and quick.

BEEF STROGANOFF

½ pound fresh mushrooms

½ cup chopped onion

1 clove garlic, chopped

½ cup butter

¼ cup flour

½ teaspoon salt

¼ teaspoon pepper

1 pound beef tenderloin (or top round)

2 tablespoons flour

¾ cup beef bouillon

2 tablespoons sherry

2 tablespoons Worcestershire sauce

1 tablespoon tomato paste

1 teaspoon salt

¼ cup sliced stuffed green olives

1 cup sour cream

Sauté mushrooms, onion and garlic in hot butter until tender. Combine ¼ cup flour, ½ teaspoon salt and pepper. Coat meat with seasoned flour. Add to vegetable mixture and brown. Remove meat and vegetables; stir 2 tablespoons flour into drippings; add bouillon. Stir to smooth paste. Add wine, Worcestershire sauce, tomato paste, 1 teaspoon salt and olives. Cook until thickened. Add sour cream, a little at a time; simmer, stirring constantly. Add meat and vegetables. Heat to serving temperature. Makes 3 or 4 servings.

Lynn Coopersmith

STUFFED STEAK SUPREME

½ cup melted butter

1 tablespoon boiling water

1 egg

2 1½-pound round steaks

Salt, pepper and paprika

3 onions, sliced

¼ pound mushrooms, sliced

1 green pepper, chopped

Bread crumbs

¼ cup butter

6 whole mushrooms

3 small onions

1 cup red wine

Beat together melted butter, boiling water and egg; set aside. Overlap steaks making one large steak. Pound thin and rub in salt, pepper and paprika to taste. Spread steaks with onions, mushrooms and green pepper. Cover with bread crumbs. Roll up and tie tightly. Flour outside and brown meat roll in ¼ cup hot butter. Place in roasting pan; add whole mushrooms and onions. Salt and pepper to taste. Add wine. Bake at 350° for 2 hours. Serve hot or cold. Serves 6.

BARBECUED STEAK

2 pounds round steak, cut 1½ to 2 inches thick

½ teaspoon salt

½ teaspoon pepper

3 tablespoons shortening

⅓ cup minced onion

⅓ cup minced celery

½ clove garlic, minced

1 can tomato soup

2 tablespoons Worcestershire sauce

2 teaspoons lemon juice

2 tablespoons brown sugar

2 teaspoons prepared mustard

Sprinkle steak with salt and pepper; pound thoroughly. Melt shortening in heaby saucepan or skillet. Brown steak, onion, celery and garlic in hot shortening. Add remaining ingredients. Cover. Bake at 350° for 1½ hours. Double last five ingredients for additional barbecue sauce to serve over fluffy rice or mashed potatoes. Serves 4.   *Allene Frost*

Place a slice of bread in the broiler pan when broiling steaks or chops to absorb grease, prevent smoke and make cleaning easier.

RAGOUT OF BEEF

3 slices middle chuck, cut 1½ inches thick

Seasoned salt

1 tablespoon shortening

2 medium onions, minced (about 1 cup)

2 beef bouillon cubes

1 chicken bouillon cube

1 tablespoon paprika

½ teaspoon garlic powder

¼ teaspoon pepper

¼ teaspoon salt

¼ teaspoon sugar

6 tablespoons Burgundy wine

3 tablespoons sherry

4 large potatoes, peeled and quartered

Cut each slice of chuck in half. Sprinkle each piece lightly with seasoned salt and sear in hot shortening. Remove from pan. Add onion; cook and stir until transparent. Return meat to pan and cook, covered, for 10 minutes. Dissolve bouillon cubes in ¾ cup boiling water. Add to meat with remaining seasonings and wine. Cover and simmer for 45 minutes, or until meat begins to get tender. Add potatoes and continue to cook until meat and potatoes are tender, adding a little boiling water as necessary. Remove meat and potatoes from pan and set aside to keep warm. Strain liquid in pan, forcing onion through sieve. Return to pan, add meat and potatoes and heat to serving temperature. Serves 6.   *Sylvia Wilson*

CHUCK WAGON BEEF STEW

2 pounds lean beef, cut in small pieces

2 tablespoons shortening

2 teaspoons flour

2 teaspoons salt

1 teaspoon granulated sugar

1 bay leaf

¼ teaspoon pepper

¼ teaspoon chili powder

¼ teaspoon thyme

2 tomatoes, quartered, or 1 small can tomatoes

1 green pepper, cut in strips

1 can beef bouillon

6 medium potatoes, quartered

6 carrots, quartered

6 small onions

3 or 4 stalks celery, sliced

1 cup fresh or frozen, cooked peas

Brown meat in hot shortening. Add flour, salt, sugar, bay leaf, pepper, chili powder, thyme, tomatoes, green pepper and bouillon. Cook about 1 hour, or until meat is almost tender. Add potatoes, carrots, onions and celery and continue cooking until vegetables are tender (about 30 minutes). Add peas just before serving. Serves 4 to 6.   *Tillie Shafer*

SAUERBRATEN WITH SPAETZLE

SAUERBRATEN:

3 to 4 pounds pot roast	½ cup sliced onion
Salt and pepper	¼ cup granulated sugar
Vinegar	2 bay leaves
Water	1 teaspoon peppercorns

Rub meat with salt and pepper. Place in crock or bowl. Heat together, but do not boil, equal parts vinegar and water (enough to more than half cover meat), onion, sugar, bay leaves and peppercorns. Pour hot mixture over meat. Cover and let stand in refrigerator 7 to 10 days, turning meat once cea hday. Cook meat in marinade until tender (about 3 hours). Remove meat from pan and thicken remaining vinegar mixture with flour. Add Spaetzle to gravy and serve with meat. Makes 6 servings.

SPAETZLE:

3 eggs	¾ to 1 cup water
3 cups sifted flour	Melted butter
½ teaspoon salt	Chopped parsley

Beat eggs well. Sift together flour and salt. Add to eggs gradually with water, using up to 1 cup as necessary to form smooth dough. Beat with wooden spoon until dough blisters (about 20 minutes). Drop from teaspoon dipped in cold water into boiling salted water. Cook for 15 minutes, or until tender. Drain; rinse in cold water. Drain; toss with melted butter and parsley.

Alice B. Weitzenfeld

HUNGARIAN GOULASH

6 tablespoons shortening	¼ cup tomato paste
2 cups sliced onions	1 bay leaf
4 pounds round steak, cut into squares	4 tablespoons paprika
2 cups (1 No. 303 can) tomatoes	4 teaspoons salt
2 green peppers, cut up	½ teaspoon pepper
½ cup dry wine	1 8-oz. package medium noodles, cooked

Sauté onions in hot shortening; add meat and brown. Cover and cook for 15 minutes. Add remaining ingredients and simmer for 1½ to 3 hours until meat is tender. Serve on noodles. (If gravy is too thin, thicken with a little cornstarch.) Serves 8.

Ione Comess

BRISKET BEAN POT

2 cups uncooked navy beans

½ teaspoon salt

2 pounds beef brisket, cut up

¼ cup brown sugar

3 tablespoons chili sauce

1 tablespoon molasses

1 tablespoon mild mustard

1 teaspoon salt

Soak beans overnight in water to cover. Place in pot with soaking water; add ½ teaspoon salt; cover; heat slowly to boiling point, then simmer until skins break. Drain; return liquid to heat and keep hot. Place beef in 4-quart casserole; add beans. Combine brown sugar, chili sauce, molasses, mustard, and salt with 1 cup bean liquid. Pour over beans. Add enough hot liquid to cover mixture in casserole. Cover and bake at 275° for 5 hours, or until meat is tender. Makes 6 servings.   *Ruth Pollak*

VIENNESE POT ROAST

1 4-pound top round of beef, rolled, with a little fat on top

2 teaspoons salt

⅛ teaspoon pepper

1 whole carrot

1 stalk celery

8 small sprigs parsley

1 bay leaf

Pinch of thyme

Pinch of marjoram

2 tablespoons butter or margarine, melted

1 medium onion, chopped

3 shallots, chopped

2 tomatoes, peeled and quartered

1 cup bouillon

1 cup red or white wine

¼ cup whiskey

2 tablespoons sherry

1 head cabbage, quartered

3 tablespoons flour

3 tablespoons water

1 tablespoon heavy cream

Wipe meat, sprinkle with salt and pepper. Place in Dutch oven with carrot, celery, parsley, bay leaf, thyme and marjoram. Sauté onion and shallots in melted butter until golden. Add to meat with tomatoes, bouillon, wine, whiskey and sherry. Cover tightly and simmer for 3 hours. About 20 minutes before end of cooking time, add cabbage. When meat is tender, remove meat and cabbage. Strain liquid and boil down to 2½ cups. Thicken with paste made from flour and water. Add cream. Serves 8.   *Sally Anne Lerner*

NEW YORK POT ROAST

1 3-pound boned, rolled chuck, rump or round steak	1 6-oz. bottle horse-radish
2 tablespoons shortening	6 medium onions, peeled
1 teaspoon garlic salt	3 tablespoons flour

In Dutch oven, brown meat well on all sides in hot shortening. Sprinkle with garlic salt. Add enough water to horse-radish to make 1 cup. Pour over meat. Cover and simmer for about 2 hours. Add onions and continue cooking for about 30 minutes. Remove meat and onions. Add enough water to drippings to make 2 cups liquid. Place 3 tablespoons drippings in pan and blend in flour. Add liquid, cook over low heat, stirring constantly, until thickened. Makes 6 servings.   *Lore Kirchheimer*

BARBECUED POT ROAST

1 3-pound pot roast	2 cloves garlic, minced
2 teaspoons salt	¼ cup lemon juice
¼ teaspoon pepper	¼ cup vinegar
3 tablespoons shortening	2 tablespoon brown sugar
1 8-oz. can tomato sauce	2 tablespoons flour
½ cup water	1 tablespoon Worcestershire sauce
3 medium onions, sliced	½ teaspoon dry mustard

Rub meat with salt and pepper. Brown in hot shortening. Add tomato sauce, water, onions and garlic. Cook, covered, over low heat for 1½ hours. Combine remaining ingredients; pour over meat. Cover and cook for 1 hour, or until tender. Serves 4 to 6.   *Lucille Yellen*

BRISKET OF BEEF

1 5-pound brisket of beef	Paprika
1 medium onion	1 bay leaf
1 small clove garlic, cut into pieces	

Place brisket in Dutch oven with onion and garlic. Sprinkle generously with paprika; add bay leaf. Cover. Bake at 325° for 1 hour. Baste with pan drippings; cover and bake for 1 hour. Uncover and bake for ½ to 1 hour longer, or until meat is tender. Makes 6 to 8 servings.   *Frieda Deutsch*

OLD-FASHIONED PRUNE TZIMMES

4 pounds beef brisket	½ cup granulated sugar
4 large potatoes, peeled	½ lemon, sliced (or sour salt)
1 pound large prunes	4 ginger snaps
½ teaspoon cinnamon	1 cup thin white sauce
½ teaspoon paprika	

Place brisket in pot with enough water to cover; cook until soft. Add potatoes, prunes, cinnamon and paprika. Cook for 5 minutes. Add sugar, lemon slices and ginger snaps. Cook until meat is tender and potatoes are done. Add thin white sauce. Bake at 350° for 15 minutes. Serves 8 to 10.

Mrs. William Schero

CARROT TZIMMES

	KNAIDLE:
2 pounds carrots, coarsely grated	1 cup sifted flour
1 pound shortribs or brisket	1 tablespoon granulated sugar
3 sweet potatoes, pared and quartered	½ teaspoon baking powder
½ cup honey	⅛ teaspoon salt
¼ cup brown sugar	2 tablespoons shortening
Salt and pepper	3 tablespoons water

Combine carrots, shortribs, potatoes, honey, brown sugar, salt and pepper to taste with enough water to cover in large heavy saucepan. Simmer for 1 to 1½ hours, or until carrots and potatoes are almost tender and water is absorbed. Meanwhile, sift together flour, sugar, baking powder and salt. Cut in shortening; add water, stirring, until soft dough is formed. Shape into a ball. About 40 minutes before end of cooking period, tuck knaidle (dumpling) into center of tzimmes close to meat. Cover pan and continue cooking until dumpling has expanded. Place in casserole. Bake at 350° for 30 minutes, or until thick and browned. Serves 6. *Florence Collen*

BRISKET OF BEEF WITH HORSE-RADISH SAUCE

2 pounds brisket of beef, all fat removed

2 onions

2 carrots

2 stalks celery

1 bay leaf

Salt and pepper to taste

HORSE-RADISH SAUCE:

¼ cup grated fresh horse-radish

1 small onion, finely chopped

1 bay leaf

1 clove

5 grains non-caloric sweetener, crushed

1 tablespoon wine vinegar

Salt and pepper to taste

1 teaspoon chopped fresh parsley

Cover brisket with boiling water. Add onions, carrots, celery, 1 bay leaf, salt and pepper. Bring to boiling and simmer for 4 hours, adding boiling water as necessary to keep meat covered. Meanwhile, combine horse-radish, chopped onion, 1 bay leaf, clove, sweetener, vinegar, salt and pepper. Cook for 10 minutes. Sprinkle with parsley. Drain meat; discard vegetables. Cut meat in thin slices and serve with *hot* horse-radish sauce. Serves 4.

If gravy will not brown without scorching, and no bottled gravy sauce is at hand, add a little coffee (it will not affect the flavor).

GINGER SNAP BEEF

2 tablespoons flour

1½ teaspoons salt

⅓ teaspoon pepper

3 pounds beef brisket, rump, round or sirloin

1 onion, thinly sliced

2 cups water

¾ cup vinegar

2 tablespoons catchup

3 bay leaves

3 cloves

1 cup raisins

10 ginger snaps

Combine flour, salt and pepper. Rub into meat. Brown meat and onions in small amount of shortening in saucepan. Add water, vinegar, catchup, bay leaves, cloves and raisins. Cover. Simmer for 2 hours. Dissolve ginger snaps in lukewarm water. Add to meat and cook 30 minutes longer, stirring occasionally. (*Do not scorch.*) Serves 6.   *Florence Collen*

BARBECUED SHORTRIBS

16 beef shortribs or flanken (very lean)   1 large bottle prepared barbecue sauce

Trim ribs well. Place on rack in roasting pan. Bake at 325° for 1 hour. Baste thoroughly with sauce. Bake 15 minutes longer. Turn ribs and repeat basting. Continue to bake until ribs are very tender (total baking time: 2 hours). Just before serving, place under broiler for 2 minutes until crisp. Makes 6 servings.   *Helen Galnik*

BAKED SHORTRIBS

4 pounds shortribs	1 teaspoon pepper
½ cup dry red wine	½ teaspoon granulated sugar
¼ cup olive oil	½ teaspoon brown sugar (optional)
½ cup catchup (optional)	½ teaspoon chili powder
1 tablespoon lemon juice	1 clove garlic, mashed
2 tablespoons dry mustard	2 onions, cut into thick slices
1 tablespoon salt	

Place ribs in large bowl. Combine wine, oil, catchup, lemon juice, mustard, salt, pepper, sugars, chili powder and garlic. Pour over ribs. Marinate in refrigerator for several hours. Place ribs in one layer in large baking dish. Bake at 475° for 15 minutes. Reduce oven temperature to 350° and add marinade. Top with onions. Cover and bake 1 hour. Bake uncovered last 15 to 20 minutes. Serves 3 or 4.   *Lorraine Pohn*

HAWAIIAN BAKED SHORTRIBS

3 pounds shortribs	½ cup catchup
3 tablespoons brown sugar	¼ cup vinegar
3 tablespoons cornstarch	1 tablespoon soy sauce
2 8-oz. cans tomato sauce	1 teaspoon salt
1 9-oz. can crushed pineapple	

Broil shortribs until brown. Mix together brown sugar and cornstarch. Add tomato sauce, pineapple, catchup, vinegar, soy sauce and salt. Cook, stirring frequently, until thick. Place layer of shortribs in 2-quart casserole and cover with sauce. Repeat until all ribs are used. Cover tightly. Bake at 350° for 1½ hours. Serves 4.   *Jean Kowitt*

SHORTRIBS AND BEAN CASSEROLE

2 cups uncooked navy beans

2 to 2½ pounds shortribs

1 medium onion

½ cup molasses

⅓ cup catchup

¼ cup brown sugar

1 tablespoon Worcestershire sauce

1 tablespoon dry mustard

2 teaspoons salt

Soak navy beans overnight in water to cover. Drain dry. Place shortribs in Dutch oven; add onion. Combine molasses, catchup, brown sugar, Worcestershire sauce, mustard and salt; blend well. Pour beans over meat in Dutch oven. Pour over molasses mixture; cover with water to about ¼ inch above top of beans. Cover. Bake at 300° for 6 to 7 hours, or until liquid is absorbed. Makes 6 generous servings.   *Ida Goldberg*

CHOLNT (Baked Beans and Beef)

2 pounds neck meat, chuck, shortribs or flanken, cut into small pieces

2 pounds uncooked large navy beans

1 cup Scotch barley

1 medium onion

1 carrot

1 8-oz. can tomato sauce

2 tablespoons chicken fat (if meat is lean)

2 tablespoons paprika

1 tablespoon salt

1 teaspoon pepper

Combine meat, beans and barley with enough water to cover; bring to boil. Add onion, carrot, tomato sauce, fat, paprika, salt and pepper. Simmer for 30 to 45 minutes. Cover. Bake at 375° for 2 to 2½ hours. After 1½ hours, if liquid has cooked down, add water and continue baking. Test beans for tenderness. Turn off oven and add more water. Keep warm in oven until ready to serve. Can be reheated and served again. Serves 8.   *Pearl Sherman*

BARBECUED BEEF (from leftover beef)

1½ cups beef stock, gravy or water

1 8-oz. can tomato sauce

½ bottle catchup

½ cup firmly packed brown sugar

1 teaspoon lemon juice

1 teaspoon dry mustard

2 bay leaves

Few drops Worcestershire sauce

Leftover beef, thinly sliced

Combine all ingredients except beef, simmer for 15 minutes. Add leftover brisket or roast beef. Serves 6. *Edith Karasik*

QUICK PEPPER STEAK (from leftover beef)

¾ cup chopped onion

2 tablespoons salad oil

2 small green peppers, cut into long thin strips

2 pounds (4 cups) leftover cooked beef, cut into long thin strips

2 to 3 tablespoons soy sauce

¼ cup water

1 can small white potatoes, drained

Sauté onions in hot oil. Add green peppers and cook for 3 minutes more. Add beef, soy sauce and water; simmer for 5 minutes. Add potatoes and simmer for 10 minutes. Serves 6. *Lorry Silverman*

GROUND BEEF

SALISBURY STEAK

1¾ pounds finely ground lean beef

2 tablespoons grated onion

2 tablespoons minced green pepper

1½ tablespoons snipped chives

1 tablespoon snipped parsley

1 clove garlic, mashed

Salt and pepper to taste

1 tablespoon salad oil

SAUCE:

⅓ cup catchup

2 tablespoons sherry

1 tablespoon lemon juice

1 teaspoon Worcestershire sauce

1 teaspoon prepared mustard

Few drops Tabasco sauce

Salt and pepper

Mix together meat, onion, green pepper, chives, parsley, garlic, salt and pepper. Shape mixture into 6 patties; sprinkle with a little flour and brush with oil. Broil 3 inches from heat for 4 to 6 minutes on each side, depending on desired doneness. Meanwhile, combine ingredients for sauce. Bring almost to boiling. When patties are done, pour sauce over them and serve immediately. Serves 6. *Dee Stein*

CARNATZLACH (Rumanian Broiled Hamburgers)

1½ pounds ground beef	2 teaspoons poultry seasoning
1 onion, grated	1 teaspoon salt
1 carrot, grated	⅛ teaspoon pepper
1 clove garlic, minced	3 tablespoons flour
2 eggs, slightly beaten	¼ teaspoon paprika

Combine all ingredients except flour and paprika. Mix well. Shape into rolls ¾ inch in diameter, 2 to 3 inches long and tapered at each end. Roll in flour seasoned with paprika. Broil 3 inches from heat for 8 to 12 minutes, turning to brown all sides. Serves 6.   *Libbie R. Frost*

SUPREME MEAT BALLS

1 8-oz. jar grape jelly	1 egg
1 bottle chili sauce	½ cup crushed corn flakes
½ cup water	Pinch salt
2 tablespoons lemon juice	⅛ teaspoon pepper
2 pounds ground beef	

Combine jelly, chili sauce, water and lemon juice. Simmer for 1 hour, or until thick. Mix together beef, egg, corn flakes, salt and pepper. Shape into small balls; add to sauce and cook 30 minutes longer. Serve in chafing dish. Makes 6 servings.   *Mrs. Jack Frost*

QUICK SPANISH MEAT BALLS

1 pound ground round steak	1 No. 1 can stewed tomatoes
1 8-oz. can Spanish rice	1 6-oz. can tomato paste
1 8-oz. can tomato sauce	1 cup water

Mix together meat and Spanish rice; shape into walnut-size balls. Mix together tomato sauce, stewed tomatoes, tomato paste and water in saucepan. Bring to boiling; drop in meat balls. Reduce heat and simmer for 45 minutes. Serve over white rice. Makes 6 servings.   *Gerry Freedman*

MEAT BALLS IN GINGER SNAP SAUCE

1½ pounds ground beef

1 egg

3 tablespoons brown sugar

2 tablespoons vinegar

1 medium onion, grated

1 hard roll or 2 slices bread, soaked in water

Salt and pepper

1 onion, diced

1 clove garlic

SAUCE:

1 8-oz. can tomato sauce

1 cup water

½ cup firmly packed brown sugar

Scant ½ cup vinegar

¼ cup catchup

6 ginger snaps

Mix together beef, egg, 3 tablespoons brown sugar, 2 tablespoons vinegar, grated onion, soaked roll, salt and pepper. Shape into small balls. Sauté diced onion and garlic in small amount of shortening. Add meat balls and brown, turning frequently. Mix together tomato sauce, water, ½ cup brown sugar, scant ½ cup vinegar and catchup. Add meat balls and simmer for 1½ hours. Add ginger snaps; cook for 30 minutes longer. Makes 6 servings.

Rose Gontovnick

SWEET-AND-SOUR CABBAGE ROLLS

1 pound ground beef

¼ cup uncooked rice

1 egg

Salt and pepper

1 head cabbage

Sliced onions

1 cup dark corn syrup

Water

Sour salt to taste

1 tablespoon mixed pickling spices

6 to 8 ginger snaps

Mix together beef, rice, egg, salt and pepper. Separate cabbage leaves by pouring boiling water over head. Fill cabbage leaves with meat mixture and roll up; secure with wooden picks. Cover bottom of deep pot with sliced onions; place cabbage rolls in pot. Pour corn syrup mixed with enough water to cover over rolls. Sprinkle with sour salt. Tie pickling spices in small cheesecloth bag; add to pot. Bring syrup to boil; simmer until cabbage rolls are tender. Remove rolls and set aside. Discard spice bag. Place ginger snaps in bowl with just enough water to make a paste. Bring gravy in pot to boiling; add ginger paste slowly, stirring constantly, until gravy is thickened. Return rolls to pot and heat thoroughly, turning them over and over to coat thoroughly with gravy. (Remove wooden picks before serving.) Serves 6 to 8.

Gert Horwitz

STUFFED GREEN PEPPERS

1½ pounds ground beef

⅓ cup uncooked rice

Salt and pepper

1 onion, chopped

4 green peppers, tops removed

1 8-oz. can tomato sauce

2 tablespoons brown sugar

Mix beef with rice; season to taste with salt and pepper; add onion. Wash and seed green peppers; stuff with meat mixture. Bring 1 inch salted water to boiling in Dutch oven. Arrange stuffed peppers in Dutch oven carefully (any remaining meat mixture may be shaped into balls and cooked with peppers). Cover. Cook over medium heat for 1 hour. Combine tomato sauce with brown sugar. Pour over peppers and simmer for 30 minutes longer. Serves 4.   *Marge Singer*

QUICK CHILI

1 small onion, chopped

1 small green pepper, chopped

2 tablespoons shortening

1 6-oz. can mushrooms

1 pound ground beef

1 No. 2 can dark red kidney beans

1 8-oz. can tomato sauce

Sauté onion and green pepper in hot shortening. Add mushrooms and beef; brown. Drain liquid from beans, reserving ⅓ cup. Add reserved liquid to meat with tomato sauce and beans; simmer 10 minutes. Serves 4.
Mildred Coleman

MEATZZA PIE

1 pound ground beef

⅔ cup evaporated milk

¼ cup fine dry bread crumbs

1 teaspoon garlic salt

⅓ cup catchup or tomato paste

1 2-oz. can sliced mushrooms

1 cup shredded Cheddar or Mozzarella cheese

¼ teaspoon finely crushed orégano

2 tablespoons grated Parmesan cheese

Mix meat, milk, crumbs and garlic salt together well. Pat mixture evenly into bottom and sides of 9-inch pie plate. Spread catchup evenly over top; cover with mushrooms. Sprinkle with shredded cheese, then with orégano. Top with grated cheese. Bake at 450° for 20 minutes. Wrain off any excess grease. Cut into wedges. Serves 4.

ONIONBURGER PIE

1 pound ground beef

1 egg

1 onion, finely chopped

½ cup dry bread crumbs

¼ cup tomato juice

1½ teaspoon salt

½ teaspoon monosodium glutamate

¼ teaspoon pepper

¼ cup chili sauce

FILLING:

2 cups thinly sliced onions

¼ cup shortening

½ teaspoon salt

¼ teaspoon paprika

¼ teaspoon pepper

Mix meat and egg. Add chopped onion, crumbs, tomato juice, 1½ teaspoons salt, monosodium glutamate and ¼ teaspoon pepper. Divide mixture into 2 parts. Pat one part into 10-inch pie plate to about ½-inch thickness. Sauté sliced onions in hot shortening for several minutes. Add ½ teaspoon salt, paprika and ¼ teaspoon pepper. Cover and steam for about 8 minutes. Cool. Place onion mixture on meat in pie plate, leaving ½-inch rim of meat around edge. Shape remaining meat into flat patty; place on onion mixture. Seal to bottom meat layer. Spread chili sauce over top. Bake on lower oven rack at 450° for 15 to 18 minutes. Place under broiler for last 2 or 3 minutes, if desired. Cut into wedges. Serves 4 to 6. *Debby Hayden*

Have beef for meat loaf ground twice for a more compact loaf—which makes for easier, neater slicing.

DUTCH MEAT LOAF

2 pounds ground beef

1 large onion, grated

1 cup crisp rice cereal, crushed

1 egg, beaten

1 8-oz. can tomato sauce

SAUCE:

1 8-oz. can tomato sauce

3 to 4 tablespoons brown sugar

1 tablespoon vinegar

1 tablespoon prepared mustard

Salt and pepper

Mix beef and onion together; add rice cereal. Add egg and tomato sauce. Mix gently. Shape into loaf and place in 9x5x3-inch pan. Combine all ingredients for sauce. Mix and pour on top of loaf. Bake at 325° for 1½ hours. Makes 6 to 8 servings. *Dorothy Grafman*

PIQUANT MEAT LOAF

⅔ cup dry bread crumbs

1 cup water or stock

1½ pounds ground beef

2 eggs, beaten

¼ cup grated onion

1 teaspoon salt

⅛ teaspoon pepper

⅛ teaspoon sage

PIQUANT SAUCE:

½ cup catchup

3 tablespoons brown sugar

1 teaspoon dry mustard

¼ teaspoon nutmeg

Soak bread crumbs in water; add beef, eggs, onion, salt, pepper and sage. Mix well. Shape into loaf; place in 9x5x3-inch pan. Combine ingredients for sauce; spread over loaf. Bake at 350° for 1 hour. Serves 4 to 6.   *Rose Mazer*

BEEF AND NOODLES

1 pound ground beef

2 8-oz. cans tomato sauce

1 8-oz. package noodles, cooked

1 cup creamed cottage cheese

¼ cup sour cream

⅓ cup chopped green onions

½ green pepper, chopped

¼ cup melted butter

Brown beef in skillet in small amount of shortening. Pour off any excess grease. Add tomato sauce. Mix well and remove from heat. Place half of noodles in greased 2-quart casserole. Combine cottage cheese, sour cream, onions and green pepper. Pour over noodles. Add remaining noodles and melted butter. Top with beef and tomato mixture. Bake at 350° for 30 minutes. Serves 6.

BALI BEEF CASSEROLE

1½ pounds ground beef

1½ cups cooked rice

1 No. 303 can tomatoes

½ cup finely chopped onion

2 teaspoons Worcestershire sauce

1½ teaspoons salt

1 teaspoon curry powder

1 clove garlic, minced

Cook beef until lightly browned. Pour off any excess grease. Combine beef with other ingredients and turn into 2-quart casserole. Cover. Bake at 350° for 30 minutes. Makes 6 to 8 servings.

MEAT LOAF À LA CHEESEBURGER

1½ pounds ground beef

1 small can evaporated milk

½ cup bread crumbs

½ green pepper, diced

1 egg

Grated onion

Salt and pepper

¼ pound Cheddar cheese, grated

2 teaspoons chili sauce

Mix together beef, milk, crumbs, green pepper, egg, onion and salt and pepper. Place half of meat mixture in 9x5x3-inch pan. Combine cheese and chili sauce. Spread over meat mixture in pan; top with remaining meat. Bake at 350° for 1 hour. Just before serving, sprinkle with additional cheese; return to oven, or place under broiler, until cheese melts. Makes 6 servings.

Francine Isaacson

BEEF MEXICANA

1 pound ground beef

¼ cup shortening

¼ cup chopped onion

¼ cup chopped green pepper

1 can tomato soup

1 cup milk or water

3 cups cooked medium noodles

2 cups whole-kernel corn

1 cup grated Cheddar cheese

Salt and pepper

Garlic and chili powders

Brown beef in hot shortening; add onion and green pepper; cook until tender. Add soup, milk, noodles, corn and cheese. Season to taste. Pour into greased 2-quart casserole. Bake at 350° for about 30 minutes. Makes 6 servings.

Isabelle Dinitz

SLOPPY JOE'S CHILI

1 large onion, diced

1 green pepper, diced

1 cup chopped celery

4 tablespoons shortening

3 pounds ground beef

1 bottle catchup

1 bottle chili sauce

Hamburger buns

Sauté onion, green pepper and celery in hot shortening. Add meat; cook until all pink color has disappeared. Add catchup and chili sauce. Simmer for 30 minutes. Spoon off excess grease. Serve on hamburger buns. Makes 16 to 18 servings.

Helen Ettinger

MEAT KNISHES

2 cups sifted flour	½ cup minced onion
1 cup shortening	2 tablespoons shortening or chicken fat
½ cup flour	2 cups ground cooked meat
3 egg yolks	½ cup mashed potatoes
3 tablespoons vinegar or lemon juice	1 egg, beaten
3 tablespoons water	½ teaspoon salt
1 teaspoon salt	¼ teaspoon pepper

Cut 1 cup shortening into 2 cups flour with pastry blender or 2 knives. Combine ½ cup flour, egg yolks, vinegar, water and 1 teaspoon salt; beat slightly. Add to flour mixture; stir with fork until just blended. Shape dough into a ball; set aside. Sauté onion in 2 tablespoons hot shortening for about 5 minutes. Combine with meat, potatoes, egg, ½ teaspoon salt and pepper. Divide dough into 3 parts. Roll out each part to ¼-inch thickness; cut into 2-inch squares. Place teaspoonful of meat mixture in center of each square. Fold sides together and pinch to seal. Repeat until all dough and filling are used. Place squares on greased baking sheet. Bake at 350° for 20 to 25 minutes, or until lightly browned. Makes 6 to 8 servings.　　*Judy Goldberg*

VEAL

QUICK VEAL PARMESAN

¼ cup flour	¼ cup grated Parmesan cheese
1 teaspoon salt	1 egg, beaten
½ teaspoon garlic salt	2 tablespoons olive or salad oil
½ teaspoon paprika	4 thin slices Mozzarella cheese
Dash pepper	1 can small white potatoes
4 loin veal chops, cut ¾ inch thick	1 8-oz. can tomato sauce
½ cup fine dry bread crumbs	1 teaspoon orégano

Combine flour, salts, paprika and pepper. Coat chops with seasoned flour. Mix crumbs with Parmesan cheese. Dip chops in egg, then in crumb mixture. Brown slowly in hot oil. Place 1 slice Mozzarella cheese on each chop; arrange potatoes around meat. Pour tomato sauce over top; sprinkle with orégano. Cover and simmer for 50 minutes, or until meat is tender. Makes 4 servings.　　*Janice Tatz*

STUFFED VEAL

1 3 to 4-pound veal breast (breast bone removed)

½ cup chopped onion

¼ cup shortening

1½ cups toasted bread cubes (about 4 slices)

1 package frozen mixed vegetables, cooked

¼ teaspoon salt

¼ teaspoon celery seed

Dash pepper

1 cut clove garlic

Salt and pepper

Have meatman remove breast bone and cut pocket between ribs and meat of veal breast. Sauté onion in hot shortening until soft. Add toasted bread cubes; toss well. Add drained, cooked vegetables, salt, celery seed and pepper. Fill pocket in veal breast with bread-vegetable mixture; secure with skewers. Rub top of stuffed veal breast with garlic and season with salt and pepper. Place on rack in roasting pan. Bake at 325° for 30 to 35 minutes per pound. Makes 6 servings. *Debby Hayden*

BROILED VEAL CHOP DINNER

¼ cup catchup

4 tablespoons salad oil

3 tablespoons soy sauce

1 tablespoon vinegar

1 tablespoon sugar

¼ teaspoon pepper

1 small clove garlic, mashed

4 loin veal chops, cut 1 inch thick

2 cups peas

3 large cooked potatoes, cut into ¼-inch slices

¼ cup melted butter

Salt and pepper

Caraway seeds (optional)

Combine catchup, oil, soy sauce, vinegar, sugar, ¼ teaspoon pepper and garlic in bowl. Beat with fork until well blended. Curl ends of chops and fasten with skewers. Arrange chops in shallow baking dish; pour marinade over top. Cover and chill in refrigerator for several hours; turn occasionally. About 20 minutes before serving, put peas in bottom of broiler pan. Sprinkle with half of melted butter, salt and pepper. Grease broiler rack; arrange chops on rack; brush with some of marinade. Broil 3 inches from heat for 10 to 12 minutes. Turn chops; brush with marinade. Place sliced, cooked potatoes on rack with meat; brush with remaining melted butter; sprinkle with salt and pepper to taste, and caraway seeds, if desired. Broil for 5 to 6 minutes, or until meat is tender and potatoes lightly browned. Makes 4 servings. *Marilyn Eager*

VEAL PAPRIKA

1½ pounds boneless veal, cut into 1-inch cubes

¼ cup flour

1 teaspoon salt

Dash pepper

¼ cup chopped onion

1 teaspoon paprika

½ cup shortening

2 medium tomatoes, cut into small pieces

½ cup hot water

½ cup sour cream

Combine flour, salt and pepper. Coat veal with seasoned flour. Sauté veal, onion and paprika in hot shortening until meat is well browned; stir frequently. Combine tomatoes with hot water; force through sieve. Add to meat; cover and simmer for 1½ hours, or until meat is tender. Add sour cream; simmer for 15 minutes longer. Add more paprika to taste. Serves 6.

Mrs. Herman Shaffer

EASY VEAL SCALLOPINI

1 small clove garlic

2 tablespoons shortening

1 pound thinly sliced veal steak, cut into squares

1 tablespoon flour

1 teaspoon salt

⅛ teaspoon pepper

1 small onion, thinly sliced

½ cup tomato juice or pureé

¼ cup sauterne wine

½ pound fresh mushrooms, sliced

1 tablespoon butter

3 tablespoons sliced stuffed green olives

Sauté garlic in hot shortening for about 5 minutes. Remove garlic and discard. In same skillet, brown meat on both sides. Sprinkle with flour, salt and pepper; add onion, tomato juice and wine. Cover and simmer for about 20 minutes, turning meat several times. Sauté mushrooms in hot butter. When meat is tender, add mushrooms and olives. Cover and cook for about 8 minutes. Makes 4 servings.

Arlene Munvez

VEAL AND TOMATOES

½ pound whole green beans

½ pound fresh mushrooms

2 onions

2 pounds lean boneless veal

1 No. 2 can plum tomatoes

½ teaspoon basil

Salt and pepper

Cook beans in salted water to cover until tender. Cool and shred. Clean mushrooms; slice thin. Cover with water and cook until soft. Drain. Slice onions; separate into rings. Cut veal into 2x½-inch strips. Brown under broiler on both sides. Mix beans, mushrooms and onion rings with tomatoes. Add basil, salt and pepper. Simmer over low heat until onions are soft. Add browned meat. Cook several minutes longer. Makes 4 servings.

VEAL SCALLOPINI

1½ pounds lean veal, sliced very thin

1 cup butter

SAUCE:

8 medium fresh mushrooms, sliced

½ large cucumber, peeled, cored and diced

½ cup Madiera wine

4 tablespoons chives, snipped fine

4 tablespoons shallots or onions, finely chopped

2 cloves garlic, crushed

1 tablespoon butter

Salt and pepper

Cut veal into 16 strips. Sauté in 1 cup hot butter in skillet, browning on both sides. Remove to serving dish and keep warm while preparing sauce. In same skillet sauté mushrooms. Add cucumber and cook for 1 minute. Add wine and cook until mixture is reduced to half. Remove skillet from heat; add chives, shallots and garlic which has been mixed with 1 tablespoon butter. Salt and pepper to taste. Pour sauce over meat and serve immediately. Makes 4 servings.   *Isabelle Dinitz*

 LAMB

GLORIFIED LAMB CHOPS

6 shoulder lamb chops

2 tablespoons shortening

2 cups chopped celery

½ green pepper, finely chopped

1 No. 2 can tomatoes

2 teaspoons Worcestershire sauce

½ teaspoon salt

Brown chops on both sides in hot shortening; remove from skillet. Sauté celery and green pepper in same skillet; add tomatoes, Worcestershire sauce and salt. Return chops to skillet; cover and cook slowly for 30 minutes, or until chops are tender. Remove chops to serving dish and serve with sauce. Serves 6.   *Alice B. Weitzenfeld*

LEG OF LAMB

1 leg of lamb (¼ to ½ lb. per serving)	Salt
1 cut clove of garlic	Paprika
Juice of ½ lemon	1 cup water
Flour	1 teaspoon soy sauce

Rub lamb with garlic; sprinkle with lemon juice, flour, salt and paprika. Roast at 500° for 30 minutes. Reduce oven temperature to 325°. Combine water and soy sauce; pour over lamb. Roast uncovered for 30 to 35 minutes per pound. (Total roasting time should include first 30 minutes at 500°.) Baste with sauce as necessary.   *Jeanne Berkowitz*

BROILED STUFFED LAMB CHOPS

¼ pound fresh mushrooms	Dash pepper
¼ pound chicken livers	2 tablespoons butter
2 tablespoons minced green onions	6 thick (double) loin lamb chops, slit
¼ teaspoon salt	

Reserve 6 large mushroom caps; chop remainder. Sauté chopped mushrooms, livers and onions in hot butter for 10 minutes. Season with salt and pepper. Chop fine and cool. Stuff lamb chops. Place chops on broiler rack and broil 3 inches from heat for 9 to 11 minutes on each side, depending on doneness desired. Season to taste with salt and pepper. About 3 minutes before chops are done, place mushroom cap on each chop, brush with drippings; finish broiling. Serves 6.   *Lee Bateman*

LAMB KAPAMA (Lamb with Tomato Sauce)

1 2½-pound lamb steak	Juice of 1 lemon
Salt and pepper	¼ cup butter
¼ teaspoon cinnamon	1 No. 2 can tomatoes

Cut lamb into serving-size pieces; season with salt and pepper. Sprinkle with cinnamon and lemon juice. Allow to stand a few minutes; drain, reserving juice. Brown meat in hot butter. Remove meat from pan; add tomatoes and bring to boiling; simmer for 5 minutes. Add meat and reserved juice. Cook slowly for 2 hours, adding hot water as needed. Serve with macaroni, rice or potatoes. Makes 4 or 5 servings.   *Lois Polales*

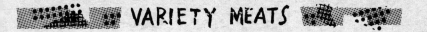

VARIETY MEATS

LIVER AND ONIONS WITH RED WINE SAUCE

6 slices calves liver	Seasoned flour
Red wine	1 tablespoon flour
3 medium onions, sliced	Pinch of orégano
6 tablespoons olive oil	Salt and pepper

Place liver on pie plate; cover with wine. Chill in refrigerator for 1 hour. Brown onions lightly in 4 tablespoons hot oil; remove. Drain wine from liver; set aside. Dust liver with seasoned flour. Add remaining 2 tablespoons oil to skillet used for browning onions; brown liver quickly (3 to 4 minutes on each side). Place liver on heated serving dish and cover with onions. Add flour and orégano to skillet; stir until smooth. Slowly add reserved wine and cook, stirring constantly, until sauce is smooth and thickened. Add salt and pepper to taste; pour over liver and onions. Makes 4 to 6 servings.

Dee Stein

SPANISH TONGUE

1 large pickled tongue	2 tablespoons shortening
3 medium onions, chopped	1 large can mushrooms, drained
2 small stalks celery, chopped	2 cans tomato soup
1 large green pepper, chopped	2 No. 2 cans peas

Cook tongue until tender. Peel and dice. Sauté onions, celery and green pepper in hot shortening. Cover and cook for 10 minutes until tender and clear. Add diced tongue, mushrooms, tomato soup and peas. Serve in patty shells, if desired. Makes 8 servings. *Mrs. Phillip Mitchell*

BARBECUED BOLOGNA ROLL

6 pounds bologna, in one piece	½ bottle catchup
1 7-oz. bottle barbecue sauce	½ bottle chili sauce

Skin bologna and score. Place in roatsing pan. Combine barbecue sauce, catchup and chili sauce; pour over bologna. Bake at 350° for 45 minutes, basting often with sauce. When ready to serve, place under broiler for 2 minutes. Serve cut into thick slices. Serves 15 to 18. *Mrs. Jack Frost*

MEAT SAUCES

ITALIAN SPAGHETTI SAUCE

1½ pounds ground beef

1 large or 2 medium onions, cut into pieces

1 clove garlic, minced

1 8-oz. can mushrooms, drained

1 No. 2½ can plum tomatoes

2 6-oz. cans tomato paste

2 paste cans water

3 bay leaves

6 chili peppers

2 tablespoons brown sugar

Salt and pepper

Brown beef, onions, garlic and mushrooms in large skillet. Combine remaining ingredients in large saucepan or kettle. Add meat mixture; cook over low heat for about 4 hours. Serve over spaghetti. Serves 8. *Shirley Goldberg*

SAUCE FOR FRANKFURTERS

1 pound ground beef

2 onions, minced

2 green peppers, chopped

1 clove garlic, minced

2 tablespoons salad oil

1 cup barbecue, chili or tomato sauce

½ teaspoon Tabasco sauce

½ teaspoon cayenne pepper

Sauté beef, onions, green peppers and garlic in hot oil until lightly browned. Add remaining ingredients; cook until thoroughly heated.

Marian D. Horwitz

QUICK BARBECUE SAUCE

1 cup catchup

1 cup water

2 tablespoons soft butter

1 tablespoon vinegar

1½ teaspoons prepared mustard

1 teaspoon Worcestershire sauce

Juice of 1 lemon

Salt and pepper to taste

Blend all ingredients together well.

Elizabeth Diamond

BARBECUE SAUCE FOR BEEF

1 onion, diced	¼ cup lemon juice
½ cup chopped celery	2 tablespoons vinegar
2 tablespoons shortening or salad oil	2 tablespoons brown sugar
Salt and pepper	1 teaspoon Worcestershire sauce
½ cup catchup	1 teaspoon prepared mustard
½ cup chili sauce	¼ teaspoon chili powder
½ cup water	

Sauté onion and celery in hot shortening. Add salt and pepper to taste. Add remaining ingredients; bring to boiling. Reduce heat and simmer for 20 minutes. *Charlene Lieberman*

EASY SPAGHETTI SAUCE

1 pound ground beef	1 cup water
1 package spaghetti sauce mix	1 6-oz. can tomato paste
1 8-oz. can tomato sauce	1 paste can water

Brown meat in small amount of hot shortening. Add remaining ingredients. Mix well; simmer for 1 hour. Serve over spaghetti. Serves 6. *Estelle Wolf*

SWEET-AND-SOUR SAUCE

2 tablespoons cornstarch	1 tablespoon Worcestershire sauce
¼ cup cold water	1 teaspoon mustard
½ cup wine vinegar	1 green pepper, chopped
½ cup sherry	1 tomato, cut into pieces
½ cup water	1 9-oz. can pineapple slices, drained
1 cup firmly packed brown sugar	1 cup canned, pitted dark sour cherries, drained
4 tablespoons chili sauce	

Combine cornstarch and cold water; mix until smooth. Add vinegar, sherry, water, brown sugar, chili sauce, Worcestershire sauce and mustard. Cook until thoroughly heated. Add green pepper, tomato, pineapple and cherries; cook only until thickened (about 1 to 2 minutes longer). *Do not overcook.* Serve with meat or poultry. *Belle D. Guralnik*

POULTRY DISHES AND STUFFINGS

...I hope to make France so prosperous that every peasant will have a chicken in his pot on Sunday.

Henry IV of France (1553-1610)

CHICKEN

CHICKEN MARENGO

1 2½ to 3-lb. ready-to-cook broiler-fryer, cut up

2 tablespoons butter or salad oil

2 medium onions, finely chopped

1 tablespoon flour

½ cup chicken broth or consommé

¼ cup dry white wine

3 tablespoons tomato paste

1 clove garlic, minced

½ teaspoon salt

¼ teaspoon thyme

Dash pepper

1 bay leaf

½ pound mushrooms, sliced

1 tablespoon finely chopped parsley

Sauté chicken in hot butter in heavy skillet until golden brown on all sides. Add onions; cook, stirring, until onions are transparent. Sprinkle with flour and cook, stirring constantly, for 3 minutes. Add broth, wine, tomato paste, garlic, salt, thyme, pepper and bay leaf. Bring to boiling; cover and simmer for 30 to 35 minutes, or until chicken is almost tender. Add mushrooms; cover and cook for 10 to 15 minutes longer. Remove chicken pieces to warm serving platter; pour sauce over top. Serves 4.   *Esther Madian*

CHICKEN CACCIATORE

1 4 to 5-lb. roasting chicken, cut up	1 No. 303 can stewed tomatoes
½ cup flour	½ cup chopped green pepper
1 tablespoon salt	½ cup chopped onion
1 teaspoon paprika	½ cup chopped celery
½ teaspoon thyme or orégano	1 clove garlic, mashed
¼ teaspoon pepper	1 teaspoon Worcestershire sauce
¼ cup chicken fat	Grated Parmesan cheese
1 4-oz. can mushrooms (stems and pieces)	

Combine flour, salt, paprika, thyme and pepper; coat chicken pieces well with flour mixture. Melt fat in large skillet or Dutch oven; brown chicken pieces well. Drain mushrooms, reserving liquid. Combine tomatoes, green pepper, onion, celery, garlic, Worcestershire sauce and mushroom liquid. Heat for 5 minutes. Pour over chicken in skillet. Cover and simmer for about 2 hours, or until chicken is fork tender. Baste chicken with sauce several times during cooking period. Remove chicken to serving platter. Stir mushrooms into sauce; heat and pour over chicken. Serve with spaghetti or noodles. Makes 6 servings. *Elaine Thomas*

HUNTER-STYLE CHICKEN

1 4-lb. roasting chicken, cut up	Salt to taste
2 cups tomatoes, fresh or canned	12 small whole onions
1 clove garlic, minced	4 carrots, cut up
1 cup dry white wine or water	8 stalks celery, cut into 1½-inch pieces
6 peppercorns, crushed	12 mushroom caps
1 bay leaf	Curry powder, chili powder or Worcestershire sauce (optional)
½ teaspoon marjoram or orégano	
Pinch thyme	

Set aside neck, wings and giblets for soup. Place remaining chicken pieces in large saucepot or kettle having a tight-fitting cover. Add tomatoes, garlic, wine, peppercorns, bay leaf, marjoram, thyme and salt. Simmer, covered, until chicken is almost tender, or about 1½ hours. Remove from heat; let stand for 10 minutes. Skim as necessary. Add onions, carrots, and celery. Bring to boiling; simmer for 15 minutes. Add mushrooms and curry powder, if desired, and simmer for 15 minutes longer, or until chicken and vegetables are tender. Makes 4 to 6 servings. *Dee Stein*

SPICED CHICKEN

1 cup orange juice

1½ cups sliced canned peaches

2 tablespoons brown sugar

2 tablespoons vinegar

1 teaspoon mace or nutmeg

1 teaspoon basil

1 clove garlic, minced

1 3-lb. ready-to-cook frying chicken, cut up

½ cup flour

1 teaspoon salt

⅛ teaspoon pepper

Combine orange juice, peaches, brown sugar, vinegar, mace, basil and garlic in saucepan; cook over low heat for 10 minutes. Combine flour, salt and pepper; coat chicken pieces well with flour mixture. Pour salad oil into skillet to ½-inch depth. Brown chicken pieces thoroughly in hot oil. Pour off oil; add fruit mixture to skillet; cover and simmer for about 20 minutes. Serves 4.

Pearl Litowsky

SOUTHERN FRIED CHICKEN

1 2½ to 3½-lb. ready-to-cook frying chicken, cut up

¼ cup flour

¼ cup corn meal

1 teaspoon salt

⅛ teaspoon pepper

Shortening

¼ cup water

2 tablespoons flour

1 cup light cream

Salt and pepper

Pinch mace

Combine ¼ cup flour, corn meal, 1 teaspoon salt and ⅛ teaspoon pepper. Coat chicken pieces well with flour mixture. Melt enough shortening in heavy skillet to make ½-inch depth. Brown chicken pieces in hot shortening over medium heat. Add water; cover and simmer for about 40 minutes, or until chicken is tender. Remove chicken to warm serving platter. Pour off all but 1 tablespoon shortening from skillet; add 2 tablespoons flour and blend well. Gradually add cream and cook, stirring, until thickened. Season to taste with salt, pepper and mace. Serve with chicken pieces. Serves 4. *Dee Stein*

CHICKEN KIEV

½ cup unsalted butter

¼ cup finely chopped parsley

Seasoned salt

6 boned, skinned chicken breasts

1½ cups fine dry bread crumbs

3 eggs, beaten

Combine butter with parsley and seasoned salt; chill in refrigerator until firm but not hard. Flatten chicken breasts with rolling pin; wipe with damp cloth. Divide butter into 4 parts; shape each part into roll about ½ inch thick. Place roll on each chicken breast; fold over so that butter is completely enclosed. Chill in refrigerator for 1 to 2 hours. Roll chicken breasts in bread crumbs; dip into egg, then roll in bread crumbs again. Let stand 10 minutes to "seal" in butter. Fry, two at a time, in deep hot fat (375°) for 5 or 6 minutes, or until golden, turning only once. Drain on absorbent paper. Repeat until all are fried. Place chicken breasts in baking dish. About 30 minutes before serving, bake at 350° for 10 to 12 minutes, or until chicken is tender. *Erika Brodsky*

CHICKEN ITALIENNE

1 3 to 4-lb. roasting chicken, cut up	1 6-oz. can tomato paste
Salt and monosodium glutamate	1 No. 2 can plum tomatoes
¼ cup olive oil	1 teaspoon salt
2 onions, minced	1 teaspoon sugar
1 or 2 large green peppers, chopped	½ teaspoon pepper
1 red pepper, chopped	4 bay leaves
½ pound fresh mushrooms	1 pound spaghetti, cooked

Season chicken pieces with salt and monosodium glutamate. Brown chicken pieces in hot oil in large skillet with onions and peppers. Sauté mushrooms in a little butter; add to chicken. Combine tomato paste, tomatoes, salt, sugar and pepper. Pour over chicken pieces. Add bay leaves; cover and simmer for 1 to 1½ hours, or until chicken is tender. Place cooked spaghetti on large platter; spoon chicken and sauce over top. Serves 4 to 6. *Hilda Eisen*

BROILED BAKED CHICKEN

2 1½ to 2-lb. ready-to-cook broiler-fryers, halved	½ cup orange juice
	½ cup grapefruit juice
Butter	½ cup chili sauce
Salt and pepper	

Dot chicken halves with butter; season with salt and pepper. Place under broiler until golden brown, turning as necessary to brown all sides. Mix together juices and chili sauce. Pour over chicken halves. Bake at 350° for 1 hour, basting frequently with sauce. Serves 4. *Mrs. Jack Levin*

GLAZED ROAST CHICKEN

2 3 to 4-lb. ready-to-cook roasting
chickens

Melted butter

Almond Stuffing, page 106

2 tablespoons cornstarch

½ teaspoon ground ginger

¾ cup light corn syrup

1 teaspoon grated orange rind

1½ cups orange juice

⅓ cup slivered blanched almonds

Stuff chickens with Almond Stuffing. Truss; place in roasting pan. Roast at 325° for about 3 hours, basting with butter frequently. Meanwhile, combine cornstarch with ginger in saucepan; stir in corn syrup, orange rind and juice. Cook over medium heat, stirring constantly, for about 8 minutes, or until thick. Add slivered almonds. Spoon glaze over chickens during last 15 minutes of roasting time. Makes 6 to 8 servings.　　　*Eve Scheff*

OVEN-FRIED CHICKEN WITH HERBS

1 3-lb. ready-to-cook frying chicken,
cut up

¾ cup sour cream

1½ teaspoons salt

½ teaspoon garlic salt

½ teaspoon paprika

½ teaspoon thyme

½ teaspoon tarragon

1 cup finely crushed corn flakes

¼ cup butter

2 cups milk

Rinse chicken pieces in cold water; pat dry. Combine sour cream with salt, garlic salt, paprika, thyme and tarragon. Dip chicken pieces in sour cream mixture, then roll in crumbs until well coated. Melt butter in shallow baking pan. Place chicken, skin-side down, in pan. Pour 1 cup milk over chicken. Bake at 400° for 30 minutes. Turn chicken pieces; add remaining milk. Bake for 30 minutes longer, or until tender. Serves 4.　　　*Lee Bateman*

CHICKEN PARISIENNE

12 small chicken breasts

2 8-oz. jars currant jelly

1 cup water

¼ cup lemon juice

2 tablespoons Worcestershire sauce

1 tablespoon cornstarch

1 tablespoon salt

2 teaspoons allspice

1 teaspoon pepper

Place chicken breasts in roasting pan so they do not overlap. Combine all other ingredients in saucepan; bring to boiling. Simmer for 5 minutes. Pour sauce over chicken breasts. Bake at 450° for 15 minutes. Reduce oven temperature to 375° and continue baking for 1 hour longer, basting frequently. If sauce becomes too thick, add water. Serve on heated platter with wild rice. Makes 4 to 6 servings.   *Alice B. Weitzenfeld*

❖❖

To coat chicken evenly, place flour and seasonings in plastic or paper bag; add chicken pieces and shake vigorously. Reserve any remaining flour mixture for use in thickening gravy.

❖❖

PEACHY BAKED CHICKEN

1 2½ to 3-lb. ready-to-cook frying chicken, cut up

Melter butter or salad oil

2 cups bread crumbs

¼ cup grated Parmesan cheese

¼ cup chopped parsley

1 tablespoon seasoned salt

1 clove garlic, minced

1 No. 2 can sliced peaches, drained

Coat chicken pieces well with melted butter; combine crumbs, cheese, parsley, seasoned salt and garlic. Roll chicken pieces in crumb mixture until well coated. Place in one layer in shallow baking pan. Bake at 350° for 45 minutes, or until done. Place peach slices on chicken pieces. Place under broiler for several minutes until peaches are slightly browned and hot. Serves 4.

Erika Brodsky

EASY CHICKEN PAPRIKA

4 chicken breasts, split

Salt, pepper and paprika

1 medium onion, sliced

½ cup butter

1 can cream of chicken soup

1 4-oz. can sliced mushrooms, drained

1 cup sour cream

Season chicken breasts with salt, pepper and paprika to taste. Sauté onion slices in hot butter; add chicken and brown lightly. Pour soup over chicken; sprinkle mushrooms over top. Cover and bake at 375° for 35 minutes.* Remove from oven; add sour cream and stir; bake for 10 minutes longer. Serves 4.   *Mrs. William Robinson*
*Or brown in electric skillet early in the day; bake just before serving.

CHICKEN CONTINENTAL

2 2 to 2½-lb. ready-to-cook frying chickens, cut up

½ cup flour

Salt and pepper

½ cup butter

2 tablespoons flour

2 tablespoons butter

1 cup chicken bouillon

½ pound mushrooms, sliced

3 tomatoes, quartered

1 cup sliced stuffed green olives

½ cup white wine

1 teaspoon Beau Monde seasoning

½ teaspoon ground coriander (or curry powder)

½ cup slivered almonds

Butter

1 package cooked frozen peas

1 3-oz. can chow-mein noodles

Combine ½ cup flour, salt and pepper; coat chicken pieces well with flour mixture. Brown chicken pieces in ½ cup hot butter. Remove chicken pieces to rack and bake at 325° for 40 minutes. Meanwhile, add to drippings in skillet, 2 tablespoons flour, 2 tablespoons butter, bouillon, mushrooms, tomatoes, olives, wine, Beau Monde seasoning and coriander. Mix well and simmer for 5 minutes. Place chicken pieces in large saucepan; pour sauce over top and simmer for 5 minutes. Sauté almonds in butter. Toss with peas. Serve chicken on chow-mein noodles with almonds and peas over top. Makes 6 servings.   *Serene Flax*

CHICKEN JUBILEE

4 1½ to 2-lb. ready-to-cook frying chickens, quartered

2 teaspoons salt

1 teaspoon garlic salt

¼ teaspoon pepper

½ cup melted butter

1 cup water

1½ cups chili sauce

2 medium onions, sliced

½ cup raisins

½ cup firmly packed brown sugar

1 tablespoon Worcestershire sauce

1 cup sherry

1 No. 303 can Bing cherries, drained

Place chicken pieces in shallow baking pan, skin-side up. Season with salt, garlic salt and pepper; drizzle with melted butter. Place under broiler until brown. Combine water, chili sauce, onions, raisins, brown sugar and Worcestershire sauce. Mix thoroughly. Pour over chicken in pan; cover with aluminum foil. Bake at 325° for 1 hour. Add wine and cherries last 15 minutes of baking period. Serves 8.   *Lee Bateman*

HAWAIIAN CHICKEN

1 2 to 3-lb. ready-to-cook frying
chicken, cut up

½ cup flour

2 teaspoons ground ginger

1 teaspoon salt

⅛ teaspoon pepper

¼ cup shortening

1 cup water

1 13-oz. can pineapple chunks

1 onion, cut into small pieces

1 green pepper, cut into 1-inch pieces

2 tablepoons vinegar

1 tablespoon brown sugar

¼ teaspoon garlic powder

Combine flour, ginger, salt and pepper. Coat chicken pieces well with flour
mixture, reserving flour. Brown chicken pieces in hot shortening in heavy
skillet. Remove chicken to casserole. Mix 2 tablespoons reserved flour mixture with drippings in skillet. Add water and stir until smooth. Drain pineapple, reserving liquid. Add pineapple, onion, green pepper, vinegar, brown
sugar, garlic powder and ¼ cup reserved pineapple liquid to mixture in
skillet. Bring to boiling. Pour over chicken in casserole. Bake at 325° for
about 45 minutes. Serve over fluffy white rice. Serves 4.   *Mrs. Abe Fertel*

---

*Look for the "Acronized" label on ready-to-cook poultry. This
is your guide to "fresh-killed" flavor and good quality.*

CHICKEN MARRAKESH

1 2½ to 3-lb. ready-to-cook frying
chicken, cut up

1 cup corn flake crumbs

1 tablespoon seasoned salt

½ cup shortening

2 large onions, sliced

1 3-oz. can mushrooms, drained

1 8-oz. can chopped ripe olives

½ cup seedless raisins

1 8-oz. can tomato sauce

½ cup vermouth or dry wine

Sprinkle chicken pieces with seasoned salt; roll in crumbs to coat well.
Sauté in hot shortening until lightly browned, about 5 minutes on each side.
Remove chicken pieces from skillet. Sauté onions in drippings in skillet
until golden. Turn off heat; add mushrooms, olives, raisins and tomato sauce
and stir well. Place chicken pieces in shallow baking dish. Pour sauce over
top. Bake at 350° for 1½ hours. Add wine and bake for 30 minutes longer.
Place under broiler for 5 minutes to brown, if desired. Serve over rice or
noodles. Serves 3 or 4.   *Bea Spilky*

CHICKEN EXTRAORDINAIRE

2 3-lb. ready-to-cook frying chickens, cut up

¾ cup sauterne

Salt, pepper and paprika

2 tablespoons dried parsley

2 tablespoons chopped green onions

¼ cup melted butter

Pour wine over chicken pieces; chill in refrigerator for 3 to 4 hours. Remove chicken pieces from wine; sprinkle with salt, pepper and paprika. Combine wine, parsley, onions and butter. Place chicken pieces in shallow baking dish, skin-side down; pour wine mixture over top. Bake at 350° for 20 minutes; turn chicken over and continue baking until tender, basting with wine as necessary. Serves 6 to 8.   *Jeanne Berkowitz*

SESAME CHICKEN IMPERIALE

1 3½-lb. ready-to-cook frying chicken, cut up

1½ cups soda cracker crumbs

1½ cups grated Parmesan cheese

¼ cup chopped parsley

¼ cup chopped onion

1 tablespoon salt

½ teaspoon pepper

½ cup melted butter

3 tablespoons butter

Sesame, poppy or celery seeds

Rinse chicken pieces in cold water; pat dry. Combine crumbs, cheese, parsley, onion, salt and pepper. Dip chicken pieces in melted butter, then roll in crumb mixture, coating thoroughly. Place chicken pieces, skin-side up, in one layer in shallow baking pan. Dot with 3 tablespoons butter; sprinkle generously with sesame seeds. Bake at 350° for 1 hour, or until tender. Makes 4 or 5 servings.   *Poppy Brooks*

CHICKEN AMANDINE

2 2½ to 3-lb. ready-to-cook broiler-fryers, quartered

2 cans cream of chicken soup

½ teaspoon seasoned salt

¼ teaspoon salt

¼ teaspoon pepper

½ cup slivered blanched almonds

Place chicken pieces skin-side down one layer deep in shallow baking dish. Combine soup with seasoned salt, salt and pepper; pour over chicken pieces. Sprinkle with slivered almonds. Bake at 350° for 1½ hours, or until chicken is tender. Makes 8 servings.   *Barbara Grahn*

CHICKEN RICE CASSEROLE

1 2½ to 3-lb. ready-to-cook frying
chicken, cut up

½ cup flour

1 teaspoon salt

¼ teaspoon pepper

1 teaspoon paprika

½ cup butter

1 cup chopped onion

½ cup diced green pepper

1 clove garlic, minced

⅓ cup pimiento strips

1 cup uncooked rice

1½ cups chicken bouillon

1 3-oz. can mushrooms, drained

Combine flour, salt, pepper and paprika; coat chicken pieces well with flour mixture. Brown chicken in hot butter. Remove chicken; add onion, green pepper and garlic to skillet; cook until onion is golden brown. Add pimiento and rice; cook, stirring, over low heat for 2 minutes. Add bouillon and mushrooms; bring to boiling. Pour into 2-qt. casserole. Place chicken pieces on top. Bake at 350° for 1½ hours, adding water every 30 minutes. Makes 4 servings. *Annette Katz*

CHICKEN BURGUNDY

2 2½ to 3-lb. ready-to-cook frying
chickens, cut up

½ cup flour

Salt and pepper

⅓ cup salad oil

1 bunch carrots, sliced or cut into strips

1 pound white onions

1 cup water

2 cloves

1 bay leaf

⅓ teaspoon marjoram

¼ teaspoon rosemary

Dash mace

2 3-oz. cans broiled sliced mushrooms

2 cups cooked lima beans (canned or
frozen)

1 cup Burgundy wine

Combine flour with salt and pepper; coat chicken pieces well with flour mixture. Brown chicken in hot oil in large skillet. Remove chicken pieces to casserole. Sprinkle with any remaining flour. Add carrots and onions to casserole. Combine water, cloves, bay leaf, marjoram, rosemary and mace with drippings in skillet. Boil for 5 minutes; strain over chicken and vegetables. Bake, covered, at 325° for 1 hour. Add mushrooms, lima beans and wine. Increase oven temperature to 400° and continue baking for 1 hour longer. Makes 8 servings. *Marian Peterman*

CHICKEN TETRAZINI

1 3-lb. ready-to-cook stewing chicken	2 cups cream
2 cups water	Salt and pepper
¼ pound cooked thin spaghetti	Garlic
1 teaspoon salt	1 cup sauterne
Grated Parmesan cheese	½ pound fresh mushrooms, sliced
2 tablespoons melted butter	2 tablespoons butter
⅓ cup sifted flour	Salt and pepper
¼ cup melted butter	Garlic

Place chicken and water in kettle; simmer for about 3 hours, or until tender. Cool chicken in cooking water; remove chicken, reserving stock. Remove chicken from bones; cut into 1½-inch pieces. Set aside. Place spaghetti in casserole; season with salt and cheese to taste. Toss with 2 tablespoons melted butter. Combine flour with ¼ cup melted butter. Gradually add cream and 1 cup reserved chicken stock, stirring constantly. Cook until smooth; add salt, pepper and garlic to taste; stir in wine. Pour 1 cup of this mixture over spaghetti in casserole. Sauté mushrooms in 2 tablespoons hot butter. Season with salt, pepper and garlic to taste. Place on top of spaghetti. Add more sauce. Arrange chicken pieces over mushrooms; add remaining sauce. Sprinkle with cheese. Bake at 350° for 30 minutes. Place under broiler until top browns. Serves 8.   *Natalie Levin*

CLUB CHICKEN

¼ cup butter	2½ cups diced cooked or canned chicken
¼ cup flour	3 cups cooked rice
1 15-oz. can evaporated milk	1 3-oz. can broiled sliced mushrooms, drained
1 cup chicken broth (or 1½ chicken bouillon cubes dissolved in 1 cup hot water)	¼ cup chopped pimiento
½ cup water	¼ cup chopped green pepper
1½ teaspoons salt	½ cup slivered toasted blanched almonds

Melt butter; stir in flour. Gradually add milk, broth and water; cook, stirring constantly, over low heat until thick. Add salt; mix well. Add chicken, rice, mushrooms, pimiento and green pepper; toss to coat well. Turn into greased 11½x7½x1½-inch baking dish. Bake at 350° for about 30 minutes. Sprinkle toasted almonds over top. Makes 8 to 10 servings.   *Gretl Loewenthal*

CHICKEN COTELETTES

1 cup cooked or canned chicken   Salt and pepper

1 egg, separated

Grind chicken 3 times. Add egg white and mix well. Season to taste with salt and pepper. Shape into 4 small or 2 large round patties. Beat egg yolk until thick and lemon-colored. Brush over patties. Place under broiler and brown on both sides. Bake at 325° for 15 to 20 minutes. Makes 2 servings.

VELVET CHICKEN

1 4 to 5-lb. cooked roasting chicken	¼ teaspoon ground ginger
2 egg whites	¾ cup small peas
½ teaspoon salt	½ cup sliced mushrooms
½ teaspoon monosodium glutamate	½ cup diced celery
Dash pepper	½ cup finely cut green beans
3 tablespoons salad oil	⅓ cup slivered almonds

Remove skin from chicken; cut meat away from bones. Cut into thin slices. Pound slices with flat surface of knife. Beat egg whites with salt, monosodium glutamate and pepper; coat chicken slices well with egg white mixture. In skillet, heat 2 tablespoons oil with ginger; sauté chicken slices over high heat, turning frequently, for 2 or 3 minutes. Remove to warm platter. Add 1 tablespoon oil to skillet; sauté peas, mushrooms, celery, beans and almonds in hot oil for about 8 minutes, or until just tender. Return chicken to skillet; mix gently with vegetables and cook for 1 minute longer. Serves 6 to 8.

Dee Stein

CHICKEN-BROCCOLI CASSEROLE

1 package frozen broccoli	2 cups cooked or canned chicken, in large pieces
1 can cream of chicken soup	
¼ cup liquified nonfat dry milk	⅛ teaspoon savory
	¼ cup grated Cheddar cheese

Cook broccoli as directed on package, just until tender. Drain. Combine soup, milk, chicken pieces and savory. Place layer of broccoli in each of 4 individual casseroles. Cover with chicken mixture; top with remaining broccoli. Sprinkle with cheese. Bake, covered, at 350° for 20 minutes, or until bubbly. Makes 4 servings.

CHICKEN AND MUSHROOMS IN CHEESE

½ cup butter

½ cup plus 2 tablespoons flour

4⅓ cups hot milk

⅓ cup sherry

1 teaspoon monosodium glutamate

¼ teaspoon saffron

⅔ pound very sharp cheese, cubed

1¾ pounds mushrooms, sliced

6 cups cooked or canned chicken, cut into bite-size pieces

Melt butter; stir in flour and cook for 2 minutes, stirring constantly. Add milk and wine; mix in monosodium glutamate, saffron and cheese. Cook until cheese is melted and sauce is almost boiling. Season to taste with salt and pepper. Sauté mushrooms in a little hot butter. Add to cheese mixture with chicken. Heat thoroughly. Serve on buttered rice or noodles. Makes 12 servings. *Mrs. Marshall Paskind*

CHICKEN À LA ROSE

3 tablespoons chicken fat

¼ pound mushrooms, minced

1 medium onion, minced

1 clove garlic, minced

½ cup dry white wine

1½ teaspoons celery salt

1 teaspoon salt

⅛ teaspoon white pepper

3 cups chicken broth

⅓ cup flour

¾ cup light cream

4 cups cooked chicken

Melt chicken fat in large skillet or saucepan. Add mushrooms, onion, garlic, wine, celery salt, salt and pepper. Simmer for 5 minutes. Add broth; simmer for 15 minutes. Stir flour into mixture; cook until thick, stirring constantly. Stir in cream. Add chicken and cook until just heated. Serves 12.

Rose Krichiver

SHERRIED CHICKEN LIVERS

½ pound mushrooms

1 medium onion, sliced

3 tablespoons butter

Seasoned flour

1 pound chicken livers

Salt and pepper

½ cup sherry

3 cups cooked rice

Sauté mushrooms and onion in hot butter in skillet. Roll chicken livers in seasoned flour. Add to skillet and brown on all sides. Season with salt and pepper to taste. Add sherry. Place layer of rice in bottom of 4 individual casseroles. Top with layer of chicken liver mixture. Repeat until all are used. Bake at 350° for 15 minutes. Serves 4.   *Rosabelle Perrye*

CHICKEN OR TURKEY DIVINE

2 packages frozen broccoli

Salt and pepper

⅓ cup butter

⅓ cup sifted flour

2¾ cups chicken stock and milk or cream

1¼ teaspoons salt

Pepper

2 tablespoons sherry

Grated Parmesan cheese

4 cups cooked or canned chicken or turkey

½ pound mushrooms, sliced and sautéed in butter

Buttered bread crumbs

Cook broccoli as directed on package, just until tender. Drain; season with salt and pepper. Place in bottom of well-greased shallow baking pan. Melt ⅓ cup butter; add flour, mixing until smooth; gradually add chicken stock and milk, stirring constantly. Bring to boiling over medium heat. Add 1¼ teaspoons salt, pepper to taste, sherry and cheese. Mix well. Pour one third of this mixture over broccoli. Arrange chicken pieces in pan; sprinkle with sautéed mushrooms; cover with remaining sauce. Top with bread crumbs; sprinkle with grated cheese, if desired. Bake at 350° for 30 minutes. Place under broiler for 10 minutes, or until golden brown. Serves 6.
Edith Karasik

CHICKEN LIVERS WITH RICE

¼ cup butter or margarine

3 tablespoons minced onion

1 5-oz. package pre-cooked rice

½ pound thawed frozen or fresh chicken livers, cut into 1-inch pieces

Seasoned flour

1 can cream of chicken soup

½ cup milk

1 tablespoon chopped parsley

Pinch basil

Melt 1 tablespoon butter in saucepan; add onion and cook until tender. Meanwhile, cook rice as directed on package. Add onion. Roll chicken livers in seasoned flour. Sauté in remaining butter in same skillet used for onions until browned on all sides. Combine rice, chicken livers, soup, milk, parsley and basil. Turn into 1½-qt. casserole. Bake at 350° for 30 minutes, or until hot and bubbly. Serves 6.   *Dee Stein*

CAPON DE ORT

1 5 or 6-lb. capon, cut into 8 pieces

Salt and pepper

¼ cup shortening

1½ cups sliced onions

½ pound mushrooms, sliced

2 cans cream of mushroom soup

1½ cups milk

1 cup sliced ripe olives

Wash capon; pat dry. Season with salt and pepper. Brown lightly in hot shortening (about 10 minutes on each side.) Drain on absorbent paper. Place in casserole. Bake at 350° for 1 hour. Meanwhile, in same skillet, sauté onions and mushrooms. Drain on absorbent paper. Combine onions and mushrooms with soup. Gradually add milk; heat almost to boiling. Add olives. Pour over chicken in casserole. Cook over low heat for 30 minutes longer. Serves 6. *Joy Reich*

ROAST CAPON OR TURKEY

1 5 to 6-lb. ready-to-cook roasting capon or turkey

½ teaspoon garlic powder or garlic clove, mashed

½ teaspoon paprika

¼ teaspoon ground ginger

Salt and pepper

½ cup pineapple, orange, pomegranate or grapefruit juice, or 1 cup consommé

Rub capon skin and cavity with garlic, paprika and ginger. Sprinkle with salt and pepper. Place on rack in roasting pan. Pour juice over top. Roast at 400° until brown, basting and turning frequently. When brown, reduce oven temperature to 350°; cover and roast until tender (about 30 minutes per pound). Baste occasionally, adding juice or water as necessary. Serves 6.

ROAST TURKEY

1 10 to 14-lb. ready-to-cook hen turkey

3 tablespoons shortening

2 tablespoons catchup

1 teaspoon paprika

1 teaspoon salt

½ teaspoon pepper

½ teaspoon dry mustard

1 clove garlic, mashed (optional)

Rinse turkey; pat dry. Prepare paste of shortening, catchup, paprika, salt, pepper, mustard and garlic. Spread over entire turkey. Wrap in dampened towel; place in refrigerator overnight. Just before roasting, stuff turkey as desired. Place on rack in roasting pan. Roast at 350° for about 1½ hours. Cover with aluminum foil; continue roasting for about 2½ hours longer. Total roasting time should be about 15 to 20 minutes per pound. Serves 10 to 12. *Faye M. Basan*

GLAZED TURKEY WITH FRUITY BARBECUE SAUCE

1 10 to 15-lb. ready-to-cook turkey	1 tablespoon grated orange rind
Salt and pepper	1 cup orange juice
Salad oil	2 tablespoons vinegar
GLAZE:	2 teaspoons soy sauce
½ cup orange marmalade	½ teaspoon ground ginger
½ cup apricot jam	

Rub cavity of turkey with salt and pepper; brush skin with oil. Place on spit and roast in rotisserie or over charcoal until tender. Test for doneness by moving thigh up and down. About 45 minutes before end of roasting period, combine remaining ingredients. Use to baste turkey. Serves 10 to 12.
Sue Weissman

DUCK

SPICED DUCK

3 4 to 5-lb. ready-to-cook ducklings, quartered	Ground ginger
	Paprika
Salt and pepper	2 No. 303 cans spiced apples, peaches or pears
Garlic powder	

Rinse ducklings; pat dry. Sprinkle on all sides with salt and pepper, garlic powder, ginger and paprika to taste. Place skin-side up in 2 shallow roasting pans. Refrigerate for 4 to 5 hours or overnight. Roast at 325° for 1 hour; drain fat from pans. Drain fruit, reserving juice; baste ducklings with fruit juice. Roast 30 minutes longer, basting occasionally. Remove ducklings to heated platter; garnish with spiced fruit. Serves 12. *Evelyn Segal*

DUCKLING WITH ORANGE SAUCE

2 4½-lb. ready-to-cook ducklings, quartered

Garlic powder

Salt and pepper

Orange marmalade

1½ cups water

1 6-oz. can frozen orange juice

3 juice cans water

3 ounces honey

Rinse ducklings; pat dry. Rub with garlic powder, salt and pepper. Spread generously with marmalade. Place on rack, skin-side up, in shallow roasting pan. Pour 1½ cups water into pan. Bake at 400° for 1 hour, or until duckling is brown. Drain excess fat from pan; reduce oven temperature to 300°. Mix orange juice with water and honey. Baste duckling. Turn duckling and continue baking, basting frequently, for 1½ hours longer. Remove duckling to serving platter. Thicken pan drippings with cornstarch. Serves 8.

Ferne Kron

ROAST DUCK

1 5 to 7-lb. ready-to-cook duck

2 3-oz. cans broiled mushrooms

1 5-oz. package pre-cooked rice

2 tablespoons shortening

¼ cup chopped onion

1 teaspoon poultry seanoning (optional)

½ teaspoon salt

½ cup orange or pineapple juice

Rinse duck; pat dry. Drain mushrooms, reserving liquid. Add enough water to mushroom liquid to make 1¾ cups. Cook rice according to directions on package, using mushroom liquid and water for liquid. Meanwhile, melt shortening in skillet; add onions and cook until soft. Add poultry seasoning, salt and mushrooms. Stir into cooked rice; mix well. Stuff duck with rice mixture. Place on rack in roasting pan. Roast at 325° for 3 to 3½ hours, basting frequently with orange juice and pan drippings. Serves 6.

Mrs. Reuben Stiglitz

DUCK DELIGHT

1 4-lb. ready-to-cook duckling

Salt

2 onions, sliced

2 apples, sliced

2 oranges, sliced

Rinse duckling; pat dry. Rub cavity with salt. Stuff with onions, apples and oranges. Broil in rotisserie at medium heat for about 30 minutes. Discard stuffing before serving. Serves 3 or 4. *Joan Florence*

DUCK JUBILEE

1 5-lb. ready-to-cook duckling, quartered	2 tablespoons cornstarch
1 tablespoon shortening	1 tablespoon lemon juice
2 tablespoons brandy	1 teaspoon salt
1 tablespoon chopped onion	¼ teaspoon pepper
1 No. 2½ can pitted Bing cherries	1 bay leaf
1 cup blanched almonds	½ cup red wine

Rinse duckling; pat dry. Brown duckling in hot shortening in skillet. Remove duckling to casserole; pour brandy over top and ignite. Sauté onion in skillet. Meanwhile, drain cherries, reserving juice. Stuff cherries with almonds; set aside. Dissolve cornstarch in ½ cup reserved cherry juice. Combine with onion, lemon juice, salt, pepper, bay leaf and wine. Pour over duckling in casserole. Bake at 350° for 1½ to 2 hours, or until duckling is tender. Add cherries just before serving. Serves 4. *Rosabelle Perrye*

GLAZED DUCKLING HAWAIIAN

1 4 to 5-lb. ready-to-cook duckling, quartered	½ teaspoon salt
	2 tablespoons soy sauce
1 13-oz. can pineapple chunks	1 teaspoon salt
⅓ cup soy sauce	2 green peppers, chopped
3 tablespoons brown sugar	2 green onions, chopped
1 teaspoon salt	3 tablespoons brown sugar
1 clove garlic, mashed	2 tablespoons cornstarch
1 cup water	¼ cup water

Rinse ducklings; pat dry. Place in shallow roasting pan. Drain pineapple chunks, reserving juice. Combine ⅓ cup soy sauce, 3 tablespoons brown sugar, 1 teaspoon salt, garlic and ⅓ cup reserved pineapple juice. Pour over duckling. Bake at 325° for 2 hours, basting occasionally. Meanwhile, simmer giblets in 1 cup water with ½ teaspoon salt until tender. Strain stock; combine with 2 tablespoons soy sauce, 1 teaspoon salt, remaining pineapple juice, pineapple chunks, green peppers, onions and 3 tablespoons brown sugar. Cook for 5 minutes. Blend cornstarch with ¼ cup water. Add to stock mixture, stirring constantly, and cook until thick and clear. Remove duckling to serving platter. Serve with sauce and rice. Serves 4. *Helen Salomon*

BROILED DUCK

2 5-lb. ducks, quartered	¼ cup olive oil
½ cup dry white wine	1 teaspoon salt
¼ cup lemon juice	½ teaspoon ground ginger

Place duck pieces skin-side down on rack in broiler pan. Broil at medium heat for 15 minutes. Meanwhile, combine wine, lemon juice, oil, salt and ginger. Baste duck with sauce; turn and continue broiling for 30 minutes. basting every 10 minutes. Serves 6.

 CORNISH HEN

GOLDEN ROCK CORNISH HENS WITH HERB BUTTER

6 1-lb. thawed frozen Rock Cornish hens	1½ teaspoons rosemary
1½ cups melted butter	1 teaspoon savory
2 teaspoons seasoned salt	1 teaspoon onion powder
1½ teaspoons paprika	¾ teaspoon freshly ground black pepper
1½ teaspoons basil	

Remove giblets from hens; set aside for use in Wild Rice-Mushroom Stuffing. Rinse hens; pat dry. Combine butter with remaining ingredients. Brush hens inside and out with herb butter. Tie legs together and fasten to tail. Arrange hens, breast-side up, in shallow baking pan lined with aluminum foil. Roast at 350° for 1 to 1¼ hours, or until tender, basting 2 or 3 times during roasting with herb butter. Serve with Wild Rice-Mushroom Stuffing, page 106. Serves 6.   *Rosabelle Perrye*

ROCK CORNISH HENS WITH WINE SAUCE

3 1-lb. thawed frozen Rock Cornish hens	1½ tablespoons cornstarch
1 tablespoon butter	⅓ cup wine vinegar
½ cup red currant jelly	1 teaspoon salt
3 tablespoons lemon juice	4 cloves

Rinse hens; pat dry. Stuff, if desired. Place in shallow roasting pan. Brush with a little melted butter. Bake at 400° for 35 minutes. Meanwhile, combine butter, jelly and lemon juice. Mix cornstarch with vinegar until smooth. Add to jelly mixture. Add salt and cloves. Simmer until thoroughly heated. Reduce oven temperature to 350°. Pour glaze over hens; bake for 20 to 30 minutes longer, basting occasionally. Serves 3.   *Marian D. Horwitz*

ROAST GOOSE WITH APRICOT STUFFING

1 10 to 12-lb. ready-to-cook goose	½ cup Burgundy
1 clove garlic, mashed	Apricot Stuffing, page 106
Salt and pepper	1 cup orange juice

Mix garlic and salt and pepper with a little Burgundy. Rub goose inside and out with this mixture. Stuff with Apricot Stuffing; truss. Prick goose all over so fat will run out. Place, breast-side up, on rack in roasting pan. Combine remaining wine with orange juice. Pour over goose. Roast at 325° until tender, basting often. Allow 25 minutes per pound. Serves 10 to 12.

STUFFED GOOSE WITH SAUERKRAUT

1 5 to 8-lb. ready-to-cook goose	Pinch salt
½ loaf day-old sliced bread	1 No. 2½ can sauerkraut
1 large onion, finely chopped	1 cup cold water
1 cup finely chopped celery	3 tablespoons brown sugar
2 unpared apples, cut into pieces	1 teaspoon caraway seeds
1 teaspoon cinnamon	1 large onion, cut into small pieces

Remove skin from back of goose. Rub lightly with salt. Soak bread in water; squeeze out. Sauté chopped onion and celery in a little shortening until golden brown. Mix with bread; add apples, cinnamon and salt. Stuff goose with bread mixture. Truss; place on rack in roasting pan. Prick breast so fat will run out. Roast, covered, at 350° for about 2½ hours, or until tender. Increase oven temperature to 500°. Pour off fat; roast, uncovered, until golden brown. Meanwhile, place gizzard, wings, neck and legs in saucepot or kettle with sauerkraut, water, catchup, brown sugar, caraway seeds and onion pieces. Bring to boiling; simmer until goose pieces are tender. Serve on platter with roast goose. Serves 6 to 8.   *Mrs. E. Friedman*

GOOSE WITH GLAZED ORANGES

Leftover goose	**GLAZED ORANGES:**
Broth or gravy	2 large oranges
Grated orange rind	½ cup granulated sugar
2 or 3 teaspoons currant jelly	3 tablespoons water
½ cup seedless raisins	1 tablespoon light corn syrup

Cut leftover goose into serving-size portions. Heat in a little broth or gravy in heavy skillet. Add orange rind to taste, jelly and raisins; cover and simmer for 15 to 20 minutes. Meanwhile, peel and section oranges. Combine sugar, water and corn syrup in saucepan. Bring to boiling; add orange sections and simmer for 5 minutes, or until orange sections are well glazed. Serve goose in broth garnished with glazed orange sections.

STUFFINGS

BRAZIL NUT STUFFING

½ cup butter	1 teaspoon poultry seasoning
½ cup chopped onion	¼ teaspoon pepper
2 cups chopped Brazil nuts	8 cups soft bread crumbs
1 cup chopped celery and leaves	2 eggs, beaten
¼ cup chopped parsley	1 cup stock or water
2 teaspoons salt	

Melt butter in large saucepan or skillet. Add onion and cook until soft but not brown. Stir in nuts, celery, parsley, salt, poultry seasoning and pepper. Add bread crumbs and toss lightly. Remove from heat and stir in eggs and stock. Makes enough to stuff 12-lb. turkey. May also be baked in aluminum foil (tightly sealed) at 350° for 35 minutes, or at 325° for 45 minutes. Serve with chicken, beef or veal.   *Maryon Goldware*

BROWN RICE STUFFING

1 cup brown rice

½ teaspoon salt

1 medium onion, diced

¼ cup butter

2 3-oz. cans sliced mushrooms, drained

Salt and pepper

Cook rice with salt according to directions on package. Sauté onion in hot butter for 5 minutes. Add mushrooms; sauté for 5 minutes longer. Grind onions and mushrooms. Add to cooked rice. Season to taste with salt and pepper. Makes enough to stuff 4 to 6 Rock Cornish hens.   *Irene Bayrach*

CORN FLAKE STUFFING

1 large onion, chopped

1 green pepper, chopped

4 stalks celery, chopped

Chicken fat

Chicken or turkey liver

8 slices toasted bread

½ cup crushed corn flakes

2 carrots, grated

2 eggs

1 teaspoon sugar

Salt and pepper

Sauté onion, green pepper and celery in hot chicken fat; cut in liver. Soak bread in water; squeeze out thoroughly. Add bread to vegetable mixture. Add corn flakes, carrots, eggs, sugar, salt and pepper to taste. Mix well. Makes enough to stuff 2 4 to 5-lb. chickens or 10-lb. turkey. May be baked in casserole at 350° for 1 hour.   *Edith Lirtzman*

Don't forget that corn flake crumbs are now packaged ready for use—no more crushing!

QUICK CORN FLAKE STUFFING

2 onions, sliced

½ cup chicken fat or butter

2 cups bread crumbs

3 cups corn flakes, crushed

1 clove garlic, minced

Salt and pepper to taste

½ cup boiling water

Sauté onions in hot fat. Add crumbs, corn flakes, garlic, salt and pepper to taste. Brown for several minutes. Add boiling water. Mix well. Makes enough to stuff 5 or 6-lb. capon or turkey.   *Marian D. Horwitz*

APRICOT STUFFING

4 cups cold cooked brown rice

6 tablespoons melted butter

½ cup chopped onion

¼ cup chopped parsley

¼ cup chopped chives

2 cups chopped dried apricots

Salt and pepper

Combine all ingredients, seasoning to taste. Chill in refrigerator for at least 1 hour before stuffing fowl. Makes enough stuffing for 10 to 12-lb. goose or turkey, or 2 5 to 6-lb. chickens or ducks.

WILD RICE-MUSHROOM STUFFING

Giblets from Rock Cornish hens

2 teaspoons salt

1 teaspoon basil

1 bay leaf

Peppercorns

1½ cups wild rice

½ pound mushrooms, sliced

4 green onions and tops, sliced diagonally

3 tablespoons butter

1 cup chicken broth

Salt and pepper

Cover giblets with water; add 2 teaspoons salt, basil, bayleaf and peppercorns. Simmer until tender. Drain and chop fine. Cook wild rice according to directions on package (about 20 to 25 minutes). Drain thoroughly. Sauté mushrooms and onions in butter for 5 minutes. Add to rice. Stir in giblets and chicken broth. Add salt and pepper to taste. Turn into 1½-qt. casserole. Bake at 350° for about 30 minutes. Pack tightly into 6 to 8 buttered custard cups. Unmold and serve with Rock Cornish hens. Serves 6 to 8.

Rosabelle Perrye

ALMOND STUFFING

4 cups bread cubes

¼ cup chopped onion

¼ cup chopped celery

2 tablespoons chopped parsley

1 cup slivered almonds

1 teaspoon salt

½ teaspoon poultry seasoning

2 tablespoons water

¼ cup melted butter

Combine all ingredients in order listed. Toss to combine well. Makes enough to stuff 2 3-lb. chickens.

Eve Scheff

ORANGE RICE STUFFING

3 tablespoons shortening	1 cup orange juice
1 cup diced celery	1½ teaspoons salt
2 tablespoons chopped onion	1½ teaspoon monosodium glutamate
1½ cups water	½ teaspoon cinnamon
2 teaspoons grated orange rind	1 cup uncooked rice

Melt shortening in heavy 2-quart saucepan. Add celery and onion; sauté until onion is transparent; set aside. Combine water, orange rind and juice, salt, monosodium glutamate and cinnamon; bring to rapid boil. Add rice gradually so boiling does not stop. Stir to blend thoroughly. Add to sautéed mixture. Cover saucepan tightly; cook over very low heat for about 25 minutes. Cool slightly. Makes enough to stuff 2 4-lb. ducklings or chickens.

Sue Weissman

CRACKER STUFFING

1 pound salted crackers	3 tablespoons chicken fat
3 eggs	Salt
1 green pepper, chopped	Garlic salt
2 medium onions, chopped	Poultry seasoning
1 stalk celery, chopped	

Soak crackers in lukewarm water. When soft, turn into colander to drain. Squeeze gently to remove as much water as possible. Place crackers in mixing bowl; add eggs and beat with fork. Sauté green pepper, onion and celery in hot chicken fat until soft but not brown. Add to crackers. Add salt, garlic salt and poultry seasoning to taste. Makes enough to stuff 12-lb. turkey. May also be baked in casserole at 350° for 1½ to 2 hours. *Rose Krichiver*

POTATO STUFFING

4 large potatoes, grated	1 teaspoon salt
1 egg	Dash pepper
1 tablespoon flour	2 tablespoons chicken fat

Drain potatoes; add egg and mix thoroughly. Add flour, salt and pepper; mix again. Add chicken fat. Makes enough to stuff 5-lb. chicken, duck, goose or turkey.

Gert Duhl

POTATO KISHKE

1 set Kishke or 4 yards beef casings

3 small onions, grated

2 large potatoes, grated

10 slices dried Chala, grated into crumbs

2 packages corn flake crumbs

10 eggs

2 cans chicken broth or consommé

½ cup chicken fat

1 tablespoon salt

1 teaspoon pepper

1 teaspoon paprika

Clean inside of casings thoroughly. Cut casings into sections. Tie one end of each section with string or thread. Mix together all remaining ingredients. Stuff casings lightly, leaving room for expansion. Tie open ends. Place in large kettle of boiling salted water; boil for 3 hours. Place in roasting pan with roast poultry or meat for last few minutes of roasting period to brown. Or bake in roasting pan at 350° until brown. Makes 1 dozen.   *Anne Gold*

KISHKE

1 12-in. beef casing

1 cup sifted flour

½ cup farina

½ cup chopped onion

½ cup ground suet

¾ teaspoon salt

½ teaspoon pepper

½ teaspoon paprika

Clean inside of casings thoroughly, removing all fat, etc. Cut casing into 4 or 6 inch lengths. Tie one end of each with thread. Combine flour, farina, onion, suet, salt, pepper and paprika. Stuff mixture lightly into casings, leaving room for expansion. Tie open ends. Place in large saucepot filled with boiling salted water; cook for at least 45 minutes, pricking casings occasionally to allow excess fat to escape. Place in roasting pan with roast fowl or meat for last hour of roasting period. Or place in roasting pan with few tablespoons chicken fat and sliced onions; bake at 325° until well browned. Serves 2 or 3.   *Roz Weissman*

For stuffings, use bread crumbs made from medium-dry bread, 2 or 3 days old. Stack slices; trim off crusts; cut into strips, then into cubes. If using unsliced bread, cut loaf in half; trim crusts. With fingers or fork break into fine, even pieces.

FISH AND SEA-FOOD DISHES AND SAUCES FOR FISH

They say fish should swim
thrice * * * first it should swim
in the sea (do you mind me?)
then it should swim in butter,
and at last, sirrah, it should
swim in good claret.

Jonathan Swift

FISH

SAUTÉ OF SMELT WITH MUSTARD

24 smelt	Salt and pepper
½ to ⅔ cup prepared mustard	3 tablespoons butter
Bread crumbs	Sauce Diable, page 125

Split smelt down back and remove large bones. Spread each smelt lightly with mustard. Coat thoroughly with bread crumbs; sprinkle with salt and pepper. Sauté in hot butter over high heat until nicely browned on all sides. Serve with Sauce Diable. Makes 6 to 8 servings.

POACHED FISH WITH VEGETABLES

2 perch, 3 slices whitefish, 3 slices trout and 1 or 2 pike (4 to 5 lbs.)	3 carrots, cut into pieces
	6 small potatoes
Salt and pepper	1 onion
2 stalks celery, sliced	

Place cleaned fish in skillet; cover with water and bring to boiling. Add salt and pepper to taste, celery, carrots, potatoes and onion. Simmer for about 25 to 30 minutes, adding a little milk for last 5 minutes of cooking period. Serves 6 to 8.

SWEET-AND-SOUR FISH

3 pounds fish, sliced

3 cups water

1 cup vinegar

¼ cup raisins

1 onion, sliced

½ cup firmly packed brown sugar

5 ginger snaps

1 lemon, sliced

Clean fish; sprinkle with salt and cover with water; set aside for at least 1 hour. Drain and rinse well. Place 3 cups water, vinegar, raisins and onion in kettle; bring to boiling and simmer for about 30 minutes, or until onion is tender. Add brown sugar, ginger snaps and fish. Cover and simmer for 10 minutes, or until fish flakes easily. Drain, reserving liquid. Serve fish garnished with lemon slices and parsley, if desired. Serve fish liquid separately. Makes 8 servings. *Roz Weissman*

TROUT BAKE

3 pounds trout, cleaned and split

Salt and pepper

Butter

1 or 2 onions, sliced

½ can tomato soup

½ soup can sour cream

1 tablespoon water

Cut fish into serving-size pieces. Wash; dry well. Salt and pepper each piece and place in greased shallow baking dish, skin-side down. Place bit of butter and onion slice on each piece. Combine soup, sour cream and water. Mix well and pour over fish. Bake at 350° for 45 to 60 minutes, or until fish flakes easily. Makes 4 to 6 servings. *Mrs. Leon Racusin*

FISH DINNER

Whitefish or pike fillets

Salt and pepper

Melted butter

Thin lemon slices

Grated Cheddar cheese

Thin potato slices

Thin onion slices

Salt and pepper

Paprika

Line broiler pan with aluminum foil. Drizzle melted butter over foil. Season fish with salt and pepper; place in center of pan. Drizzle more melted butter over fish. Place 4 or 5 lemon slices on each piece of fish; sprinkle generously with grated cheese. Line sides of pan with potato and onion slices. Season with salt, pepper and paprika. Bake at 450° for 15 minutes; baste fish and vegetables with butter; turn vegetables; bake for 15 minutes longer, or until fish flakes and vegetables are done.   *Harriet Spiesman*

HALIBUT CASSEROLE

2 pounds halibut	½ can tomato soup
Salt and pepper	1 teaspoon Worcestershire sauce
Juice of 1 lemon	½ cup sherry
2 bay leaves	½ pound mushrooms, sliced
¼ cup melted butter	¼ pound Cheddar cheese, grated
2 tablespoons flour	2 tablespoons butter
1 cup milk	Paprika

Place fish, salt and pepper, lemon juice and bay leaves in skillet with enough water to cover; bring to boil. Drain fish and break into chunks. Combine melted butter, flour, milk, soup and Worcestershire sauce in saucepan; cook for 3 minutes; add sherry. Sauté mushrooms in a little butter. Add to soup mixture. Combine with fish chunks and half of cheese. Turn into casserole; sprinkle remaining cheese over top. Dot with 2 tablespoons butter and sprinkle with paprika. Bake at 375° for 20 minutes. Serves 6.

Hattie Atkins

SAUCY FISH BAKE

1 cup chopped onion	⅛ teaspoon pepper
½ cup chopped celery and leaves	¼ cup salad oil
½ cup chopped parsley	1 teaspoon paprika
2 pounds fish fillets	2 8-oz. cans tomato sauce
1 teaspoon salt	

Combine onion, celery and parsley in greased shallow baking dish. Place fish in overlapping layers over vegetables. Season with salt and pepper. Drizzle oil over top; sprinkle with paprika. Bake at 375° for 10 minutes. Pour tomato sauce over fish. Bake for 30 to 35 minutes longer, or until fish flakes, basting frequently with sauce. Serves 5.   *Bertha Gross*

FISH BAKED IN PAPER

3 pounds fish fillets (red snapper, trout, etc.)

¼ cup olive oil

¼ cup lemon juice

Salt and pepper

1 tablespoon orégano

1 clove garlic, slivered

Thin lemon slices

Chopped parsley

Wash the fish and salt lightly; combine olive oil and lemon juice. Dip fish pieces in oil mixture; sprinkle with salt and pepper. Make small slits in each piece; place pinch orégano and sliver of garlic in each slit. Place lemon slice on each and sprinkle with parsley. Wrap fish pieces individually in heavy brown paper or parchment; seal edges by folding over and over. Place on baking sheet; bake at 350° for about 30 minutes, or until fish flakes easily. Serves 8.

MOLDED GEFILTE FISH

6 pounds fish (whitefish, pike, trout, etc.)

1 large onion

6 eggs, separated

Salt and pepper

Sugar

1 cup cream

Clean fish, discarding heads, skin and bones. Grind fish with onion. Beat egg yolks until frothy; add to fish mixture. Add salt, pepper and sugar to taste. Stir in cream. Beat egg whites until stiff; fold into fish mixture. Turn into greased mold. Bake at 350° for 1¼ hours. Serves 12 to 14.

M. Weinstock

LOX SOUFFLÉ

¼ pound lox (or more)

Hot water

1¼ cups milk

1 large onion, diced

1 green pepper, diced

½ cup sliced mushrooms

½ cup butter

4 to 6 eggs

Pour hot water over lox; let stand for 15 minutes, then drain. Cover lox with milk and let stand. Sauté onion, green pepper and mushrooms in hot butter for about 10 minutes. Place sautéed mixture in shallow oven-glass baking dish. Drain lox, reserving milk. Place lox in baking dish. Beat eggs with reserved milk. Pour over lox. Bake at 350° for 45 to 60 minutes. Makes 3 or 4 servings.

Rose Fishman

CURRIED FISH BALLS À LA CHAFING DISH

2 pounds fish fillets (any white fish)

½ cup sesame or peanut oil

2 fresh chili peppers, ground (or ½ teaspoon ground dried chili peppers)

3 onions, finely chopped

4 cloves garlic, minced

1 teaspoon grated lemon rind

1 teaspoon turmeric

2 teaspoons salt

¼ cup flour

3 tomatoes, chopped

Wash fish thoroughly; remove and discard any bones. Grind fish twice or chop very fine. Sauté in skillet chili peppers, onions, garlic, lemon rind, turmeric and salt in ¼ cup hot oil for 10 minutes, stirring frequently. Remove one third of this mixture and combine with ground fish. Shape fish mixture into walnut-size balls. Roll lightly in flour. Add remaining oil to skillet; heat. Add fish balls and brown on all sides, stirring frequently. Add tomatoes and cook over low heat for 25 minutes. Turn into chafing dish. Serve hot over fluffy white rice. Makes 6 servings.   *Sandra Kaufman*

SALMON RICE BALLS

1 1-lb. can salmon

1 cup cooked rice

2 eggs, slightly beaten

1 tablespoon minced onion

1 teaspoon salt

½ cup bread crumbs

1 can cream of mushroom soup

1 soup can water

Combine salmon, rice, eggs, onion, salt and crumbs. Mix well. Shape into balls. Place in casserole. Combine soup and water. Pour over salmon balls. Bake at 350° for 30 to 45 minutes. Serves 5.   *Lillian Bender*

SALMON-CORN BAKE

1 1-lb. can salmon, drained and flaked

1 No. 2 can cream-style corn, drained

1 can cream of mushroom soup

½ cup bread crumbs

2 eggs, beaten

1 teaspoon grated onion

Salt and pepper

Crushed corn flakes

Combine all ingredients; mix well. Turn into greased casserole. Dot with butter; top with crushed corn flakes. Sprinkle with paprika. Bake at 325° for about 1 hour. Serves 6.   *Doris Soren*

ESCALLOPED SALMON AND EGGS

¼ cup melted butter

1 tablespoon minced onion

¼ cup flour

½ teaspoon salt

Dash paprika

2 cups milk

6 hard-cooked eggs, sliced

3 7¾-oz. cans salmon

¼ cup chopped green pepper

2 tablespoons butter

½ cup fine dry bread crumbs

¼ cup grated Cheddar cheese

Sauté onion in ¼ cup hot butter until transparent. Add flour, salt and paprika; blend well. Add milk and cook, stirring, until smooth and thick. Arrange eggs, salmon and green peppers in alternate layers in greased oven-glass baking dish. Pour milk mixture over top. Melt 2 tablespoons butter; remove from heat. Mix in crumbs and cheese; sprinkle on top of salmon mixture. Bake at 350° for 1 hour. Serves 4.   *Rozella Karol*

❖❖

A tablespoon of white distilled vinegar added to the water in which fish is simmering will keep fish firm and white.

❖❖

SALMON LOAF WITH CREAM SAUCE

1 1-lb. can salmon

½ cup milk

1 cup dry bread crumbs

½ cup melted butter or margarine

3 eggs, separated

2 tablespoons lemon juice

2 tablespoons minced onion

½ teaspoon salt

Dash pepper

1 can cream of mushroom soup

1 8-oz. can small peas, drained

Line bottom of 9x5x3-inch pan with aluminum foil. Grease foil; set pan aside. Drain salmon, reserving liquid. Flake salmon, removing skin and bones. Scald milk; add crumbs and melted butter. Let stand for 5 minutes. Add reserved salmon liquid and beat until well blended. Add salmon, egg yolks, lemon juice, onion, salt and pepper. Beat egg whites until stiff but not dry; fold into salmon mixture. Turn into prepared pan. Set pan in pan of hot water. Bake at 350° for 45 minutes, or until done. Meanwhile, combine mushroom soup and peas; heat. Serve salmon loaf, sliced, with sauce. Makes 4 servings.   *Iris Rubin*

SALMON CUPCAKE PUFFS

1 1-lb. can red salmon

1 cup sour cream

½ cup melted butter

3 cups corn flakes, slightly crushed

1 egg, slightly beaten

Drain and flake salmon; combine in bowl with remaining ingredients. Mix well. Lightly pack into 6 greased custard cups. Set cups in pan of hot water. Bake at 350° for 1 to 1½ hours, or until puffy and nicely browned. Unmold and serve with cream sauce, if desired. Makes 6 servings.

Mrs. Marshall Paskind

TUNA PARISIENNE

5 stalks celery

1 small onion

¼ cup butter

1 15-oz. can tuna, drained and flaked

1 2-oz. jar pimiento

1 4-oz. can mushrooms

1 No. 303 can peas

2 tablespoons cornstarch

1 cup milk

Salt and pepper

Paprika

¼ cup butter or margarine

Grated Cheddar cheese

⅓ cup sherry

Cut celery and onion into small pieces; sauté in ¼ cup hot butter until golden brown. Drain mushrooms and peas, reserving liquid. Add tuna, pimiento, mushrooms and peas to sautéed mixture. Combine reserved liquid with cornstarch. Add milk, salt and pepper, paprika, ¼ cup butter and grated cheese to taste. Cook over medium heat, stirring until mixture thickens. Add sherry. Combine with tuna mixture and heat. Serves 6.

Janice Weil

MOCK CHOP SUEY

1 7-oz. can tuna, drained and flaked

1 4-oz. can mushrooms (stems and pieces), drained

1 No. 2 can Chinese vegetables, drained

1 8-oz. can water chestnuts

1 3-oz. can chow-mein noodles

1½ to 2 cans cream of mushroom soup

Mix together tuna, mushrooms, vegetables, water chestnuts and half of noodles. Pour undiluted soup over all and mix well. Turn into greased 2-qt. casserole. Sprinkle remaining noodles over top. Bake at 350° for 30 minutes. Serves 6 to 8.

Felicia Nadborne

TUNA CASSEROLE

1 15-oz. can water-pack tuna, drained

1 pound mushrooms

¼ cup butter

1 onion, minced

1 2-oz. jar pimiento, minced

1 green pepper, minced

3 or 4 slices Cheddar cheese, grated

1 can cream of mushroom soup

1½ cups milk

1 8-oz. package spaghetti or noodles cooked

½ cup chopped blanched almonds

Potato chips

Sauté tuna and mushrooms in butter. Add onion, pimiento, green pepper and cheese. Mix mushroom soup with milk and spaghetti. Add nuts; toss together with tuna mixture. Turn into greased 2-qt. casserole. Crush potato chips and sprinkle over top. Bake at 350° for 45 minutes. Serves 4 to 6.

Nan Potkin

TUNA ASPARAGUS BAKE

2 tablespoons flour

1 tablespoon chopped parsley

1½ teaspoons grated onion

1 teaspoon salt

½ teaspoon dry mustard

Dash pepper

1 cup skim milk or liquified nonfat dry milk

1 package frozen asparagus spears, cooked and drained

2 hard-cooked eggs, sliced

1 7-oz. can water-pack tuna, in chunks

Lemon juice

Snipped parsley

In small saucepan, combine flour, chopped parsley, onion, mustard, salt and pepper; stir in milk very slowly. Cook over low heat, stirring constantly, until smooth and thickened. Arrange asparagus, eggs and tuna in 1-qt. casserole. Pour milk mixture over top. Bake at 350° for about 30 minutes, or until hot and bubbly. Sprinkle with lemon juice and snipped parsley. Makes 4 servings.

TUNA TREASURE LOAF

1 1-lb. loaf French bread

¼ cup melted butter

2½ cups flaked tuna

1½ cups cubed process cheese

1 cup mayonnaise or salad dressing

½ cup pickle relish

Cut French bread in half lengthwise. Scoop out centers of both halves. Brush cavities with melted butter. Combine remaining ingredients; mix well. Fill bread halves with mixture. Place in shallow baking pan. Bake at 400° for 10 minutes. Cut each half into 5 slices. Serve hot. Makes 10 servings.

Evelyn G. Blum

CHILLED POACHED FISH

1 6 to 8-pound whitefish or trout (with head and tail)	Tartar Sauce, page 125
	Mayonnaise
Spice bag (mixed pickling spices tied in cheesecloth bag)	Chopped parsley
Lemon juice	Pimiento strips
Salt and pepper	Grated egg yolk
Stuffed Shrimp, page 121	

Wrap fish in cheesecloth. Place fish, spice bag, lemon juice, salt and pepper in large skillet with enough boiling water to cover. Cook over low heat for about 40 minutes, or until done. Remove fish to large platter. Discard cheesecloth. Cool fish. Meanwhile, prepare Stuffed Shrimp and Tartar Sauce. Skin fish; tuck endive around it. Frost entire fish, including head, with mayonnaise. Garnish with parsley, pimiento strips, egg yolk and, if desired, decorate with flowers made by forcing mayonnaise through a pastry tube. Arrange Stuffed Shrimp around fish; chill in refrigerator until ready to serve. Serve with Tartar Sauce. Serves 8. *Sylvea Zimmerman*

FISH IN WINE SAUCE

3 pounds whitefish, pike or carp	1½ cups raisins
½ cup firmly packed brown sugar	2 tablespoons sherry
Juice of 1 lemon	Salt
1 onion, diced	1 lemon, sliced
1 stick cinnamon	Parsley sprigs

Clean fish; sprinkle with salt. Chill in refrigerator for several hours. Slice in serving portions; cover with boiling water and simmer for about 10 minutes, or until fish flakes easily. Drain fish, reserving liquid. Place fish on serving platter. Combine 1 cup reserved liquid with brown sugar, lemon juice, onion, cinnamon stick, raisins, sherry and salt. Simmer until mixture is thick, about 10 minutes. Strain and pour over fish. Garnish with lemon slices and parsley. Chill in refrigerator until ready to serve. Makes 6 servings. *Libbie R. Frost*

FISH MARINADE

4 to 6 pounds trout, whitefish or pike

3 onions, sliced

2 carrots, sliced

1 tablespoon mixed pickling spices

2½ cups vinegar

1 cup granulated sugar

1 envelope unflavored gelatine

½ cup water

1 lemon, sliced

Salt fish; let stand overnight without washing. Next day, clean fish, reserving fish heads. Place fish heads in kettle; add onions, carrots, spices and water to cover; simmer for 30 minutes. Add vinegar and sugar and simmer for 15 minutes longer. Meanwhile, fillet fish; add fish to kettle; add water if necessary and simmer for 15 minutes. Place fish fillets on serving dish having a tight cover, reserving cooking liquid. Dissolve gelatine in ½ cup water. Strain reserved cooking liquid; add to gelatine mixture. Pour over fish. Arrange lemon slices over top. Chill in refrigerator for at least 48 hours. Keeps well in refrigerator for 2 to 3 weeks. Makes 12 servings. *Lill Raizner*

ARTICHOKE AND SEA-FOOD CASSEROLE

2 large artichokes

2 cups mixed flaked, shredded or chopped cooked sea food (shrimp, lobster or crab meat)

½ green pepper, chopped

1 teaspoon chopped parsley or dill

¼ teaspoon curry powder

¼ teaspoon ground ginger

¼ teaspoon paprika

Salt and pepper

½ cup buttermilk

Cook artichokes in 1-inch boiling salted water for about 30 minutes. Clip off tips of leaves, remove chokes and discard. Reserve hearts; line bottom and sides of greased casserole with leaves. Mix sea food with green pepper, parsley, curry powder, ginger, salt, pepper and paprika. Add buttermilk; mix well. Pour over artichocke leaves in casserole. Cut hearts into quarters; arrange in circle in center of sea-food mixture. Bake at 375° until top begins to brown. Makes 2 large or 4 small servings.

SHRIMP DE JONGHE

1 pound cleaned uncooked shrimp

1 cup dry bread crumbs

½ cup butter

1 tablespoon chopped parsley

2 cloves garlic, slivered

½ cup sherry or other white wine

Place layer of shrimp in greased casserole; top with layer of bread crumbs, reserving 2 tablespoons for topping. Dot shrimp with butter; sprinkle with parsley and garlic. Top with remaining crumbs. Pour sherry over all. Bake at 350° for 30 minutes, or until bubbly and brown on top. Makes about 4 servings.   *Sydelle Prebish*

QUICK SHRIMP CURRY

1 can frozen shrimp soup

1 soup can milk

1 6-oz. package frozen shrimp

1 teaspoon curry powder

Combine shrimp soup and milk according to directions on can. Cook frozen shrimp according to directions on package. Combine with soup and add curry powder, more or less, to taste. Serve over fluffy white rice with curry accompaniments such as chutney, chopped egg, salted nuts, etc., if desired. Makes 4 servings.

SHRIMP CREOLE

1 cup chopped celery

3 tablespoons chopped green pepper

1 small onion, chopped

3 tablespoons butter

1 6-oz. can tomato paste

1¼ cups tomato juice

⅛ teaspoon baking soda

3 tablespoons cornstarch

½ cup water

½ cup tomato juice

1 teaspoon chili powder

½ teaspoon paprika

⅛ teaspoon garlic powder

½ cup mushrooms

1½ pounds cleaned cooked shrimp

2 cups cooked rice

Sauté celery, green pepper and onion in hot butter. Combine tomato paste, 1¼ cups tomato juice and baking soda. Add to sautéed mixture. Cook slowly, covered, for about 15 minutes. Dissolve cornstarch in water and ½ cup tomato juice. Add to cooked mixture with chili powder, paprika and garlic powder. Add mushrooms and shrimp; simmer for 5 minutes. Serve over rice. Makes 4 servings.   *Elaine Thomas*

SHRIMP IN WINE SAUCE

2 pounds cleaned uncooked shrimp	1 teaspoon salt
½ cup flour	½ teaspoon pepper
½ cup olive oil	Dash cayenne pepper
½ cup dry white wine	1 tablespoon chopped parsley
2 teaspoons tomato paste	1 scallion, chopped
4 tablespoons warm water	2 teaspoons lemon juice

Roll shrimp in flour. Sauté shrimp in hot olive oil until brown on both sides. Drain shrimp, reserving oil. Return shrimp to skillet; add wine and cook over low heat until wine is absorbed. Combine reserved oil with tomato paste, water, salt and peppers in saucepan. Cook over low heat for 5 minutes. Pour over shrimp in skillet; add parsley and scallion; cook for 5 minutes. Remove from heat; sprinkle with lemon juice and serve. Makes 6 servings.

Sandra Kaufman

SHRIMP TIMBALES

½ pound cleaned cooked shrimp	½ teaspoon monosodium glutamate (optional)
½ green pepper	¼ teaspoon ground ginger
1 stalk celery	Salt and pepper
½ onion	3 tablespoons tomato sauce
1 egg	1 teaspoon freshly ground horse-radish

Grind together shrimp, green pepper, celery and onion. Mix with egg, monosodium glutamate, ginger, salt and pepper. Turn into 2 ramekins or custard cups. Bake at 350° for 30 to 40 minutes. Meanwhile, combine tomato sauce and horse-radish. Unmold shrimp mixture; top with tomato mixture. Makes 2 servings.

HOT SHRIMP SCAMPI

2 pounds cleaned uncooked shrimp	½ cup butter
Salt and pepper	1 large clove garlic

Arrange shrimp in broiler pan; sprinkle with salt and pepper. Melt butter with garlic; pour over shrimp. Place under broiler for 6 to 7 minutes, basting occasionally. Serve from a chafing dish. Serves 4 to 6.

Ethel Taub

COMPANY SHRIMP CASSEROLE

2 pounds cleaned cooked shrimp

Scant ¼ cup butter

1½ cups hot milk

1 cup bread crumbs

½ cup minced parsley

1 small clove garlic, cut fine (or ¼ teaspoon garlic salt)

1½ teaspoons salt

⅛ teaspoon pepper

¼ cup grated Parmesan cheese

½ cup soft butter

Sauté shrimp in scant ¼ cup butter. Remove to greased baking dish. Pour hot milk over bread crumbs. Mix well with fork; let stand until thick. If mixture becomes too thick, add milk as necessary (should be consistency of soft custard). Add parsley, garlic salt, pepper and soft butter. Spread over shrimp in baking dish. Sprinkle with cheese and drizzle with a little melted butter. Bake at 350° for 30 minutes. Serves 6 to 8.   *Marilyn Schiller*

STUFFED SHRIMP

Cooked jumbo shrimp

Flaked crab meat

Mayonnaise

Finely chopped celery

Salt and pepper

Mixed salad herbs

Slit backs of shrimp. Combine all other ingredients; mix well. Using teaspoon, stuff shrimp with crab meat mixture. Chill in refrigerator until ready to serve.   *Sylvea Zimmerman*

CRAB MORNAY

2 cups thick cream sauce

2 7-oz. cans crab meat, flaked

2 tablespoons sherry

2 slices mild Cheddar cheese

2 tablespoons melted butter

Paprika

Pour thin layer of cream sauce into each of 4 ramekins or shells. Into each ramekin place one-fourth of crab meat, 1½ teaspoons sherry, one-fourth of remaining cream sauce and top with ½ slice cheese. Drizzle 1½ teaspoons butter over each and sprinkle with paprika. Bake at 350° for 10 minutes. Serves 4.   *Ruth Rose*

CRAB PUFFS

8 baked Tart Shells, page 220

1 tablespoon finely chopped onion

½ clove garlic, minced

3 tablespoons butter

¼ cup flour

1¾ cups cream

¼ cup sherry

½ teaspoon salt

Few drops Tabasco sauce

1 6½-oz. can crab meat, flaked

1 cup grated sharp process cheese

1 8-oz. package soft cream cheese

1 teaspoon Worcestershire sauce

¼ cup cream

1 teaspoon baking powder

1 teaspoon dry mustard

1 teaspoon paprika

1 egg

Yellow food coloring

Sauté onion and garlic in hot butter until lightly browned. Blend in flour; gradually add 1¾ cup cream, and cook, stirring, over medium heat until mixture is smooth and thickened. Stir in sherry, salt and Tabasco sauce; add crab meat and mix well. Spoon into baked tart shells. Mix cheese, Worcestershire sauce and ¼ cup cream, beating until fluffy. Add baking powder, mustard, paprika and egg and blend well. Tint delicate yellow with few drops food coloring. Spread over crab mixture. Place under broiler for 3 or 4 minutes, or until puffy and lightly browned. If desired, prepare, cool and refrigerate a day in advance. Reheat at 350° before serving. Serves 8.   *Lee Bateman*

CRAB CASSEROLE

2 tablespoons butter

1 cup mushrooms, finely chopped

½ medium green pepper, finely chopped

1½ tablespoons flour

⅓ cup nonfat dry milk powder

½ cup water

¼ teaspoon salt

⅛ teaspoon pepper

1 egg yolk, beaten

2 7-oz. cans crab meat, in chunks

1 tablespoon grated Parmesan cheese

1 tablespoon dry bread crumbs

Sauté mushrooms and green pepper in hot butter in top of double boiler. Blend in flour; add dry milk and water, salt and pepper. Cook, stirring, over hot water until mixture thickens. Add small amount of hot mixture to egg yolk, then add egg yolk to creamed mixture. Add crab meat; mix gently. Pour into 4 ramekins or shells. Toss cheese with bread crumbs; sprinkle over crab meat mixture. Bake at 350° for 30 minutes. Serves 4.

CRAB DELIGHT

2 tablespoons chopped green pepper	½ teaspoon Worcestershire sauce
2 tablespoons butter	½ teaspoon dry mustard
2 tablespoons flour	Dash cayenne
1 cup strained tomatoes	¼ teaspoon salt
1 cup grated process cheese	⅔ cup scalded milk
1 egg, slightly beaten	1 7-oz. can crab meat, flaked

Sauté green pepper in butter for 3 minutes. Add flour and mix until smooth. Combine tomatoes, cheese, egg, Worcestershire sauce, mustard, cayenne and salt. Add to flour mixture. Cook in top of double boiler over hot water for 10 minutes. Add milk slowly, stirring constantly. Add crab meat and heat thoroughly. Serve in patty shells or on toast. Makes 4 servings.

Raye Korshak

CRAB BUNWICHES: Mix melted butter, lemon juice, salt and pepper. Roll soft-shelled crabs in mixture, then in flour. Sauté in butter in skillet and serve in toasted buns with tartar sauce.

CRAB NEWBURG

¼ cup butter	1 teaspoon salt
3 tablespoons flour	½ teaspoon celery salt
2 cups milk	¼ teaspoon pepper
2 tablespoons minced onion	2 tablespoons sherry
2 tablespoons minced green pepper	1 egg, beaten
2 tablespoons snipped parsley	3 7-oz. cans crab meat, flaked
1 pimiento, minced	½ cup bread crumbs
1 teaspoon grated orange rind	½ cup grated cheese

Melt butter in saucepan; add flour; stir until smooth; add milk gradually, stirring, until mixture is thick and creamy. Add onion, green pepper, parsley, pimiento, orange rind, salts and pepper. Remove from heat; add sherry. Pour a little of hot mixture onto egg; stirr egg into creamed mixture. Stir in crab meat. Pour into greased casserole. Toss bread crumbs with cheese; sprinkle over crab meat mixture. Bake at 350° for about 25 minutes, or until bubbly and lightly browned. Makes 6 servings. *Jeannette Kowitt*

BROILED LOBSTER TAILS

4 12-oz. thawed frozen rock lobster tails	½ teaspoon onion juice
½ cup melted butter	⅛ teaspoon salt
½ cup bread crumbs	⅛ teaspoon monosodium glutamate
2 tablespoons butter	Dash pepper
½ teaspoon lemon juice	Paprika

Remove thin under shell from lobster tails. Place on rack in broiler pan, shell-sides up. Broil 4 inches from heat for 6 to 8 minutes. Turn and brush with melted butter. Broil for 4 minutes. Meanwhile, combine bread crumbs, butter, lemon juice, onion juice, salt, monosodium glutamate and pepper. Brush lobster tails with more melted butter; sprinkle with crumb mixture. Continue to broil for 2 minutes longer, or until done. Sprinkle with paprika. Serve with lemon wedges. Serves 4.

LOBSTER NEWBURG

¼ cup butter	3 egg yolks, beaten
2 cups diced cooked lobster	1 cup light cream
½ teaspoon paprika	¼ cup sherry
¼ teaspoon nutmeg	Salt

Melt butter in top of double boiler. Add lobster and cook, stirring, for 3 minutes. Add paprika and nutmeg; cook for 1 minute longer. Add egg yolks and cream; cook, stirring, over low heat for 2 minutes. *Do not boil.* Add sherry and salt to taste. Serve over toast or rice. Serves 6.   *Edith Dratler*

LOBSTER THERMIDOR

3 lobsters (2¼ lbs. each)	2 cups heavy cream
¼ cup olive oil	3 tablespoons flour
1½ teaspoons salt	1 cup milk
Freshly ground black pepper	½ teaspoon salt
¾ cup butter	½ cup grated Parmesan cheese
¼ cup prepared mustard	

Split lobsters lengthwise. Brush with oil and sprinkle with 1 teaspoon salt and pepper. Place under broiler at 350° for 5 minutes. Remove from broiler; dot each lobster half with 1 tablespoon butter. Place on baking sheet; bake at 400° for 10 minutes. Remove lobster meat and coral from shells carefully; set coral aside. Brush inside of each shell lightly with mustard. Break lobster meat into chunks with 2 forks. Place in shells. Meanwhile, simmer cream over low heat for 30 minutes, stirring occasionally. Melt 4 tablespoons butter; stir in flour. Add milk slowly with ½ teaspoon salt; cook, stirring constantly, until mixture is smooth. Mix in cream and reserved coral. Pour over lobster meat in shells. Sprinkle with cheese and dot with remaining butter. Bake at 400° for 10 minutes. Serves 6.   *Ruth Rose*

SAUCES FOR FISH

TARTAR SAUCE

1 cup mayonnaise

¼ cup chili sauce

2 scallions, finely chopped (or 1 tablespoon chopped chives)

2 hard-cooked eggs, chopped

3 sweet pickles, finely chopped

10 stuffed green olives, sliced

2 tablespoons caviar

1 clove garlic, mashed

Dash cayenne pepper

Dash paprika

Combine all ingredients. Chill in refrigerator. Serve with hot or cold fish.

Sylvea Zimmerman

SAUCE DIABLE

⅓ cup dry white wine

3 shallots, chopped

8 peppercorns, crushed

1 cup consommé

1 teaspoon Worcestershire sauce

½ teaspoon chopped parsley

Combine wine, shallots and peppercorns in small saucepan; cook until mixture is reduced to a thick paste. Add consommé, Worcestershire sauce and parsley; cook until just blended. Serve with fish, or with broiled meat or poultry. Makes about 1¼ cups.

ORIENTAL FAVORITES

To win the heart of your husband—satisfy his stomach.

To uphold the love of your dearest ones—serve them a
good variety of food.

To expect your children to grow strong—give them
appetite.

Confucius (551-479 B.C.)

WON TON SOUP

WON TON:

1½ cup sifted flour

1 egg, slightly beaten

1 teaspoon salt

⅓ cup water

½ pound raw or cooked beef or shrimp,
finely chopped

2 teaspoons finely chopped scallions

½ teaspoon salt

Dash pepper

SOUP:

4 cups chicken bouillon

½ cup diced celery

½ cup shredded cooked meat or chicken
(optional)

1 cup tightly packed spinach

Place flour, egg and 1 teaspoon salt in bowl. Add water and mix well. Turn
out on floured surface and knead until smooth. Cover and let stand for
about 15 minutes. Roll out as thin as paper. Cut into 3-inch squares. Combine
beef, scallions, ½ teaspoon salt and pepper. Place 1 teaspoonful of mixture
in center of each square. Fold corners together diagonally; press edges
with fork to seal. Cook in 1 quart boiling salted water for 15 minutes.
Transfer to 4 soup bowls. Keep warm. Bring chicken bouillon to boiling in
saucepot; add celery. Cook over medium heat for 5 minutes; add meat and
spinach. Cook for 1 minute longer. Pour over Won Ton in soup bowls.
Makes 4 servings. *Marian Peterman*

MANDARIN BEEF

1½ pounds round steak

⅓ cup soy sauce

1 teaspoon granulated sugar

3 large tomatoes, peeled

2 green peppers

¼ cup peanut oil

1 clove garlic

¾ teaspoon ground ginger

2 teaspoons cornstarch

2 tablespoons soy sauce

Cut round steak across grain into paper-thin slices. (This is easier to do if meat is frozen.) Place meat in bowl with mixture of ⅓ cup soy sauce and sugar. Marinate for 30 minutes, turning after first 15 minutes. Cut tomatoes into eighths; cut green pepper into julienne strips about 1½ inches long. Heat oil in skillet; add garlic and ginger. Cook for several minutes; remove and discard garlic. Add green pepper strips and sauté, stirring constantly, for 3 minutes. Add beef and marinade and cook for 3 minutes longer. Add tomatoes; cover and simmer for several minutes until tomatoes are hot. Blend constarch with 2 tablespoons soy sauce; gently stir into mixture in skillet. Cook for 1 minute longer. Serves 6.   *Lois Payne*

SUKIYAKI

1 to 2 pounds flank, sirloin or tenderloin steak

1 4-oz. can mushrooms

6 stalks celery, sliced very thin

1 onion, sliced very thin diagonally

1 package thawed frozen spinach, green beans or broccoli, drained

1 No. 2 can bean sprouts, drained

8 green onions, chopped

¼ cup sliced pimiento

SAUCE:

⅔ cup consommé

½ cup soy sauce

3 tablespoons lemon juice

1½ tablespoons granulated sugar

1 tablespoon molasses

Cut meat across grain into thin diagonal strips. Drain mushrooms, reserving liquid for sauce. Place ingredients in separate piles on waxed paper. Heat a little oil in electric skillet. Sauté steak briefly; push to one side. Add celery and sliced onion; sauté only until transparent. Push aside. Add mushrooms, spinach and bean sprouts. Cook for 3 to 5 minutes, or just until heated. Add green onions and pimiento; cook for 2 minutes longer. Serve immediately over rice. *Do not overcook.* If desired, combine consommé, soy sauce, 4 tablespoons reserved mushroom liquid, lemon juice, sugar and molasses. Bring quickly to boiling. Serve sauce over Sukiyaki. Makes 4 to 6 servings.   *Marian D. Horwitz*

STEAK ORIENTAL

1 small onion, chopped	1 pound round steak, cut into pieces
1 clove garlic, minced	2 tablespoons salad oil
2 tablespoons soy sauce	1 small green pepper, chopped
1 scant teaspoon salt	1 4-oz. can mushrooms, chopped
Dash pepper	4 ounces slivered almonds, chopped

Combine onion, garlic, soy sauce, salt and pepper. Pour over steak and set in refrigerator to marinate overnight. When ready to serve, drain meat; cook for 5 to 7 minutes in hot oil. Add green pepper, mushrooms and almonds; cook for 5 minutes longer. Serve with Fried Rice, page 142, or chow-mein noodles. Serves 4. *Blossom Porter*

BEEF CANTONESE

1 pound round steak, cut into small pieces	1 can beef bouillon
2 tablespoons salad oil	2 3-oz. cans mushrooms, drained
1 teaspoon salt	2 tablespoons cornstarch
Dash pepper	2 tablespoons soy sauce
2 teaspoons chopped onion	¼ cup water
1 clove garlic, minced	

Sauté meat in hot oil; season with salt and pepper. Add onion and garlic and cook over low heat, stirring constantly, for 20 minutes. Add bouillon and mushrooms. Cover and simmer for 30 minutes. Combine cornstarch, soy sauce and water; add to meat mixture, stirring until smooth. Continue to cook for 20 minutes longer. Serve over rice seasoned with lemon juice. Serves 4. *Lucille Yellen*

CHINESE NOODLES

1 egg	½ teaspoon salt
½ cup flour	Dash garlic salt

Beat egg with flour, salt and garlic salt. Roll out on well-floured surface paper thin. Cut into strips desired width. Fry in hot oil until light brown. Drain on absorbent paper. Makes ¼ pound. *Jeanie Greene*

CANTONESE POT ROAST

1 4 to 5-lb. pot roast

2 tablespoons shortening

1 2-oz. can button mushrooms

¼ cup water

2 tablespoons soy sauce

1 teaspoon ground ginger

1 cup finely chopped onion

1 cup chopped celery

¾ cup finely chopped green pepper

GRAVY:

2 tablespoons cornstarch

2 tablespoons water

1 13-oz. can pineapple tidbits

½ cup water

Brown roast on all sides in hot shortening in Dutch oven. Drain mushrooms, reserving liquid. Combine mushroom liquid with ¼ cup water, soy sauce and ginger. Pour over roast. Add onion, celery and green pepper; cover and cook over low to medium heat for 2 to 2½ hours, or until meat is fork-tender. Remove from pan to warm serving platter; keep hot while preparing gravy. Make a paste of cornstarch and 2 tablespoons water. Drain pineapple, reserving ½ cup juice. Combine pineapple juice with ½ cup water; add to drippings in Dutch oven. Blend well; heat to boiling. Slowly stir in cornstarch mixture; bring to boiling again. Add pineapple tidbits. Serve with roast. Makes 6 to 8 servings. *Poppy Brooks*

CHOP SUEY

3 pounds beef, veal or chicken, cut into 1-inch cubes

½ cup shortening

Salt and pepper

½ cup water

4 cups sliced onions (lengthwise slices)

4 cups sliced celery (1-inch slices)

⅓ cup chopped green pepper

¼ cup pimiento strips

1 No. 2 can bean sprouts

2 4-oz. cans mushrooms, drained, or ½ pound fresh mushrooms

Salt and pepper

¼ cup soy sauce

¼ cup cornstarch

¼ cup water

Sauté beef, a little at a time, in hot shortening, until browned on all sides. Season with salt and pepper. Add ½ cup water; cover and simmer for 30 to 60 minutes, or until tender. Add more water as necessary. Combine onions, celery, green pepper, pimiento and bean sprouts. Sauté mushrooms in a little butter. Add to vegetable mixture. Season with salt and pepper. Add to meat and cook for 10 minutes longer. Combine soy sauce, cornstarch and ¼ cup water. Stir into chop suey and cook just until thickened. Serves 8 to 10. *Goldye Gordon*

QUICK CHOP SUEY (Pressure Cooked)

2 pounds stew meat, diced

1 tablespoon shortening

1 teaspoon salt

⅛ teaspoon pepper

1½ cups chopped onion

½ cup chopped green pepper

2 tablespoons soy sauce

1½ teaspoons granulated sugar

1 teaspoon concentrated meat extract

2 cups water

1 tablespoon molasses

1 No. 2 can bean sprouts

1 No. 2 can mixed Chinese vegetables

5 tablespoons cornstarch

½ cup water

Brown meat in hot shortening in pressure saucepan. Add salt and pepper, onion, green pepper, soy sauce, sugar, meat extract, water and molasses. Heat to 15 pounds pressure; cook 10 minutes. Reduce heat gradually. Add bean sprouts and Chinese vegetables. Combine cornstarch with ½ cup water; stir into mixture and cook over low heat until thickened, stirring constantly. Serve over rice or chow-mein noodles. Serves 6 to 8.   *Lucille Yellen*

The secret to successful Oriental dishes is do not overcook.

CHINESE HAMBURGERS

1 pound ground beef

3 tablespoons soy sauce

1 tablespoon Worcestershire sauce

1 teaspoon salt

1 teaspoon granulated sugar

¼ teaspoon ground ginger

2 tablespoons peanut oil

8 green onions, cut up

6 stalks celery, cut up

3 tomatoes, cut into wedges

1 green pepper, cut into ¼-inch strips

1 can consommé

2½ tablespoons cornstarch

Combine beef, soy and Worcestershire sauce, salt, sugar and ginger. Shape into thin patties about 2 inches in diameter. Brown on both sides in hot oil in large heavy skillet. Push aside. Add onions, celery and green pepper. Cook for about 5 minutes. Add ¼ of consommé. Combine remaining consommé with cornstarch; mix well. Add to skillet; cook, stirring constantly, until mixture is thick and clear. Add tomatoes; cook 1 minute longer. Serve with hot rice. Serves 4 or 5.   *Shirley Levititz*

TIM-SHUN-YOK-KOW (Sweet-and-Sour Meat Balls)

3 large green peppers, cut into sixths	1 teaspoon salt
1 pound ground beef	1 cup chicken bouillon
1 egg	4 slices canned pineapple, cut into sixths
2 tablespoons flour	½ cup sugar
½ teaspoon salt	3 tablespoons cornstarch
Dash pepper	½ cup vinegar
¾ cup salad oil or shortening	2 teaspoons soy sauce

Cook green peppers in boiling water until almost tender. Shape ground beef into 16 small balls. Combine egg, flour, ½ teaspoon salt and pepper. Dip meat balls into egg mixture. Heat oil and 1 teaspoon salt in heavy 10-inch skillet. Brown meat balls on all sides, about 10 minutes. Remove meat balls to hot platter and keep warm. Pour off all but 1 tablespoon oil. Add ⅓ cup chicken bouillon, pineapple and drained green pepper. Cook over very low heat for 10 minutes. Blend together sugar, cornstarch, vinegar, soy sauce and remaining bouillon. Add to skillet; cook, stirring constantly, until thickened and very hot, about 5 minutes. Pour over meat balls. Serve with hot rice. Serves 4. *Marian Peterman*

CHICKEN CHOW MEIN

1 green pepper, cut into thin strips	1 9-oz. can pineapple chunks
1 medium onion, cut into thin strips	4 cups slivered cooked chicken
1 cup sliced celery (1-inch slices)	1½ teaspoons salt
2 tablespoons salad oil	¾ cup chicken broth
1 2-oz. can mushrooms	2 tablespoons soy sauce
1 2-oz. jar pimiento	¼ cup cornstarch
1 No. 2 can bean sprouts	Chow-mein noodles
1 8-oz. can bamboo shoots	Toasted slivered almonds
1 8-oz. can water chestnuts	

Sauté green pepper, onion and celery in hot oil for 5 minutes. Add mushrooms, pimiento, bean sprouts, bamboo shoots, water chestnuts, pineapple, chicken and salt. (Do not drain canned vegetables.) Bring to boiling. Combine broth, soy sauce and cornstarch. Add to vegetables and cook, stirring, until mixture thickens. Serve over chow-mein noodles; sprinkle with toasted almonds. Serves 8. *Lee Bateman*

CANTONESE CHICKEN ALMOND

2 cups sliced raw chicken breast	½ cup blanched almonds
¼ cup peanut oil	2 or 3 cups consommé
1 8-oz. can bamboo shoots, drained	¼ cup soy sauce
1 No. 2 can mixed Chinese vegetables	½ teaspoon bead molasses
1 8-oz. can water chestnuts, drained	1 teaspoon monosodium glutamate
1½ cups thinly sliced celery	½ cup water
1 cup diced bok choy (Chinese chard)	¼ cup cornstarch

Sauté chicken in hot oil until all pink color has disappeared. Add bamboo shoots, drained vegetables, water chestnuts, bok choy, celery, almonds, consommé, soy sauce, molasses and monosodium glutamate. Mix well. Cover and cook for 5 minutes. Meanwhile, combine water and cornstarch; cook, stirring, until thick and clear. Add to chicken mixture and cook only until thick. Serve with rice. Serves 8.   *Marian D. Horwitz*

LUAN CHICKEN WITH ALMONDS

1 3½ to 4-lb. ready-to-cook frying chicken, cut up	½ cup finely chopped parsley
	⅔ cup finely chopped blanched almonds
Salt and pepper	½ cup soft butter or margarine
1 6½-oz. can crushed pineapple, drained	

Arrange chicken pieces in shallow baking pan. Sprinkle with salt and pepper to taste. Combine remaining ingredients, mixing into a paste. Spread over chicken pieces. Bake at 325° for 50 minutes, or until tender. Serves 4 or 5.
Lee Bateman

CHICKEN ORIENTAL

1 3½ to 4-lb. ready-to-cook broiler-fryer, cut up	2 tablespoons vinegar
	1 tablespoon soy sauce
1 teaspoon monosodium glutamate	2 green peppers, cut into strips
¼ cup shortening	2 medium onions, sliced
1 3 or 4-oz. can mushrooms	1½ tablespoons cornstarch
1 13-oz. can pineapple chunks	2 tablespoons water
2 tablespoons granulated sugar	3 cups hot cooked rice

Sprinkle flesh sides of chicken pieces with monosodium glutamate. Let stand 15 to 20 minutes. Brown chicken pieces on all sides in hot shortening in skillet. Drain mushrooms and pineapple, reserving liquids. Combine reserved liquids with enough water to make 2 cups. Add to skillet and bring to boiling. Cover, reduce heat and simmer for 1 hour. Stir in sugar, vinegar and soy sauce. Add mushrooms, pineapple, green peppers and onions. Cook for 15 minutes longer. Blend cornstarch with water; stir into chicken mixture. Cook, stirring, until slightly thickened. Serve with hot rice. Serves 6 to 8.

Jeannette Weintraub

CHINESE DUCK

1 4-lb. ready-to-cook duck, cut into 8 pieces

¼ cup peanut oil

Pinch garlic salt

Dash pepper

½ cup chopped green onions

1 3-oz. can mushrooms

2 tablespoons soy sauce

2 tablespoons water

Remove all fat from duck. Sauté in hot oil until golden brown on all sides. Season with garlic salt and pepper (no salt). Mix together onions, mushrooms, soy sauce and water. Drain duck on absorbent paper. Place in saucepan or chafing dish. Pour vegetable mixture over top. Cook, covered, over low heat for 1 hour, or until tender. Serve with hot rice. Serves 4.

Midge Strauss

When cooking regular rice to accompany Oriental dishes allow scant ¼ cup raw rice per serving. If using packaged pre-cooked allow ⅓ cup per serving.

HAR-CHOW-FON (Shrimp with Fried Rice)

2 eggs

1 teaspoon salt

Dash pepper

3 tablespoons peanut oil

1 pound cleaned shrimp, cut into thirds

½ cup sliced mushrooms

⅓ cup diced onion

4 cups cold cooked rice

2 tablespoons soy sauce

½ teaspoon granulated sugar

Beat eggs with salt and pepper. Cook in hot oil in 10-inch skillet until firm. Cut into shreds. Add shrimp, mushrooms and onions; cook over medium heat for 5 minutes. Add rice, soy sauce and sugar. Cook until rice is thoroughly heated. Serve immediately. Serves 4 to 6. *Marian Peterman*

CHOW-LOONG-HAR (Canton Lobster)

½ pound coarsely ground cooked beef	Dash pepper
1 tablespoon diced celery	2 cooked lobsters
1 tablespoon diced scallions	1 cup chicken bouillon
½ teaspoon salt	1 egg, slightly beaten
Dash pepper	2 tablespoons cornstarch
3 tablespoons peanut oil	¼ cup water
1 teaspoon salt	2 teaspoons soy sauce

Mix together beef, celery, scallions, ½ teaspoon salt and pepper. Cut lobster through shell into halves; then cut crosswise into 1-inch pieces. Heat peanut oil with 1 teaspoon salt and pepper in heavy 10-inch skillet. Place lobsters, beef mixture and bouillon in skillet. Cover and cook, over medium heat, for about 10 minutes. Add egg and cook over high heat, stirring constantly, for 2 minutes. Combine cornstarch with water and soy sauce. Add to skillet and cook, stirring, until mixture thickens and is very hot. Serve immediately over hot rice. Serves 4.   *Betty Markey*

LOBSTER CANTONESE

6 4-oz. thawed frozen rock lobster tails	1 tablespoon soy sauce
1 clove garlic, minced	4 green onions and tops, cut into 1-inch pieces
¼ cup peanut oil	
1 cup bouillon	3 eggs, slightly beaten
1 tablespoon cornstarch	Salt and pepper

Cut away underside membrane and remove lobster meat from shells. Cut into 2-inch pieces. Sauté garlic in hot oil. Add lobster meat and sauté for 3 minutes, turning only once. (Meat will turn white when cooked.) Add bouillon and simmer for 5 minutes. Mix together cornstarch and soy sauce. Stir into lobster and cook until thickened. Add green onions and cook for 5 minutes longer. Just before serving, stir in eggs, salt and pepper to taste. Serve over rice. Serves 6.   *Clare Schaeffer*

CANTONESE SHRIMP

½ cup sliced onion

¼ cup peanut oil

1 pound cleaned shrimp

1 cup bean sprouts, drained

1 8-oz. can water chestnuts, drained and sliced

1 cup sliced green pepper

½ cup chopped celery

1 cup applesauce

1 cup consommé

Dash pepper

3 tablespoons cornstarch

3 tablespoons cold water

1½ tablespoons soy sauce

3 tomatoes, quartered

½ cup chopped green onions

Sauté sliced onion in hot oil until transparent. Add shrimp, bean sprouts, water chestnuts, green pepper and celery. Mix well. Add applesauce, consommé and pepper. Combine cornstarch, water and soy sauce. Stir into shrimp mixture. Cook only until mixture thickens and is hot. Add tomatoes and green onions, cook for 2 minutes longer. *Do not overcook.* Serve with chow-mein noodles. Serves 4.   *Marian D. Horwitz*

EGG FOO YUNG

water chestnuts canned mushrooms

1 No. 2 can bean sprouts, drained

¾ cup thinly sliced onion

¼ cup diced celery

1½ to 2 cups thinly sliced cooked meat

6 to 8 eggs, beaten

¾ teaspoon pepper

½ teaspoon salt

SAUCE:

3 cups chicken broth

2 cups mushroom steak sauce

Molasses

3 tablespoons cornstarch

Combine bean sprouts, onion, celery, meat, eggs, pepper and salt. Drop by generous tablespoonfuls into hot shortening in skillet. Fry for 5 minutes on each side, turning only once. Combine broth with steak sauce. Add molasses to taste and enough cornstarch to thicken. Cook over medium heat, stirring, until thick. Pour over egg foo yung patties. Serve with rice. Serves 6.   *Lee Nathan*

NOODLES
SPAGHETTI
AND
RICE

NOODLES ROMANOFF

1 8-oz. package noodles	1 teaspoon Worcestershire sauce
1 cup large curd cottage cheese	¼ teaspoon Tabasco sauce
1 cup sour cream	Chopped pimiento or green pepper
¼ cup grated onion	½ cup grated process Cheddar cheese
1 clove garlic, mashed	

Cook noodles just until tender in boiling salted water. Drain well. Combine with cottage cheese, sour cream, onion, garlic, Worcestershire and Tabasco sauce. Add pimiento, if desired. Turn into greased casserole and top with grated cheese. Bake at 350° for 25 minutes. Serves 8.   *Alice B. Weitzenfeld*

KRAUT FLECKEL (Cabbage and Noodles)

1 pound broad noodles	3 or 4 tablespoons shortening
2½ pounds cabbage, grated	Salt and pepper

Cook noodles in boiling salted water just until tender. Drain thoroughly. Brown cabbage in hot shortening; add salt and pepper to taste. Add to noodles and toss gently to mix well. Serve hot as vegetable in place of potatoes. Serves 4 to 6.   *Lenore Goldman*

KUGEL

½ pound matzo farfel

1 cup butter or margarine

1 large onion, diced

1 cup diced celery

2 tablespoons dried or fresh chopped parsley

2 eggs

1 teaspoon sugar

Salt

Soak farfel in warm water until completely softened; drain in collander. Sauté onion and celery in hot butter until tender; add to farfel. Add remaining ingredients and mix well. Turn into greased 2-qt. casserole; dot with butter. Bake at 350° about 45 minutes. Serves 6.   *Florence M. Mayron*

KASHE AND NOODLES

⅓ package unprocessed buckwheat groats

1 egg

½ pound mushrooms, sliced

2 medium onions, cut into small pieces

⅓ package medium shell noodles, cooked

Combine groats and egg in large skillet. Cook over medium heat, stirring frequently, for 10 minutes. Add boiling water to cover and cook, covered, until groats are tender, or until all water has been absorbed. Add boiling water as necessary to keep grits from sticking to skillet. Sauté mushrooms and onions in a little butter. Add to groats with noodles and salt and pepper to taste. Turn into greased casserole. Cover and bake at 350° for about 30 minutes. Add butter as necessary to keep mixture moist. Serves 4 to 6.
Olivia Schatz

HUNGARIAN FARFEL

2 medium onions, minced

2 to 3 tablespoons chicken fat

1 8-oz. package farfel

2 teaspoons soy sauce

Salt and pepper

2 cups boiling water

½ pound mushrooms

1 tablespoon chicken fat

Sauté onion in 2 to 3 tablespoons chicken fat until tender. Add uncooked farfel, soy sauce, salt and pepper. Cook until brown. Pour boiling water over farfel mixture; simmer, covered, for 10 to 15 minutes. Sauté mushrooms in 1 tablespoon chicken fat for 10 minutes. Add to farfel mixture. Cook for 5 minutes longer. Serves 4 to 6.   *Ferne Kron*

FARFEL RING

2½ cups boiling water

2 beef bouillon cubes

1 8-oz. package farfel

1 large onion, minced

¼ pound mushrooms, chopped

½ cup butter or margarine

Dissolve bouillon cubes in boiling water; add farfel and cook until all water is absorbed. Sauté onion and mushrooms in hot butter. Add to farfel. Place in greased ring mold. Cover mold with aluminum foil and set in pan of hot water. Bake at 375° for 30 minutes. Serves 4 to 6.   *Sara Trilling*

REAL LASAGNA

SAVORY MEAT SAUCE:

1 cup chopped onion

2 cloves garlic, minced

¼ cup olive oil

2 pounds ground beef

4 No. 303 cans tomatoes

2 6-oz. cans tomato paste

½ cup water

½ cup chopped celery

¼ cup chopped parsley

2 tablespoons granulated sugar

1½ tablespoons salt

1 teaspoon basil

¼ teaspoon pepper

2 bay leaves

Sauté onion and garlic in hot oil in large saucepot or kettle for 5 minutes. Add remaining ingredients; stir to mix well. Bring mixture to boiling; reduce heat and simmer, stirring occasionally, for 3 to 6 hours, or until sauce is *very* thick. Remove bay leaves; skim off excess fat.

LASAGNA:

1 pound lasagna noodles

1 tablespoon salad oil

5 cups Savory Meat Sauce

3 cups ricotta cheese

3 8-oz. packages Mozzarella cheese slices

½ cup grated Parmesan cheese

Add oil to boiling salted water in large kettle. Place lasagna noodles in water without breaking. Cook, stirring frequently, for about 15 minutes, or until almost tender. Drain and rinse with cold water. Line bottom of greased 13x9x2-inch baking dish with layer of noodles. Spoon one third of meat sauce over noodles; top with one third of ricotta cheese and one third of Mozzarella and Parmesan cheese. Repeat layering until all noodles and cheeses are used. Bake at 350° for 45 minutes or until piping hot. Serves 10 to 12.   *Mrs. Marshall Paskind*

EASY LASAGNA

1 can prepared spaghetti sauce

1 pound lasagna noodles, cooked

2 cups ricotta or cottage cheese

3 8-oz. packages Mozzarella cheese slices

½ cup grated Parmesan cheese

Cover bottom of greased 13x9x2-inch pan with thin layer spaghetti sauce. Place layer of lasagna noodles crisscross-fashion over sauce. Cover with layer of ricotta and Mozzarella cheeses. Repeat 3 times, or until all are used. Sprinkle with Parmesan cheese. Bake at 350° for 1 hour. Let stand for 10 minutes before serving. Serves 6 to 8.   *Muriel Kahn*

PASTITSO (Lasagna in Cream Sauce)

1 pound lasagna noodles

2 onions, finely chopped

1 pound ground beef or lamb

½ cup butter

1 medium tomato, peeled and chopped

Salt and pepper to taste

½ cup grated Mozzarella cheese

CREAM SAUCE:

2 tablespoons butter

2 tablespoons flour

1 cup scalded milk

1 egg, beaten

¼ cup grated Mozzarella cheese

Cook lasagna noodles in boiling salted water until tender. Drain. Sauté onions and ground meat in ½ cup hot butter over high heat, stirring to brown evenly. Add tomato and salt and pepper. Cook over low heat until meat is tender. Remove from heat and add ½ cup cheese. Place half of lasagna noodles in greased shallow baking dish. Cover with meat mixture; top with remaining noodles. Melt 2 tablespoons butter in top of double boiler; stir in flour until smooth. Add milk and cook, stirring, until thick and smooth. Remove from heat and add egg and ¼ cup cheese. Blend well. Pour over noodles. Bake at 350° for 40 to 50 minutes, or until nicely browned. Cut into squares and serve piping hot. Serves 6.   *Dee Stein*

SPAGHETTI AU GRATIN

1 small onion, chopped	1 can tomato soup
¼ cup diced celery	½ soup can milk
¼ cup diced green pepper	¼ cup grated Cheddar cheese
3 tablespoons butter	½ teaspoon salt
1 8-oz. package thin spaghetti, cooked	¼ teaspoon pepper

Sauté onion, celery and green pepper in hot butter until golden brown. Set aside. Combine soup, milk, cheese, salt and pepper; bring to boiling over low heat. Combine with sautéed mixture and cooked spaghetti. Cook over low heat until thick, stirring frequently to prevent scorching. Serves 4.

Ruth Goodman

VEGETARIAN SPAGHETTI

½ cup butter	1½ pounds spaghetti, cooked
5 onions, thinly sliced	2 tablespoons granulated sugar
1 clove garlic, mashed (optional)	Salt
½ cup olive oil	Paprika
1 6-oz. can tomato paste	Grated Italian cheese
3 6-oz. cans tomato juice	

Melt butter in skillet. Sauté onions and garlic for 10 minutes, stirring frequently. Add olive oil; season to taste with salt, pepper and herbs. Cook for 10 minutes longer. Add tomato paste and juice and continue to cook for 20 minutes longer. Add spaghetti, salt and paprika. Mix well and serve with grated cheese. Serves 12.

Mrs. Julius Lackner

RICE PILAF

1 cup rice	2¼ cups hot chicken broth
2 tablespoons chicken fat	Salt and pepper

Brown rice in hot chicken fat. Add soup, salt and pepper to taste. Cover and simmer over low heat for 25 minutes. Serves 4.

Anne Gold

WILD RICE RING

1 small onion, minced

6 tablespoons chicken fat

1 12-oz. package wild rice

4 cups boiling water

1 tablespoon Worcestershire sauce

2 tablespoons chopped parsley

1 2-oz. jar pimientos, diced

Sauté onion in hot fat until tender. Wash rice once; add to onion. Add boiling water and Worcestershire sauce. Cover and simmer for 30 minutes, or until all water is absorbed. Remove from heat; add parsley and pimiento; mix gently. Place in greased ring mold. Bake at 300° for 30 minutes. Serves 4 to 5.   *Evelyn Yavitz*

WILD RICE CASSEROLE

1 cup wild rice

½ pound mushrooms

1 cup canned tomatoes, drained

1 cup chopped ripe olives

½ cup salad oil or butter

1 package onion soup mix

1 cup hot water

1 cup grated Cheddar cheese

Dash pepper

Soak rice overnight in water to cover. Cook according to directions on package. Set aside. Sauté mushrooms, tomatoes and olives in hot oil. Mix with rice. Dissolve soup mix in hot water. Add to rice mixture with ¾ cup cheese and pepper. Mix well and pour into greased casserole. Sprinkle remaining cheese over top. Bake at 350° for 1 hour. Serves 6.   *B. Meyer*

PEPPER RICE

½ to 1 pound mushrooms

1 large onion, minced

1 green pepper, minced

½ cup butter

1½ cups rice

4 beef bouillon cubes

4 cups boiling water

Sauté mushrooms, onion and green pepper in hot butter until golden brown. Add rice; cook, stirring, for 3 minutes. Add more butter if necessary to coat rice completely. Dissolve bouillon cubes in boiling water. Add to rice mixture; cook for 5 minutes longer. Place in greased casserole. Cover and bake at 350° for 1 hour. Serves 8.   *Mrs. Phillip Mitchell*

SPANISH RICE

1 onion, thinly sliced	2 8-oz. cans tomato sauce
½ green pepper, diced	1½ cups hot water
1⅓ cups packaged pre-cooked rice	1 teaspoon salt
¼ cup butter	¼ teaspoon pepper

Sauté onion, green pepper and rice in hot butter until lightly browned, stirring constantly. Add tomato sauce, water, salt and pepper. Mix well. Bring to boiling; reduce heat and simmer for 5 minutes. Makes 4 servings.

Arlene Pollock

RICE-MUSHROOM CASSEROLE

1⅓ cups packaged pre-cooked rice	1 4-oz. package sliced almonds
1 medium onion, sliced	3 tablespoons butter or chicken fat
1 6-oz. can mushrooms, drained	

Cook rice in water or chicken broth according to directions on package. Sauté onion, mushrooms and almonds in hot butter until golden brown. Add rice and stir for several minutes to mix thoroughly. Place in greased casserole or ring mold. Bake at 350° for 45 minutes. Serves 4.   *Florence Braverman*

FRIED RICE

1 cup rice	1 teaspoon salt
1½ cups boiling water	⅛ to ¼ cup chopped green onions and tops
¼ cup peanut oil	
1 egg, slightly beaten	1 tablespoon soy sauce

Cook rice in boiling water over low heat until tender but not soft. Heat peanut oil in large skillet; add egg, breaking up with fork as it cooks. Quickly add rice, salt, onions and soy sauce. Blend and serve at once, or place in casserole. Keep warm in oven until ready to serve. Serves 4.

To prevent boiling water from rising above top of pot when cooking noodles, spaghetti or rice, place a lump of butter or shortening in the water.

DAIRY DISHES

There is a thing called wheaten flour,
which the sulphury necromantic cooks
do mingle with water, eggs, spice
and other tragical magical enchantments,
and then they put it little by little into
a frying-pan of boiling suet, where it is
transformed into the form of a flapjack, which
in our translation is called a pancake.

John Taylor (1630)

SCRAMBLED EGGS DE LUXE

3 tablespoons butter

8 eggs

½ cup milk

1 teaspoon salt

Pepper

4 slices Swiss cheese

1 tablespoon bread crumbs

Melt 2 tablespoons butter in 9-inch skillet. Beat eggs with milk, salt and pepper. Pour into skillet; cook, stirring constantly, until eggs are creamy and thick, but still soft. Top with cheese slices; dot with remaining butter. Sprinkle with bread crumbs. Cover and cook over medium heat for 10 minutes. Serve with sausage and sliced tomatoes. Makes 4 to 6 servings.

E. Entin

SCRAMBLED EGGS WITH RICE

4 tablespoons butter

6 eggs, well beaten

1 No. 2 can bean sprouts

1 small green pepper, diced

Chopped pimiento

Salt and pepper

3 cups cooked rice

Melt butter in skillet. Pour in eggs and cook slowly over low heat, stirring with fork, until eggs are creamy and thick. Add bean sprouts, green pepper, pimiento, salt and pepper. Mix in rice; cover skillet and steam mixture for 7 to 10 minutes. Serves 6 to 8.

Jean Weiss

SPIT-IN-THE-EYE

4 slices bread

4 eggs

4 tablespoons butter

With juice glass or biscuit cutter, cut rounds from center of bread slices. Reserve rounds. Melt butter in skillet. Place bread slice in skillet; immediately break egg in center of each slice. Cook to desired doneness on each side. Serve with reserved rounds for pushers. Serves 4.   *Joan Florence*

HERB OMELET

4 eggs, separated

½ teaspoon salt

4 tablespoons milk

Dash pepper

1 tablespoon mixed dried herbs (savory, tarragon, basil, chives, orégano, etc.)

Beat egg whites until stiff but not dry. Beat egg yolks until thick and lemon-colored. Add milk, herbs, salt and pepper. Fold into egg whites. Pour into hot, buttered omelet pan or skillet. Cook over low heat until omelet is puffy and golden brown on the bottom. Bake at 350° for 5 minutes, or until top seems set when pressed with finger. Remove to warm serving plate; serve immediately. Makes 2 servings.   *Dee Stein*

ASPARAGUS OMELET

4 tablespoons butter

¼ pound fresh mushrooms

4 eggs

2 tablespoons butter

¼ cup cream

8 cooked asparagus spears

½ teaspoon salt

3 slices Swiss cheese

⅛ teaspoon white pepper

Paprika

Melt 4 tablespoons butter in 9-inch oven-proof skillet until butter sizzles but is not brown. Beat eggs with cream, salt and pepper for 30 seconds. Pour into skillet and cook over low heat until omelet is puffy and lightly browned on the bottom. Meanwhile, sauté mushrooms in 2 tablespoons butter. Place mushrooms in center of omelet; fold over. Arrange asparagus spears on top of omelet, then top with Swiss cheese; sprinkle with paprika. Place under broiler at 450° for 2 or 3 minutes, or until cheese melts. Remove to heated serving platter. Serves 2. *Shirley Sostrin*

L'OEUF À LA ROI

6 hard-cooked eggs	Dash cayenne pepper
2 tablespoons melted butter	1 tablespoon butter
1 small onion, grated	1 tablespoon flour
1 tablespoon snipped parsley	1 cup cream
¼ teaspoon salt	2 teaspoons grated Parmesan cheese
⅛ teaspoon pepper	

Halve eggs lengthwise; scoop out yolks carefully. Mix yolks with melted butter, onion, parsley, salt and pepper. Stuff egg whites with egg yolk mixture, reserving 1 tablespoonful. Place egg whites in deep baking dish. Melt 1 tablespoon butter; mix in flour and brown. Add cream and reserved egg yolk mixture. Bring to boiling and pour over stuffed egg whites in baking dish. Sprinkle cheese over top. Bake at 350° for 25 minutes. Serves 4.

Ann Metzger

CASSEROLE BRUNCH EGGS

½ cup crab meat, flaked	Salt and pepper
½ pound mushrooms, sliced	SAUCE:
¼ cup butter	2 tablespoons butter
6 hard-cooked eggs	2 tablespoons flour
Mayonnaise	1 cup milk
1 tablespoon minced fresh herbs (chives, parsley, tarragon, etc.)	½ cup grated cheese
	Salt and pepper
½ teaspoon prepared mustard	Minced herbs

Sauté crab meat and mushrooms in ¼ cup hot butter for 5 minutes. Spoon into 4 well-greased individual casseroles or ramekins. Halve eggs lengthwise. Scoop out yolks carefully; mash with a little mayonnaise; add herbs, mustard, salt and pepper. Fill egg whites with egg yolk mixture; place 3 halves in each casserole. Melt 2 tablespoons butter; stir in flour. Add milk, stirring constantly, and cook until thick and smooth. Stir in cheese, salt and pepper to taste. Pour over egg halves in casseroles. Sprinkle with minced herbs. Bake at 425° for 10 minutes. Serves 4. *Rosabelle Perrye*

FLUFFY BREAKFAST PANCAKES

4 eggs, separated

4 teaspoons granulated sugar

1 scant tablespoon matzo cake flour

Beat egg whites until stiff but not dry. Beat egg yolks with sugar until thick and lemon-colored. Gently stir cake flour into egg yolks. Fold in egg whites. Drop by tablespoonfuls into hot, buttered skillet. Cook for about 1 minute on each side. Makes about 12 pancakes.   *Rosabelle Perrye*

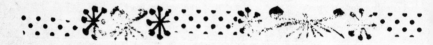

BLINTZES

2 eggs

1 teaspoon granulated sugar

½ teaspoon salt

½ cup water

1 cup flour

¼ teaspoon baking powder

½ cup milk

FILLING:

1½ cups dry cottage cheese

½ cup creamed cottage cheese

1 egg

Sugar to taste

Pinch salt

Beat 2 eggs with 1 teaspoon sugar and ½ teaspoon salt. Add water; mix well. Stir together flour and baking powder. Add to egg mixture. Add milk. Lightly butter heavy 6-inch skillet; heat. Pour only enough batter into skillet to cover bottom. Brown on one side only. Turn out, browned-side up, on board. Repeat. Mix together cheese, 1 egg, sugar and salt. Place rounded teaspoonful cheese mixture on each pancake. Fold edges into center, slightly overlapping. Just before serving, fry or bake until golden brown. Serve hot with sour cream and cinnamon-sugar. Serves 6.   *Charlene Lieberman*

CHEESE BLINTZES

4 eggs, well beaten

1 cup sifted flour

1 teaspoon salt

1 cup milk

Butter

3 cups dry cottage cheese

2 egg yolks

1 tablespoon butter

1 tablespoon granulated sugar

1 tablespoon cinnamon

Add flour, salt and milk to eggs, mixing well. (This may be done on the blender.) Heat heavy 6-inch skillet until water dropped on skillet "dances." Butter lightly, then pour in only enough batter to cover bottom of skillet. Cook until bubbly and lightly browned. Turn onto board, browned-side up. Repeat until all batter has been used, lightly buttering skillet for each pancake. Blend together cottage cheese, egg yolks, butter, sugar and cinnamon. Mix well. Place teaspoonful of cheese mixture on each pancake. Roll up and turn ends in. Fry in hot butter until golden brown on all sides. Or place in greased baking pan; bake at 350° until lightly browned. Serve hot with dab of sour cream; sprinkle with cinnamon-sugar, if desired. Makes about 10 blintzes.   *Barbara Ackerman*

GRANDMOTHER'S CHEESE PANCAKES

2 egg whites	¼ teaspoon baking powder
Pinch salt	Dash pepper
2 egg yolks, beaten	Cinnamon (optional)
⅓ cup flour	2 tablespoons dry cottage cheese, mashed

Beat egg whites with salt until foamy. Fold egg yolks into whites. Sift together flour and baking powder. Add to egg mixture with pepper and cinnamon, if desired. Add cottage cheese and mix well. If mixture seems thin, add a little flour. Drop by tablespoonfuls into hot, buttered skillet; cook over low heat, being careful not to burn. Turn only once. Makes 12 small pancakes.   *Dee Stein*

COTTAGE CHEESE PANCAKES

1 cup dry cottage cheese	1 teaspoon caraway or poppy seeds
2 large eggs	Salt
Dash pepper	1 cup buttermilk
1 teaspoon chopped chives or parsley	1 teaspoon lemon juice

Place cheese in mixing bowl and mash with fork. Break eggs over cheese; add pepper and mix well with fork or beat until smooth. Add chives and caraway seeds; mix well. Heat cast iron or heavy aluminum skillet over low heat until water dropped on skillet sizzles. Sprinkle salt into skillet, covering entire bottom lightly. Drop batter by tablespoonfuls into hot skillet. Brown lightly on both sides. Meanwhile, combine buttermilk and lemon juice and beat until thick. Serve pancakes with buttermilk mixture. Makes 8 pancakes.

SOUR CREAM PANCAKES

1 egg, beaten

1 cup sour cream

½ cup sifted flour

Pinch salt

Combine egg, sour cream, flour and salt. Drop by tablespoonfuls onto lightly buttered hot griddle. When lightly browned on bottom and bubbly on top, turn with spatula. Sprinkle with confectioners' sugar. Makes 1 dozen.

Selma Melvoin

RARE-BIT ON RYE

1 can cream of mushroom soup

½ pound sharp cheese, grated (Wisconsin brick)

¼ cup chopped ripe olives

¼ cup chopped green pepper

Combine soup and cheese in top of double boiler or chafing dish. Heat, stirring occasionally, until cheese melts. Add olives and green pepper. Heat thoroughly. Serve hot over rye toast or chow-mein noodles. Serves 4 or 5.

Anabel Berliner

BAKED CHEESE KREPLACH

1 cup sifted flour

1 tablespoon sour cream

1 teaspoon salt

2 eggs

¼ cup cold water

2 cups dry cottage cheese

2 eggs

1 teaspoon salt

¼ teaspoon pepper

SAUCE:

½ cup melted butter

2 cups sour cream

1 teaspoon salt

¼ teaspoon pepper

Sift flour into a bowl. Make well in center; drop 1 tablespoon sour cream, 1 teaspoon salt, 2 eggs and water in well. Mix until dough is hard and not sticky, adding more flour as necessary. Turn onto floured surface and knead for 10 to 15 minutes until hard ball is formed. Roll out dough into long thin rectangle; cut into 2-inch squares. Blend together cheese, 2 eggs, 1 teaspoon salt and ¼ teaspoon pepper until smooth. Place 1 teaspoonful of mixture in center of each square. Pinch edges of squares together to form triangles. Place in 3-qt. casserole. Combine cooled melted butter with 2 cups sour cream, 1 teaspoon salt and ¼ teaspoon pepper. Pour over kreplach in casserole. Mix lightly. Bake at 350° for 1¼ hours, or until golden brown. Serves 4 to 6.

Rhoda Rock

VEGETABLES

Oh, potatoes they grow
small,

In Kansas.

Oh, potatoes they grow
small,

For they plant them in
the fall,

And they eat 'em skins
and all,

In Kansas.

Anon.

ASPARAGUS AU GRATIN

¼ cup butter

¼ cup flour

2 cups milk

Salt and pepper

2 packages frozen asparagus, cooked

4 hard-cooked eggs, sliced

1 cup grated process cheese

Buttered bread crumbs

Melt butter in skillet; add flour, stirring until smooth. Add milk and cook, stirring, until thickened. Season with salt and pepper. Alternate layers of sauce, asparagus, egg slices and cheese in greased 1-qt. casserole. Top with crumbs. Bake at 350° until brown on top. Serves 6.   *Jean Kowitt*

LIMA BEAN CASSEROLE

1 pound dried lima beans

¼ cup butter or margarine

½ cup catchup

½ cup firmly packed brown sugar

¼ teaspoon dry mustard

Soak lima beans in salted water to cover overnight. Cook in soaking liquid for 1 hour. Drain. Pour into casserole. Add remaining ingredients; mix well. Bake at 350° for 1½ hours. Serves 6.   *Jean Weiss*

WESTERN BARBECUED BEANS

2 cups large dried lima beans	1½ teaspoons chili powder
½ pound shortribs, cut into small pieces	1 teaspoon Worcestershire sauce
2 tablespoons butter or margarine	1 teaspoon salt
1 large onion, minced	¼ cup firmly packed brown sugar
1 clove garlic, mashed	1 can tomato soup
2 teaspoons prepared mustard	¼ cup vinegar

Soak beans in salted water to cover overnight. Bring to boiling; add short-ribs and simmer for 1½ to 2 hours, or until beans are almost tender. Drain, reserving liquid. Melt butter in skillet; add onions and garlic and cook until onions are transparent. Add mustard, chili powder, Worcestershire sauce and salt. Mix and add brown sugar, soup, vinegar and 1 cup reserved bean liquid. Add lima beans; mix thoroughly and turn into 1½-qt. casserole. Cover tightly. Bake at 350° for about 2 hours, or until beans are tender and well-flavored with sauce. Uncover casserole for last 30 minutes of baking period to brown top. If beans become too dry, add bean liquid to casserole as necessary. Serves 6 to 8. *Alice B. Weitzenfeld*

GREEN BEANS FAR EAST

2 cans cream of mushroom soup	2 packages thawed French-style green beans
1 cup grated Cheddar cheese	
1 small onion, grated	1 8-oz. can water chestnuts, drained and sliced
2 teaspoons soy sauce	
1 teaspoon salt	1 No. 2 can bean sprouts, well drained
1 teaspoon monosodium glutamate	1 can French fried onions

Heat soup; add cheese, onion, soy sauce, salt and monosodium glutamate. Mix well. Place half of green beans in greased casserole; cover with water chestnuts and bean sprouts; pour half of mushroom-cheese sauce over top.

Top with remaining green beans; top with remaining cheese sauce. Crumble French fried onions over top. Bake at 350° for 20 minutes.   *Dena Slotky*

GREEN BEAN CASSEROLE

2 packages frozen French-style green
beans

¾ can cream of mushroom soup

1 can French fried onions

1 2-oz. jar pimiento, diced

Salt and pepper

Cook beans according to directions on package only enough to thaw, about 3 minutes. Drain. Mix with mushroom soup. Crush half of onions; mix with beans. Add pimiento and salt and pepper to taste. Place in greased casserole; sprinkle with remaining onions. Bake at 325° for 35 minutes. Serves 8.
     Vivian Kaz

GREEN BEANS À LA DILL

1 package frozen French-style green
beans

1 3-oz. package soft cream cheese

1 tablespoon light cream or milk

¾ teaspoon dill seed

¼ teaspoon salt

Cook beans as directed on package. Drain. Combine cheese, cream, dill seed and salt. Pour over beans and toss lightly until cheese melts. Serve immediately. Serves 4.   *Cele Weinberger*

BROCCOLI NEW ORLEANS

¼ cup finely chopped onion

¼ cup butter

2 tablespoons flour

½ cup water

1 8-oz. jar process cheese spread

2 packages thawed frozen chopped
broccoli, drained

3 eggs, well beaten

½ cup cracker crumbs

2 tablespoons butter

Sauté onions in ¼ cup hot butter until soft. Stir in flour until smooth; add water. Cook over low heat, stirring constantly, until thick. Blend in cheese. Remove from heat and add broccoli. Add eggs and mix gently. Turn into greased 1½-qt. casserole. Sprinkle with crumbs; dot with 2 tablespoons butter. Bake at 325° for 30 minutes. Serves 6 to 8.   *Grayce Dorf*

PARTY BROCCOLI CASSEROLE

4 packages frozen broccoli

2 medium onions, minced

¼ cup butter

2 cans cream of chicken soup

1 8-oz. can or ½ pound fresh mush-rooms

Salt and pepper

Butter

Cook broccoli according to directions on package for 3 minutes. Drain. Sauté onions in hot butter until transparent, but not brown. Combine with broccoli. Add soup, mushrooms, salt and pepper to taste; toss gently to mix well. Place in 2-qt. casserole. Dot with butter. Bake at 325° for 1 hour. Serves 12.

June Steinberg

CABBAGE PEPPER HASH

1 small head cabbage, grated

1 large onion, grated

1 green pepper, grated

1 teaspoon salt

1 cup granulated sugar

1 cup vinegar

1 tablespoon mustard seed

1 tablespoon celery seed

1 2-oz. jar pimiento, diced

Combine cabbage, onion, green pepper and salt. Allow to stand for 3 hours. Combine sugar, vinegar, mustard and celery seed in saucepan; bring to boiling and cook for 3 minutes. Pour over cabbage, toss to coat well; add pimiento and serve immediately. Serves 4.

Ruth Schwartz

CARROT MOLD

1 cup salad oil

½ cup firmly packed brown sugar

1½ cups sifted flour

1 teaspoon baking powder

½ teaspoon baking soda

½ teaspoon salt

½ teaspoon cinnamon

½ teaspoon nutmeg

1 egg

1 tablespoon water

2 cups grated carrots

Mix together oil and sugar until creamy. Sift together flour, baking powder, soda, salt, cinnamon and nutmeg. Combine with egg, water and carrots. Combine with creamed mixture and mix well. Turn into greased 1½-qt. mold. Bake at 350° for 1 hour. Serves 10 to 12.

Lillian Bender

CARROT RING

½ cup soft butter or shortening

1 cup firmly packed brown sugar

1 cup sifted flour

1 teaspoon baking soda

½ teaspoon baking powder

Pinch salt

2 cups grated carrots

Grated rind of 1 lemon

3 tablespoons lemon juice

3 eggs

½ cup chopped pecans

Cream butter and brown sugar well. Sift together flour, soda, baking powder and salt. Add to creamed mixture with carrots, lemon rind and juice and eggs. Mix well. Place pecans in bottom of greased 1-qt. ring mold. Pour carrot mixture into mold. Bake at 350° for about 45 minutes. Makes 8 to 10 servings.

Rose Fishman

CARROT PUDDING

1 cup shortening

½ cup firmly packed brown sugar

1 egg

1½ cups cake meal

1 tablespoon potato starch

1 teaspoon cinnamon

⅛ teaspoon salt

1½ cup grated carrots

Grated rind of 1 lemon

Juice of 1 lemon

Cream shortening and sugar on electric mixer; add egg and mix well. Sift together cake meal, potato starch, cinnamon and salt. Add alternately to creamed mixture with carrots. Add lemon rind and juice; mix in. Turn into greased mold or baking pan. Bake at 350° for 1 hour. Serves 6 to 8.

Evelyn Yavitz

CARROT-CORN PUDDING

2 bunches carrots, cooked and mashed

1 No. 2 can cream-style corn

1 teaspoon granulated sugar

Dash nutmeg

Salt and pepper to taste

4 eggs, well beaten

2 tablespoons melted butter

Combine cooked carrots with corn, sugar, nutmeg, salt and pepper. Add eggs; fold in melted butter. Turn into greased 2-qt. casserole. Bake at 350° for 40 to 50 minutes. Serves 8 to 12.

Florence Collen

CARROT PUFF

3 tablespoons butter	2 cups mashed cooked carrots
3 tablespoons flour	Peas (optional)
1 cup milk	1 5-oz. can chopped ripe olives
1 teaspoon salt	3 tablespoons chopped parsley
¼ teaspoon pepper	2 eggs, separated

Melt butter in skillet; stir in flour until smooth. Add milk and cook, stirring, until thick. Add salt and pepper. Blend in carrots, peas, olives and parsley. Beat egg yolks until frothy. Add to vegetable mixture. Beat egg whites until stiff but not dry. Fold in vegetable-egg yolk mixture. Turn into greased 1½-qt. casserole. Bake at 350° for 45 minutes. Serves 6 to 8.   *Libby Strauss*

CAULIFLOWER-MUSHROOM CASSEROLE

1 large head or 2 packages frozen cauliflower	1 soup can milk
	½ teaspoon salt
½ pound mushrooms	¼ teaspoon pepper
1 small green pepper, diced	4 slices pimiento cheese
3 tablespoons butter	Paprika
2 cans cream of mushroom soup	

Cook cauliflower until just tender. Sauté mushrooms and green pepper in hot butter until tender. Mix together soup and milk; add mushrooms and green pepper. Season with salt and pepper. Arrange cauliflower in bottom of greased casserole; place 2 slices cheese over cauliflower. Cover with soup mixture. Top with remaining cheese slices; sprinkle with paprika. Bake at 350° for 30 to 40 minutes, or until bubbly and slightly browned. Serves 6 to 8.
Rosalyn Greenberg

KASHE CASSEROLE

1½ cups unprocessed buckwheat groats	Salt
¼ cup butter or ½ cup chicken fat	3 cans chicken broth

Melt butter in casserole over medium heat. Sauté buckwheat groats in butter

until bleached and sizzling. Add salt to taste. Pour in chicken soup. Bake
at 350° for 1½ to 2 hours. Serves 6.   *Lee Bateman*

CORN PUDDING

1 No. 2 can cream-style corn	1 teaspoon granulated sugar
4 eggs, slightly beaten	½ teaspoon salt
2 cups scalded milk	½ teaspoon pepper
2 tablespoons melted butter	½ teaspoon chopped pimiento

Combine all ingredients; stir to blend well. Pour into greased 1½-qt.
casserole. Set in pan of hot water. Place in oven. Bake at 325° for 1½ hours
or until set. Serves 6.   *Mina Siegel*

CORN FRITTERS

1 cup sifted flour	¾ cup light cream
2 teaspoons baking powder	¼ cup melted butter
½ teaspoon salt	1 No. 303 can cream-style corn, drained
2 eggs, well beaten	½ cup shortening

Sift together flour, baking powder and salt. Add eggs, cream, butter and
corn. Stir until well mixed. Melt shortening in heavy skillet. Drop batter
into hot shortening, using about ¼ cup for each fritter. Fry until brown on
each side, turning only once. Makes 6 servings.   *Millie Bows*

EGGPLANT ITALIANO

1 large eggplant	1 6-oz. can pizza sauce
2 eggs, beaten	1 6-oz. package Mozzarella cheese slices
1 cup water	

Pare eggplant and cut into ½-inch slices. Coat with seasoned flour. Dip into
combined eggs and water. Coat with flour. Fry in hot salad oil until golden
brown on both sides. Drain on absorbent paper. Arrange eggplant slices in
shallow baking pan; cover with thin layer pizza sauce, then with cheese.
Repeat layering if necessary. Bake at 325° for 45 minutes, or until cheese is
melted. Serves 4 to 6.   *Meryl Eisenberg*

FRIED EGGPLANT

1 medium eggplant	Flour, or egg and cracker crumbs
Salt	Butter

Pare eggplant and slice very thin. Sprinkle slices with salt. Stack slices on plate or pie plate and cover with weight, such as cutting board or heavy pan, to press out juice. Let stand about 1 hour. Coat slices with flour or dip into egg and crumb mixture. Fry slowly in a little hot butter, or fry in hot deep fat (375°) for 6 to 8 minutes. Serves 4.   *Bertha Gross*

MIXED VEGETABLES MORNAY

2 packages frozen mixed vegetables	¼ cup grated Parmesan cheese
1 teaspoon salt	1 teaspoon salt
¼ teaspoon garlic salt	⅛ teaspoon garlic salt
2 tablespoons butter	Pinch nutmeg
MORNAY SAUCE:	Pinch thyme
¼ cup butter	2 tablespoons white wine
¼ cup flour	2 cups buttered bread crumbs
Milk	

Cook vegetables according to directions on package. Drain, reserving cooking liquid. Season vegetables with 1 teaspoon salt, ¼ teaspoon garlic salt and 2 tablespoons butter. Place in greased baking dish. Melt ¼ cup butter; stir in flour until smooth. Combine reserved vegetable liquid with enough milk to make 2 cups. Add to flour mixture slowly, stirring constantly; cook until thick and smooth. Add cheese, 1 teaspoon salt, ⅛ teaspoon garlic salt, nutmeg, thyme and wine. Mix until cheese melts. Pour over vegetables. Top with buttered crumbs. Bake at 350° for 30 minutes. Place under broiler for several minutes until crumbs are brown. Serves 8.   *Sylvia Klow*

MIXED VEGETABLE BAKE

2 packages frozen mixed vegetables	2 or 3 slices Cheddar cheese, grated
2 tablespoons flour	Salt and pepper
1 cup milk	1 package prepared poultry stuffing

Cook vegetables as directed on package; drain. Combine flour, milk, cheese, salt and pepper in saucepan. Cook, stirring constantly, until thick and smooth. Add to vegetables. Turn into greased casserole. Prepare stuffing according to directions on package. Spoon over vegetables in casserole. Bake at 325° for 20 minutes. Serves 8.   *Therese Dillon*

BROILED MUSHROOMS

1 onion, grated	2 tablespoons wine vinegar
2 tablespoons chopped parsley	1½ pounds mushrooms
1 clove garlic, mashed	¼ cup butter
1 teaspoon salt	½ cup bread crumbs
¼ teaspoon pepper	1 tablespoon grated Parmesan cheese
⅛ teaspoon basil	¼ cup butter
⅓ cup olive oil	

Combine onion, parsley, garlic, salt, pepper, basil, oil and vinegar in a bowl. Add mushrooms; toss to mix well; set aside to marinate for 3 hours, turning frequently. Drain, reserving marinade for other food preparation. Melt ¼ cup butter in skillet; add mushrooms and cook over high heat for 1 minute. Reduce heat and cook for 10 minutes, stirring occasionally. Place mushrooms in well-greased baking dish. Sprinkle with bread crumbs and cheese; dot with ¼ cup butter. Place under broiler until browned. Makes 6 servings.
                                                                  Sandra Kaufman

---

Attention calorie-watchers! Place a can of grated Parmesan cheese on the table and use it on vegetables instead of butter.

CREAMED ONIONS

3 tablespoons butter	1 8-oz. can small boiled onions
2 tablespoons flour	1 2-oz. jar sliced pimiento
1½ cups milk	½ pound Cheddar cheese, cubed
½ teaspoon salt	

Melt butter in skillet; add flour, stirring until smooth. Slowly add milk and cook over low heat until thick, stirring constantly. Add salt, onions, pimiento and cheese. Mix and turn into casserole. Bake at 350° for about 35 minutes. Serves 4.   *Mrs. Maurice Spilky*

POTATOES DELICIOUS

4 medium potatoes, sliced	Salt and pepper
1 cup heavy cream	

Place potatoes in greased casserole; add cream and salt and pepper. Bake at 350° for 1 hour, or until potatoes are done. Serves 4.   *Emily Kron*

POTATO PUDDING

4 medium potatoes	4 tablespoons buttermilk or skim milk
2 eggs	Salt and pepper

Pare, wash and quarter potatoes. Cook until soft in salted water to cover. Mash; whip with eggs, buttermilk, salt and pepper. Place in oven-glass baking dish or casserole. Bake at 350° until top is browned. Serves 4.

MUSHROOM SCALLOPED POTATOES

5 cups sliced potatoes	1 tablespoon minced onion
1 can cream of mushroom soup	½ teaspoon salt
½ cup milk	Dash pepper

Mix soup with milk, onion, salt and pepper. Place potatoes and soup mixture in alternate layers in greased 2-qt. casserole. Dot with butter. Bake at 350° for 30 to 40 minutes, or until potatoes are done. Serves 6.   *Beverly Kaluzna*

POTATO LOAF

3 tablespoons butter	1 tablespoon minced parsley
3 tablespoons flour	1 teaspoon grated onion
1 cup milk	6 medium potatoes, cooked and cut into ½-inch cubes
1½ teaspoons salt	
¼ teaspoon pepper	1 cup grated sharp cheese

Melt butter; blend in flour, mixing until smooth. Add milk, salt and pepper, and cook, stirring constantly, until thick and smooth. Stir in parsley and onion; mix lightly with potatoes. Turn into greased 9x5x3-inch pan. Chill in refrigerator for several hours or overnight. Unmold onto buttered oven-proof platter. Bake at 350° for 45 minutes. Remove from oven; sprinkle cheese over top. Return to oven and continue to bake for 15 minutes longer. Serves 6 to 8.   *Lee Bateman*

POTATO KUGEL

3 eggs, slightly beaten	Dash pepper
1 teaspoon grated onion	1 cooked potato, mashed
¼ cup matzo meal	5 large potatoes, grated
1 teaspoon baking powder	½ cup shortening
1 teaspoon salt	

Mix together eggs, onion, matzo meal, baking powder, salt and pepper. Combine mashed and grated potatoes. Mix with egg mixture. Place shortening in 11½x7½x1½-inch pan. Set in oven at 350° until shortening is melted, and pan is hot. Pour potato mixture into pan. Bake for 1 hour, or until brown crust has formed on top. Serves 6.   *Dorothy Salkin*

POTATO BALLS

6 potatoes	Corn flake crumbs
1 tablespoon chicken fat	

Cook potatoes in salted water. Mash with chicken fat. Season as desired. Cool; shape into small balls; roll balls in corn flake crumbs until well coated. Place on greased baking sheet. Bake at 350° for about 30 minutes. Serves 6.
Shirley Crane

POTATO PANCAKES

6 medium potatoes, grated	1 teaspoon salt
1 small onion, grated	½ teaspoon baking powder
2 eggs	¼ teaspoon pepper
3 tablespoons flour	

Combine all ingredients and mix well. Drop by tablespoonfuls into hot well-greased heavy skillet. Fry over medium heat until brown on all sides. Serves 6.   *Shirley Crane*

POTATO PUFFS

2 cups mashed potatoes	½ teaspoon salt
1 egg	⅛ teaspoon pepper
½ cup grated cheese	1 cup fine bread crumbs

Combine potato, egg, cheese, salt and pepper. Shape mixture into small balls; roll balls in bread crumbs. Fry in hot deep fat (370°) until golden brown on all sides. Drain on absorbent paper and serve piping hot. Makes 4 servings.

Sara Slutsky

STUFFED BAKED POTATOES

6 large baked Idaho potatoes	¾ cup sour cream
2 tablespoons butter	6 tablespoons chopped green onions
2 tablespoons flour	6 to 12 tablespoons chopped shrimp, lobster or crab meat
1 cup milk	
1 cup grated Cheddar cheese	Butter

Keep baked potatoes hot. Melt 2 tablespoons butter; add flour, stirring until smooth. Add milk and cheese; cook, stirring until cheese is melted and mixture begins to thicken. Season with salt and pepper. Set aside and keep warm. Blend sour cream with onions and shrimp. Split baked potatoes; dot with butter; season with salt and paprika. Spoon sour cream sauce over tops. Pour cheese mixture over potatoes and place under broiler until cheese bubbles. Or place potatoes in oven for a few minutes before serving. Serves 6.

Alice B. Weitzenfeld

MEAT STUFFED POTATOES

6 large round potatoes	1 teaspoon salt
1 pound ground beef	¼ teaspoon onion powder
½ cup water	¼ teaspoon pepper
1 egg	Paprika
1 large clove garlic, minced	

Pare potatoes; scoop out deep well in each. Set aside in cold water to cover to soak. Mix together beef, water, egg, garlic, salt, onion powder and pepper.

Sprinkle potatoes inside and out with paprika. Stuff with meat mixture (shape any remaining mixture into small balls and bake with potatoes). Place potatoes in greased shallow baking pan. Bake at 350° for 1 hour, or until potatoes are done. Makes 6 servings.   *Mary Leibovitz*

SWEET POTATO TZIMMES

4 pounds sweet potatoes	¾ cup firmly packed brown sugar
¾ cup water	Juice of 2 lemons
1½ teaspoons salt	Juice of 1 orange
1 pound dried prunes	

Pare potatoes and cut into pieces. Place in stainless steel saucepan having a cover. Add water and salt; place prunes on top. Cover and cook over low heat for 20 to 25 minutes. Add brown sugar and mix with wooden spoon. Add lemon and orange juices. Mix again. Makes 12 servings.   *Lisa Lev*

NOTE: Mixture may be made in advance and refrigerated. Reheat just before serving. Or cool, then freeze; thaw and reheat just before serving.

SWEET POTATO BALLS

1½ cups mashed sweet potatoes	2 tablespoons granulated sugar
¼ cup orange juice	½ cup chopped pecans

Combine potatoes, orange juice and sugar. Blend well; shape mixture into 12 balls, using about 2 tablespoonfuls for each. Roll in chopped pecans. Place on greased baking sheet. Bake at 325° for 20 minutes. Serves 4 to 6.

Lois Payne

PINEAPPLE-MARSHMALLOW SWEET POTATOES

2 cups mashed sweet potatoes	2 tablespoons butter
1 cup pineapple juice	½ teaspoon cinnamon
1 cup drained crushed pineapple	Marshmallows

Mix together potatoes, pineapple juice, crushed pineapple, butter and cinnamon. Beat until light and fluffy, adding more juice if necessary. Turn into well-greased casserole. Bake at 350° for 30 minutes. Remove from oven; cover top with marshmallows. Return to oven and bake until marshmallows are browned. Serves 4.   *Irma Silberman*

BRANDIED SWEET POTATOES

1½ cups dried apricots	3 tablespoons melted butter
2 cups hot water	1 teaspoon grated orange rind
6 medium sweet potatoes	2 teaspoons orange juice
½ to 1 cup apricot brandy	Pecan halves
1 cup firmly packed brown sugar	

Soak apricots in water to cover for 1 hour. Add 2 cups hot water and cook until apricots are plump. Cool and drain well, reserving liquid. Cook potatoes until tender. Drain; pare and slice lengthwise. Dip each slice in apricot brandy, coating thoroughly. Arrange alternate layers of potato slices, apricots and brown sugar in greased baking dish. Combine reserved apricot juice, butter, orange rind and juice. Pour over potatoes and apricots. Bake at 375° for 45 minutes, basting occasionally with syrup in dish. About 5 minutes before end of baking period, place pecan halves on top. Serves 8.

Sue Weissman

GERMAN SAUERKRAUT

3 tablespoons flour	1 No. 2½ can sauerkraut
1 can tomato soup	Sugar or vinegar (optional)
3 tablespoons brown sugar	

Brown flour in heavy skillet, stirring constantly; *do not burn.* Add soup; stir well. Add brown sugar and mix well. Add sauerkraut. If desired, add sugar or vinegar to taste. Place mixture in baking dish. Bake at 325° until brown and thoroughly heated. Serve as accompaniment for duck or any fowl. Serves 4.

Jeanne Rosenhouse

SPINACH TIMBALES

2 packages frozen chopped spinach	1 can cream of mushroom soup
1 medium onion, finely chopped	½ cup milk
2 tablespoons butter	½ teaspoon salt
½ cup bread crumbs	Dash pepper
3 eggs, separated	Dash nutmeg

Cook as directed on package only until thawed; drain well. Sauté onion in hot butter; stir in bread crumbs. Beat egg yolks. Combine soup and milk.

Mix together spinach, egg yolks and soup mixture. Season with salt, pepper and nutmeg. Beat egg whites until stiff; fold into spinach mixture. Turn into 8 greased custard cups or 2-qt. casserole. Set in pan of hot water. Bake at 350° for 50 to 60 minutes, or until knife inserted in center of casserole comes out clean. Serves 8.   *Shirley Levititz*

CREAMED SPINACH

1 package frozen chopped spinach	2 tablespoons flour
½ clove garlic, mashed	1 cup warm milk
2 tablespoons butter	

Cook spinach as directed on package. Drain; add garlic. Melt butter; stir in flour until smooth. Add milk, stirring constantly; cook, stirring, until thick. Season with salt and pepper to taste. Add spinach. Serves 4.   *Shirley Crane*

SPINACH PATTIES

½ pound cooked fresh or 1 No. 303 can spinach, drained	½ teaspoon salt
1 egg	Cracker meal

Combine spinach, egg and salt with enough cracker meal to hold mixture together. Shape into patties and fry until golden on both sides in hot butter. Serves 3.   *Mrs. Harry Kreiter*

SPINACH SUPREME

2 packages frozen chopped spinach	1 package onion soup mix
2 tablespoons butter	1 beef bouillon cube
2 tablespoons flour	2 tablespoons sour cream
1 cup hot milk	

Cook spinach as directed on package; drain well. Melt butter; add flour, stirring until smooth. Add hot milk slowly, stirring constantly, and cook over low heat for 3 minutes. Add onion soup mix and bouillon cube. Add spinach and mix gently. Pour into greased 9-inch pie plate. Top with dabs of sour cream. Sprinkle with paprika. Bake at 275° for 20 minutes. Serves 4 to 6.   *Ruth Schwartz*

SPINACH MOLD

2 packages frozen chopped spinach	Grated onion
1 8-oz. package soft cream cheese	Salt and pepper

Cook spinach as directed on package; drain well. Toss with cream cheese and grated onion. Season to taste with salt and pepper. Turn into greased ring mold. Bake at 350° for 30 minutes. Serves 6 to 8.   *Isabel Fiddler*

SPINACH-MUSHROOM CASSEROLE

1 3-oz. can mushrooms, drained	Butter
1 onion, chopped	Garlic salt
2 tablespoons butter	1 4-oz. can evaporated milk
2 packages cooked frozen spinach ·	1 cup grated Cheddar cheese
1 teaspoon salt	

Sauté mushrooms and onions in 2 tablespoons hot butter. Line greased casserole with spinach seasoned with 1 teaspoon salt and butter. Arrange mushrooms and onions over spinach. Sprinkle with garlic salt. Combine milk and cheese and simmer for 2 or 3 minutes. Spoon over spinach carefully. Bake at 350° for 20 minutes. Place under broiler for several minutes until top is brown. Serves 8.   *Sylvia Klow*

SPINACH ITALIANO

2 packages frozen chopped spinach	½ cup light cream
2 tablespoons butter	Salt, pepper and nutmeg
1 clove garlic	½ cup seedless raisins
1 scant tablespoon flour	½ cup pine nuts or slivered almonds

Cook spinach as directed on package just until thawed. Drain thoroughly. Melt butter in iron or earthenware casserole with garlic. Remove and discard garlic. Add flour and spinach; blend well. Add cream, salt, pepper and nutmeg to taste. Keep hot. Soak raisins in cold water for 10 minutes. Meanwhile, sauté pine nuts in a little butter. Drain raisins and add to nuts. Mix with spinach and serve hot. Serves 8 to 10.   *Rachel Long*

SQUASH PATTIES

1 1-lb. summer squash	2 tablespoons melted butter
2 eggs	½ teaspoon salt
½ cup matzo meal	Dash pepper

Cut slice from stem and blossom ends of squash; cut into pieces. Grate squash very fine and combine with remaining ingredients. Mix well. Shape into patties and fry in deep hot fat until golden brown on all sides. Or place mixture in greased casserole. Bake at 375° for 40 to 45 minutes. Makes 3 or 4 servings. *Sara Slutsky*

ZUCCHINI CAKES

3 cups chopped zucchini	1 egg
3 tablespoons parsley	Salt and pepper
1 small clove garlic, mashed	1 cup biscuit mix
½ cup grated Parmesan cheese	

Combine zucchini, parsley, garlic, cheese, egg, salt and pepper with enough biscuit mix to make a thin batter. Drop from tablespoon into ½ inch hot oil and fry until brown. May be prepared in advance and heated in oven before serving. Makes 4 servings. *Della Becker*

STUFFED ZUCCHINI

1½ pounds small zucchini	2 tablespoons chopped parsley
1 teaspoon salt	1¼ teaspoons salt
Boiling water	⅛ teaspoon pepper
1½ cups fresh bread crumbs	2 eggs, beaten
½ cup grated Cheddar cheese	2 tablespoons butter or margarine
¼ cup minced onion	¼ cup grated Cheddar cheese

Cook whole zucchini with 1 teaspoon salt in 1-inch boiling water, covered, for 5 to 7 minutes. Cut zucchini in halves lengthwise; carefully scoop out squash; set shells aside. Chop squash and combine with bread crumbs, ½ cup cheese, onion, parsley, 1¼ teaspoons salt, pepper and eggs. Fill shells lightly with mixture; dot with butter and top with ¼ cup cheese. Bake at 350° for 30 minutes. Makes 4 servings. *Alice B. Weitzenfeld*

BAKED ACORN SQUASH

1 small acorn squash	1 tablespoon butter
2 fresh or canned peach halves	1½ teaspoon brown sugar

Split squash lengthwise; remove seeds. Place in saucepan with 1-inch boiling salted water; cover and cook for 25 minutes. Place peach half in cavity of each squash half. Place half of butter and brown sugar in each peach cavity. Bake at 350° for 30 minutes. Serves 2.   *Natalie Abrams*

ZUCCHINI CANTONESE

½ cup peanut oil	1 clove garlic
3 pounds zucchini, cut into ½-inch slices	½ cup water
3 onions, thinly sliced	3 tablespoons soy sauce

Heat oil in skillet; add zucchini, onions and garlic. Sauté until onions are soft but not brown. Add water; cover and cook until zucchini is tender, but crisp. Discard garlic. Just before serving, toss mixture with soy sauce. Serves 4 to 6.   *Alice B. Weitzenfeld*

TOMATO PUDDING
toast

4 slices white bread, cubed	2 8-oz. cans tomato sauce
¼ cup melted butter	6 tablespoons brown sugar

Pour melted butter over bread cubes in casserole. Heat tomato sauce to boiling; add brown sugar and stir until sugar is dissolved. Pour mixture over bread cubes. Cover and bake at 375° for 45 to 60 minutes. If pudding is too thin, remove cover for last 15 minutes of baking period. Serves 4.
Jeanne Berkowitz

❖❖❖

*Different and delicious! Crumb topping for cooked vegetables —
sauté ½ to 1 cup fresh bread crumbs in 2 to 4 tablespoons butter
until light brown. Add salt, pepper and paprika and 1 tablespoon
lemon juice, or ½ cup grated cheese.*

❖❖❖

SALADS
AND
SALAD DRESSINGS

Oh, herbaceous treat!
'Twould tempt the dying anchorite to eat;
Back to the world he'd turn
   his fleeting soul,
And plunge his fingers in
   the salad bowl,
Serenely full the epicure would say,
"Fate cannot harm me,—I have dined today."

Sidney Smith (1810)

VEGETABLE SALADS

BEET SALAD

1 No. 2 can diced or shoestring beets, drained

1 8-oz. can small peas, drained

2 hard-cooked eggs, diced

½ cup mayonnaise

Juice of ½ lemon

Salt and pepper

Combine all ingredients and mix well. Chill in refrigerator. Serve in lettuce cups. Makes 4 servings.

Ferne Kron

SPINACH SURPRISE

1 teaspoon baking soda

½ pound spinach

2 hard-cooked eggs, chopped

3 tomatoes, quartered

1 8-oz. can white asparagus, drained

1 8-oz. can chopped ripe olives

Surprise Dressing, page 193

Dissolve baking soda in cold water; wash spinach well. Then wash again in clear cold water; pat dry and cut leaves into 1-inch squares. Place in large wooden salad bowl; add eggs. Garnish with tomato quarters and place asparagus around edges. Just before serving, top with olives. Pour Surprise Dressing over all and toss gently. Serves 4.

Sharon Hockman

GREEN BEANS VINAIGRETTE

2 10-oz. packages frozen French-style green beans

1 cup cocktail onions, drained

Vinaigrette Dressing, page 194

Cook green beans in small amount of salted water for 5 minutes. Drain. Combine with onions. Pour Vinaigrette Dressing over all and toss gently to mix. Marinate in refrigerator for several hours. Drain and serve on lettuce, or fill center of tomato aspic ring. Serves 6.   *Alice B. Weitzenfeld*

ST. CLAIR ROQUEFORT SALAD

1 clove garlic, cut into pieces

Pinch salt

1 can anchovy fillets

1 3-oz. wedge Roquefort or Blue cheese

Olive oil

2 tablespoons red wine vinegar

Salad herbs

Salt

2 quarts salad greens

1 hard-cooked egg, chopped

6 to 8 medium shrimp, chopped

Freshly ground black pepper

Mash garlic with salt in bottom of large wooden salad bowl. Drain anchovies, reserving oil. Mash half of anchovies with garlic. Crumble two-thirds of cheese into bowl. Combine reserved anchovy oil with enough olive oil to make ½ cup. Pour into bowl, stirring well. Add salad herbs and salt to taste. Toss washed, crisp salad greens in bowl until well coated with dressing. Top with remaining anchovies, egg, shrimp and remaining cheese. Sprinkle with freshly ground black pepper and toss together just before serving. Serves 6.   *Dee Stein*

SOUR CREAM POTATO SALAD

4 cups diced cooked potatoes

½ cup diced cucumber

1 tablespoon minced onion

3 hard-cooked eggs, diced

1½ cups sour cream

½ cup mayonnaise

¼ cup vinegar or pickle juice

1 teaspoon prepared mustard

1 teaspoon celery seed

Salt and pepper

Combine all ingredients; mix well to coat vegetables and eggs with sour cream and mayonnaise. Chill in refrigerator until ready to serve. Makes 6 to 8 servings.   *Dee Stein*

TOMATO, PARSLEY AND DILL SALAD

2 large tomatoes, quartered	1 tablespoon chopped dill
½ cup wine vinegar	1 bay leaf
1 tablespoon snipped parsley	Salt and pepper

Place tomatoes in bowl. Add remaining ingredients; toss gently to mix. Marinate in refrigerator for at least 1 hour. Makes 2 servings.

CABBAGE BOWL: Cut off top half or third of cleaned cabbage head. With a sharp knife, scoop out center and core end, leaving a shell. Use scooped out cabbage and top to make coleslaw. Then serve coleslaw in scooped out cabbage "bowl."

COLESLAW

1 medium head cabbage, shredded	¼ cup vinegar
1 9-oz. can crushed pineapple, drained	6 tablespoons granulated sugar
1 orange or apple, grated	1 teaspoon salt
1 cup sour cream	1 teaspoon dry mustard

Combine all ingredients, mixing well. Chill in refrigerator until ready to serve. Makes 6 servings. *Jeanie Greene*

ELEGANT COLESLAW

1 small head cabbage	½ teaspoon salt
½ cup sliced radishes	Dash pepper
1 small red onion, diced	¾ cup sour cream
3 tablespoons vinegar	⅓ cup granulated sugar
1 tablespoon water	

Shred cabbage; soak in iced water. Add radishes. When ready to serve, drain well. Add onion, vinegar, water, salt and pepper; mix well. Combine sour cream and sugar; pour over cabbage mixture; toss until well mixed. Serves 6. *Rose Krichiver*

CRISPY CRACKER SALAD

½ cup mayonnaise

1 tablespoon wine vinegar

¼ teaspoon Worcestershire sauce

2 cloves garlic, crushed

¾ teaspoon salt

Salad greens (bibb, Boston and ice-berg lettuce, Romaine, etc.)

2 7-oz. cans tuna, chicken or salmon

8 radishes, quartered

1 cup small cheese crackers

4 tomatoes, quartered

Combine mayonnaise, vinegar, Worcestershire sauce, garlic and salt. Toss greens with tuna, radishes and crackers. Pour mayonnaise mixture over greens; toss until well coated. Garnish with tomatoes. Serves 4.

Tillie Shafer

RICE SALAD

2 cups cooked rice

4 tomatoes, peeled and cubed

2 green peppers, thinly sliced

2 pimientos, finely chopped

2 tablespoons chopped onion

2 tablespoons chopped parsley

¾ cup olive oil

¼ cup wine vinegar

1½ teaspoons salt

½ teaspoon pepper

1 clove garlic, minced

Combine rice, tomatoes, green peppers, pimientos, onion and parsley in a bowl. Mix lightly with 2 forks. Combine oil, vinegar, salt, pepper and garlic; beat well. Pour over rice mixture and toss gently to coat well. Chill in refrigerator; serve very cold. Serves 6.

Sandra Kaufman

HOT VEGETABLE SALAD

2 tablespoons shortening

3 cups shredded cabbage or celery cabbage

1 cup thinly sliced celery

1 cup sliced green pepper

¼ cup thinly sliced onion

1½ teaspoons salt

⅛ teaspoon pepper

Heat shortening in skillet; add cabbage, celery, green pepper and onion. Cover and cook over low heat for 5 minutes. Uncover; add salt and pepper and continue to cook for 1 minute longer, stirring with fork. Serve at once. Serves 6.

Ruth Kiver

EGG SALADS

EGG SALAD

1½ dozen hard-cooked eggs, mashed

½ small onion, finely chopped

½ cup mayonnaise

½ teaspoon prepared mustard

Paprika

Combine eggs and onion. Mix together mayonnaise and mustard. Add to egg mixture. Sprinkle with paprika. Chill in refrigerator until ready to serve. Serves 12.   *June Steinberg*

EGG SALAD MOLD

12 hard-cooked eggs, chopped

2 3-oz. packages soft cream cheese

¼ cup mayonnaise

1½ tablespoons chili sauce

½ cup chopped celery

2 tablespoons chopped green pepper

2 tablespoons chopped pimiento

1 teaspoon grated onion

Salt and pepper

Mix together cheese, mayonnaise, chili sauce, celery, green pepper, pimiento, onion, salt and pepper. Add to eggs. Line mold with waxed paper. Turn egg mixture into mold and chill in refrigerator overnight. Unmold onto serving plate; garnish with greens. Serves 8.   *Marcey Glass*

 CHICKEN SALADS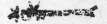

PARTY CHICKEN SALAD

2 cups diced cooked chicken

1 cup pineapple tidbits, drained

1 cup finely chopped celery

¾ cup slivered blanched almonds

Salad dressing

Salt

Combine chicken, pineapple, celery and almonds. Fold in enough salad dressing to moisten; season with salt to taste. Chill in refrigerator. Serve on crisp lettuce leaves. Serves 6 to 8.   *Florence Goldenson*

MOLDED CHICKEN SUPREME

2½ cups diced cooked chicken	¼ teaspoon pepper
1 cup seedless grapes	1 envelope unflavored gelatine
1 cup chopped celery	¼ cup cold water
½ cup slivered almonds	½ cup chicken broth
2 tablespoons minced parsley	½ cup heavy cream, whipped
1 teaspoon salt	1 cup mayonnaise

Combine chicken, grapes, celery, almonds, parsley, salt and pepper. Dissolve gelatine in cold water; melt over hot water. Combine gelatine with broth, whipped cream and mayonnaise; stir until mixture begins to thicken. Add to chicken mixture. Pack into greased ring mold. Chill in refrigerator until firm. Unmold onto serving plate. Garnish with olives, sliced hard-cooked eggs, radish roses, etc. Serves 8 to 10.   *Libby Friedman*

MOTHER'S MOLDED CHICKEN SALAD

1 envelope unflavored gelatine	½ teaspoon dry mustard
½ cup cold water	½ teaspoon paprika
1 cup chicken broth or milk	½ teaspoon salt
2 egg yolks, slightly beaten	1 cup diced cooked chicken
¼ cup vinegar	½ cup diced celery
1 teaspoon granulated sugar	

Soften gelatine in cold water. Combine broth, egg yolks, vinegar, sugar, mustard, paprika and salt in top of double boiler. Cook over hot water, stirring constantly, until mixture coats spoon. Add gelatine and stir until dissolved. Chill in refrigerator until partially set. Fold in chicken and celery. Turn into individual molds and chill until firm. Unmold onto lettuce leaves. Makes 4 servings.   *Mrs. Richard Blair*

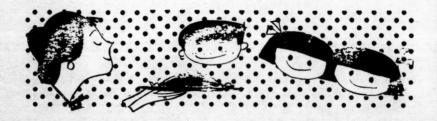

FISH AND SEA-FOOD SALADS

HAWAIIAN TUNA SALAD

1 7-oz. can tuna	3 green onions and tops, chopped
1 13-oz. can pineapple chunks, drained	1/3 cup mayonnaise
1/2 cup sliced stuffed green olives	Pinch salt
1/2 cup slivered almonds	

Wash and drain tuna. Mix with remaining ingredients lightly so that tuna is in large chunks. Place in lettuce cups. Chill and serve. Serves 4.

Sunny Satten

TUNA SALAD MOLD

1 envelope unflavored gelatine	1 green pepper, chopped
1/2 cup cold water	1/4 cup finely chopped celery
1 cup mayonnaise	1/4 cup chopped sweet pickles
1 13-oz. can tuna	Salt to taste
2 hard-cooked eggs, chopped	

Dissolve gelatine in cold water; melt over hot water. Cool. Combine with mayonnaise. Combine tuna, eggs, green pepper, celery, pickles and salt. Add to gelatine mixture; mix well. Turn into greased mold. Chill in refrigerator until firm. Unmold onto serving plate. Serves 8. *Gertrude Lewin*

CRAB MEAT SALAD

2 6½-oz. cans crab meat, flaked	1/2 cup mayonnaise
2 hard-cooked eggs, chopped	2½ teaspoons lemon juice
1/4 cup chopped green olives	3/4 teaspoon salt
2 tablespoons chopped onion	1/2 teaspoon paprika
1 teaspoon chopped parsley	Dash pepper
2 tablespoons chopped sweet pickle	Pimiento strips

Toss all ingredients except pimiento strips together well. Turn into salad bowl; garnish with pimiento strips. Chill in refrigerator until ready to serve. Serves 4 or 5. *Mrs. E. Shafer*

LOBSTER OR CRAB MEAT MOUSSE

2 envelopes unflavored gelatine

1 cup cold water

1 can tomato soup

¼ pound cream cheese

1 tablespoon lemon juice

2 teaspoons instant minced onion

1 cup mayonnaise

1 cup chopped celery

¼ cup chopped green olives

3 tablespoons finely chopped green pepper

1 cup diced cooked lobster, or 1 6½-oz. can crab meat, flaked

Soften gelatine in ½ cup cold water. Heat tomato soup; add gelatine and cream cheese and stir until smooth. Add remaining cold water, lemon juice and instant onion. Chill in refrigerator until mixture is partially set. Fold in mayonnaise, celery, olives, green pepper and lobster. Turn into greased 1¼-qt. mold. Chill until firm. Unmold; garnish with radish roses, parsley sprigs and mayonnaise, if desired. Serves 6 to 8.   *Jean Kowitt*

SEA-FOOD SALAD

1 cup lobster, shrimp or crab meat

¼ cup finely chopped celery

¼ cup finely chopped green pepper

½ cup buttermilk

1 tablespoon tomato sauce

½ teaspoon Worcestershire sauce

1 teaspoon basil

¼ teaspoon garlic powder

Pinch cayenne pepper

Salt and pepper

Flake lobster or crab meat; break shrimp into small pieces. Mix with celery and green pepper. Beat buttermilk with tomato sauce; add remaining ingredients; mix well. Pour over sea-food mixture; toss gently until well coated. Serve on lettuce leaves, or stuff hollowed-out tomatoes, green peppers or cucumbers. Makes 2 servings.

MOLDED SHRIMP SALAD

1½ pounds cleaned cooked shrimp, split

⅓ cup French dressing

1 envelope unflavored gelatine

¼ cup cold water

1¼ cups mayonnaise

3 cups finely chopped celery

½ cup chopped green onions and tops

1 tablespoon chopped pimiento

5 hard-cooked eggs, sliced

Pour French dressing over shrimp; toss to coat well. Set aside. Dissolve gelatine in cold water; melt over hot water. Combine with mayonnaise. Add remaining ingredients and marinated shrimp. Mix well. Turn into greased mold. Chill in refrigerator for 10 hours or longer. Unmold onto serving plate. Serves 8 to 10. *Edith Lirtzman*

CRAB MEAT SALAD IN AVOCADO CUPS

1 6½-oz. can crab meat, flaked

¼ cup finely chopped celery

2 tablespoons finely chopped green pepper

2 tablespoons pimiento pieces (about 1 inch)

1 hard-cooked egg, sliced

3 tablespoons mayonnaise

¼ teaspoon salt

⅛ teaspoon freshly ground black pepper

1 avocado

Lemon juice

Combine crab meat with celery, green pepper, pimiento, egg, salt, pepper and mayonnaise. Toss gently to mix well. Split avocado lengthwise; remove stone and peal off skin. Brush with lemon juice. Place each avocado half on lettuce leaf. Pack crab meat mixture into custard cup or ½ cup of measuring cup set; unmold onto avocado half. Garnish with pimiento or green pepper strips, if desired. Serve Thousand Island or French dressing separately. Serves 2. *Shirley Sostrin*

FRUIT SALADS

SOUR CREAM MOLD

1 cup mandarin oranges

1 cup pineapple chunks

1 cup sour cream

1 cup miniature marshmallows

½ cup shredded coconut

Combine all ingredients; mix gently but thoroughly. Turn into lightly greased mold. Chill in refrigerator overnight. Serves 6 to 8. *Lorrayne Schwartz*

MELON SURPRISE

1 package strawberry-flavored gelatin

1 9-oz. can fruit cocktail, drained

1 large ripe honeydew melon

1 3-oz. package soft cream cheese

2 teaspoons milk

Prepare gelatin according to directions on package; add fruit cocktail. Pare melon; cut off 1 inch from narrow end. Stand melon upright in bowl. Scoop out seeds; fill cavity with gelatin mixture. Chill in refrigerator until gelatin is set. Combine cream cheese with milk until mixture is of spreading consistency. Place melon on plate; frost entire melon with cream cheese. Chill in refrigerator. When ready to serve, cut into ½-inch crosswise slices. Place each slice on lettuce leaf. Serves 5 or 6.   *Mrs. Harold Kaplan*

MELON RINGS WITH FROSTED GRAPES

1 medium honeydew melon

1 pound green seedless grapes

½ cup granulated sugar

1 lime, cut into 6 wedges

Cut melon into 6 wedges; remove seeds. Chill in refrigerator. Wash grapes and divide into 6 clusters. Sprinkle with sugar; place in freezer or freezing compartment of refrigerator for 20 to 30 minutes. Serve melon wedges on salad plates with cluster of grapes on top. Garnish each with wedge of lime. Makes 6 servings.   *Cele Malvin*

FROZEN FRUIT SALAD

1 No. 2½ can fruits for salad, drained

1 cup seeded grapes

16 large marshmallows, quartered

6 maraschino cherries, halved

1 cup shredded coconut

½ cup mayonnaise

½ cup sour cream

2 bananas, sliced

½ cup slivered almonds

¼ cup chopped pecans

2 tablespoons granulated sugar

2 cups heavy cream, whipped

Mix together in large bowl, fruits for salad, grapes, marshmallows, cherries, coconut, mayonnaise and sour cream. Chill in refrigerator overnight. Early next day, add bananas, almonds, pecans, sugar and whipped cream. Toss gently to mix well. Turn into large ice-cube tray and place in freezing compartment of refrigerator for several hours. Serve on lettuce or other greens. Serves 14 to 16.   *Sylvea Zimmerman*

AMBROSIA FRUIT SALAD

1 large jar fruits for salad, drained

1 pint berries

2 cups sour cream

1 4-oz. can shredded coconut

16 large marshmallows, cut up, or 1 4-oz. package miniature marshmallows

12 maraschino cherries

Place fruits for salad in bowl; add other ingredients in order listed. Mix gently. Chill in refrigerator overnight. Serve on salad greens or melon wedges. Serves 10. *Merle Rosenbaum*

FROZEN CRANBERRY SALAD

1 cup sour cream

1 cup crushed pineapple, well drained

3 ounces chopped pecans

1 can whole cranberry sauce

Mix all ingredients together well. Turn into ice-cube tray and place in freezing compartment of refrigerator for several hours. Cut into squares and serve on salad greens. Serves 6. *Isabel Fiddler*

MOLDED FRUIT SALADS

FROSTED FRUIT MOLD

1 No. 2 can fruit cocktail

1 package lemon-flavored gelatin

3 tablespoons lemon juice

1 cup ginger ale

1 banana, sliced

1 cup halved strawberries

1 3-oz. package soft cream cheese

3 tablespoons milk

Drain fruit cocktail, reserving juice. Dissolve gelatin in heated juice; stir. Blend in lemon juice and ginger ale. Chill in refrigerator until partially set. Fold in fruit cocktail, banana and strawberries. Turn into greased mold; chill until firm. Unmold onto greens on serving plate. Whip together cream cheese and milk until fluffy. Frost fruit mold and chill until ready to serve. Serves 6. *Lila Pizer*

CINNAMON APPLESAUCE SALAD

2 packages lemon-flavored gelatin

½ cup red cinnamon candies

2 cups boiling water

2 cups unsweetened applesauce

1 teaspoon lemon juice

½ cup broken walnuts

2 3-oz. packages soft cream cheese

¼ cup milk or light cream

2 tablespoons mayonnaise

Dissolve gelatin and candies in boiling water. Stir in applesauce and lemon juice. Chill in refrigerator until partially set. Stir in walnuts. Pour into greased 8x8x2-inch pan. Combine cream cheese, milk and mayonnaise until well blended. Spoon onto gelatin; swirl with back of spoon to give marbled effect. Chill until firm. Cut into squares and serve on crisp greens. Serves 12.

Alice B. Weitzenfeld

GINGER ALE FRUIT SALAD

2 packages lemon-flavored gelatin

¼ cup granulated sugar

1 cup boiling water

½ cup orange juice

1 tablespoon lemon juice

2 cups ginger ale

1 No. 2 can crushed pineapple, drained

1 tablespoon grated orange rind

½ cup slivered almonds

Dissolve gelatin and sugar in boiling water. Cool and add orange juice, lemon juice and ginger ale. Chill in refrigerator for about 1 hour. Add remaining ingredients; turn into greased mold and chill until firm. Unmold onto serving plate. Serves 12.

Pauline Piel

FESTIVE CRANBERRY MOLD

1 No. 303 can grapefruit sections

1 package cherry-flavored gelatin

1 package frozen cranberry relish

1 apple, chopped

½ cup chopped nuts

Drain grapefruit sections, reserving juice. Dissolve gelatin in heated reserved juice combined with enough water to make 1½ cups liquid. Cool; thaw cranberry relish slightly. Mix relish with apple and nuts. Combine with gelatin mixture. Arrange grapefruit sections in bottom of lightly greased mold. Spoon gelatin mixture carefully into mold. Chill in refrigerator until firm. Unmold onto serving plate. Serves 8.

Esther Levine

JELLIED CRANBERRY MOLD

4 cups cranberries

¼ cup non-caloric sweetening solution

2 cups water

2 envelopes unflavored gelatine

¼ cup cold water

Combine cranberries, sweetening solution and water in saucepan. Cook for 8 to 10 minutes, or until skins pop. Soften gelatine in cold water. Add to cranberries, stirring until gelatine is dissolved. Pour into greased mold and chill in refrigerator until firm. Unmold and serve with assorted fruit. Serves 8 to 10.   *Ruth Knapp*

CRANBERRY-PINEAPPLE MOLD

2 packages raspberry, strawberry or cherry-flavored gelatin

2 cups hot water

2 cups sour cream

1 No. 303 can crushed pineapple, drained

1 No. 303 can whole cranberry sauce, drained

Dissolve gelatin in hot water. Chill in refrigerator until partially set. Whip with electric mixer, gradually adding sour cream, until fluffy and well blended. Fold in pineapple and cranberry sauce. Mix thoroughly. Turn into mold and chill until firm. Unmold onto serving plate. Serves 8 to 10.

Estelle Meyers

CHERRY WINE MOLD

2   1 No. 2½ can pitted Bing cherries

4   2 packages cherry-flavored gelatin

4   2 cups boiling water

C   ½ cup sweet wine

C   ½ cup walnut halves

2½ c - 1¼ c. cherry juice

Dissolve gelatin in boiling water. Drain cherries, reserving juice. Combine reserved cherry juice with wine and enough water to make 4 cups liquid. Add to gelatin; pour into mold and chill in refrigerator until partially set. Meanwhile, stuff pitted cherries with walnut halves. Fold cherries into gelatin. Chill until firm. Unmold onto salad greens on serving plate. Serves 12.   *Queenie Lerman*

Moisten the serving plate—then if salad unmolds a bit off-center it can be coaxed into position.

LIME-PINEAPPLE MOLD

1 No. 303 can crushed pineapple   1 cup sour cream

2 packages lime-flavored gelatin

Drain pineapple, reserving juice. Prepare gelatin according to directions on package, substituting reserved pineapple juice for part of water. Chill gelatin in refrigerator until partially set. Add sour cream, mixing well with electric mixer; fold in crushed pineapple. Pour into lightly greased mold; chill until set. Unmold onto serving plate. Serves 12.   *Thelma Disson*

PINEAPPLE-CUCUMBER RING

2 No. 303 cans crushed pineapple   2 packages lime-flavored gelatin

2 large cucumbers, chopped

Drain pineapple and cucumber thoroughly, reserving liquid. Combine 1 cup heated reserved liquid with gelatin. Add remaining liquid and enough water to make 2½ cups; stir. Chill in refrigerator until partially set; fold in pineapple and cucumber. Pour into greased 2-qt. ring mold. Chill in refrigerator until firm. Unmold onto serving plate. Makes 12 servings.   *Perle Jacobs*

PINEAPPLE-VEGETABLE MOLD

1 No. 303 can crushed pineapple   2 carrots, grated

1 package lemon-flavored gelatin   ¾ cup chopped celery

Drain pineapple well, reserving juice. Prepare gelatin according to directions on package, substituting reserved pineapple juice for part of water. When gelatin mixture has cooled slightly, add pineapple, carrots and celery. Pour into greased 8-inch ring mold. Chill in refrigerator until firm. Unmold onto serving plate. Serves 8.   *Ruth Rose*

ORANGE FROTH MOLD

3½ cups orange juice   1 cup sour cream

2 packages orange-flavored gelatin   ½ cup sliced toasted almonds

Heat orange juice. Add to gelatin and stir until gelatin is dissolved. Chill in refrigerator until partially set. Add sour cream; beat on electric mixer until frothy. Add nuts and mix gently but thoroughly. Pour into greased mold and chill until firm. Unmold onto serving plate. Serves 8.

Rochelle Braverman

MANDARIN ORANGE-SHERBET MOLD

3 packages orange-flavored gelatin

3 cups boiling water

2 11-oz. cans mandarin oranges

2 teaspoons lemon juice

1 pint orange sherbet

Dissolve gelatin in boiling water. Drain oranges, reserving syrup. To reserved syrup, add enough water to make ¾ cup liquid. Add lemon juice; stir into gelatin mixture. Stir in orange sherbet just until sherbet melts. Add oranges; turn into greased mold and chill in refrigerator until firm. Unmold onto serving plate. Serves 12.

Bett Wein

PEAR SEA-FOAM MOLD

1 No. 2½ can Bartlett pears

1 package lime-flavored gelatin

2 3-oz. packages soft cream cheese

2 tablespoons cream

½ cup heavy cream, whipped

Drain pears, reserving juice. Combine reserved juice with enough water to make 1 cup liquid. Heat to boiling. Dissolve gelatin in hot liquid. Cool. Mix cream cheese with cream until smooth; add to gelatin mixture. Beat until well blended. Chill in refrigerator until partially set. Mash pears; add to gelatin mixture and blend well. Fold in whipped cream and pour mixture into greased mold. Chill until firm. Unmold onto serving plate. Serves 8.

Mabel Koffay

ICED MILK MOLD

1 15-oz. can ice cold evaporated milk

3 packages raspberry-flavored gelatin

½ cup hot water

½ cup sugar

¼ cup lemon juice

2 cups sliced strawberries or other fruit

Whip evaporated milk in large bowl with electric mixer until stiff and at least doubled in volume. Dissolve gelatin in hot water; add sugar and lemon juice, stirring until sugar is dissolved. Add to whipped milk and beat until well mixed. Fold in fruit by hand. Turn mixture into greased 1½-qt. mold. Chill in refrigerator for at least 4 hours. Serves 12 to 15.   *Erika Brodsky*

LIME LAYER SALAD

1 package lime-flavored gelatin	1 tablespoon lemon juice
¼ teaspoon salt	½ cup diced orange sections
1 cup hot water	¼ cup diced celery
1 cup cold water	1 3-oz. package soft cream cheese

Dissolve gelatin and salt in hot water; add cold water and lemon juice. Chill 1 cup of this mixture in refrigerator until partially set; fold in orange sections and celery. Pour into 1-qt. mold and chill until almost set. Add cream cheese to remaining gelatin; beat until smooth. Chill until partially set, then pour over gelatin mixture in mold. Chill until firm. Unmold and serve on crisp greens. Serves 5.

Lila Pizer

BLUEBERRY-LEMON LAYERS

1 No. 2 can blueberries	1 package lemon-flavored gelatin
1 package raspberry, strawberry or cherry-flavored gelatin	1 cup sour cream

Drain blueberries, reserving juice. Dissolve raspberry-flavored gelatin in ½ cup boiling water; add reserved juice and water combined to make 1¼ cups liquid. Cool; add blueberries. Pour into 1½-qt. mold; chill in refrigerator until firm. Dissolve lemon-flavored gelatin in ½ cup boiling water. Cool; add 1 cup cold water. Mix in sour cream, blending until well mixed on low speed of electric mixer. Pour into mold; chill until firm. Unmold onto serving plate; garnish with blueberries, if desired. Serves 8 to 10.

Eve Eisenstein

FROZEN LEMON-BLUEBERRY MOLD

1 package lemon-flavored gelatin	1 No. 303 can blueberries
1 cup boiling water	1 package raspberry-flavored gelatin
1 No. 303 can fruits for salad	1 cup boiling water
1 3-oz. package cream cheese	

Dissolve lemon gelatin in 1 cup boiling water. Drain fruits for salad, reserving juice. Combine juice with enough cold water to make 1 cup liquid. Add to gelatin mixture. Cool; beat in cream cheese. Add fruits for salad and pour into greased mold. Freeze. Drain blueberries, reserving juice. Dissolve raspberry gelatin in 1 cup boiling water. Combine blueberry juice with enough cold water to make 1 cup liquid. Add to gelatin mixture. Cool; add blueberries and pour over frozen mixture. Chill in refrigerator until firm. Unmold. Serves 12. *Shirley Crane*

APRICOT SUPREME

2 packages orange-flavored gelatin

1 cup boiling water

1 No. 2 can apricots

¾ cup sour cream

1 large banana, sliced

Dissolve gelatin in boiling water. Place apricots and juice in blender container and blend until mushy. Add to gelatin. Pour half of gelatin mixture into greased mold. Chill in refrigerator until firm (about 2 hours). Beat remaining gelatin mixture with ½ cup sour cream. Arrange banana slices on gelatin in mold. Spread with remaining sour cream. Pour remaining gelatin mixture carefully over top. Chill in refrigerator until firm. Unmold onto serving plate. Serves 10 to 12. *Florence Kite*

RASPBERRY-CREAM CHEESE RIBBON MOLD

1 package lemon-flavored gelatin

½ cup hot water

1 8-oz. package soft cream cheese

2 teaspoons confectioners' sugar

1 cup heavy cream

1 teaspoon vanilla

1 package thawed frozen raspberries

Hot water

2 packages raspberry-flavored gelatin

Dissolve lemon-flavored gelatin in hot water. Chill in refrigerator until partially set. Meanwhile, combine cream cheese with confectioners' sugar, creaming thoroughly. Whip cream with vanilla. Blend cream cheese and whipped cream into gelatin on low speed of electric mixer. Pour into mold and chill until firm (about 3 hours). Drain raspberries, reserving juice. Combine raspberry juice with enough hot water to make 3¼ cups liquid. Dissolve raspberry-flavored gelatin in hot juice mixture; cool. Arrange raspberries over layer in mold; pour raspberry gelatin mixture over berries. Chill in refrigerator overnight. Unmold onto serving plate. May be served as dessert. Serves 10. *Sandra Kaufman*

STRAWBERRY STRIPE

4 packages strawberry-flavored gelatin

1 9-oz. can crushed pineapple, drained

1 package thawed frozen strawberries, drained

1 cup sour cream

Prepare gelatin as directed on package. Pour half of gelatin into greased 2-qt. mold. Chill in refrigerator until firm. Add fruits to remaining gelatin. When first layer is firm, spread with sour cream. Chill in refrigerator for 20 to 30 minutes. Spoon gelatin-fruit mixture on top of sour cream. Chill until firm. Unmold onto serving plate. Serves 12.   *Mickey Mandel*

STRAWBERRY-BANANA MOLD

3 packages strawberry-flavored gelatin

4 cups hot water

2 packages thawed frozen strawberries, drained

1 No. 2 can crushed pineapple, drained

2 bananas, sliced

1 cup sour cream

Dissolve gelatin in hot water. Chill in refrigerator until partially set. Add strawberries and pineapple. Pour half of gelatin mixture into greased mold. Chill until firm. Arrange banana slices on gelatin; dab sour cream over bananas. Pour remaining gelatin mixture carefully over top. Chill in refrigerator until firm. Unmold onto serving plate. Serves 16.

Helen Metnick

SPLASH MOLD

2 packages strawberry-flavored gelatin

1 cup hot water

1 package thawed frozen strawberries

2 packages lemon-flavored gelatin

1¾ cups hot water

1 3-oz. package soft cream cheese

1 No. 303 can crushed pineapple

2 packages lime-flavored gelatin

1 No. 303 can applesauce

2 packages orange-flavored gelatin

1½ cups hot water

1 No. 303 can strained apricots

Dissolve strawberry gelatin in 1 cup hot water. Chill in refrigerator until partially set. Fold in strawberries. Dissolve lemon gelatin in 1¾ cups hot water; chill until partially set. Add cream cheese and beat until smooth and well blended; fold in pineapple. Dissolve lime gelatin in 1½ cups hot water; chill until partially set. Fold in applesauce and whip until frothy. Dissolve orange gelatin in 1½ cups hot water; chill until partially set; fold in strained apricots. Spoon gelatin into 2 greased 2-qt. molds, alternating colors; chill in refrigerator until firm, or overnight. Unmold onto crisp greens. Serves 32.   *Edith Karasik*

MELON-PINEAPPLE MOLD

1 envelope unflavored gelatin

½ cup pineapple juice

1 cup sherry or orange juice

4 cups melon balls

Soften gelatin in ¼ cup pineapple juice. Heat remaining pineapple juice to boiling; dissolve gelatin mixture in hot juice. Add wine; stir to mix. Chill in refrigerator until partially set. Drain melon balls thoroughly. Pour a little of partially set gelatin into 1½-qt. mold; arrange melon balls in mold. Mix remaining balls with remaining gelatin. Pour into mold. Chill until firm. Unmold onto greens; serve with whipped cream-mayonnaise dressing. Serves 6.   *Jeannette Kowitt*

MOLDED CHEESE SALADS

CHEESE MOLD TROPICANA

2 envelopes unflavored gelatine

½ cup pineapple juice

3 cups dry cottage cheese

3 cups creamed cottage cheese

1 cup sour cream

2 tablespoons plus 1½ teaspoons granulated sugar

1 tablespoon salt

2 tablespoons orange juice

1 tablespoon pineapple juice

¼ cup red and green candied cherries

1 teaspoon vanilla

Dissolve gelatine in ½ cup pineapple juice; melt over hot water. Cool. Put cheeses through food mill or force through sieve; mix well with sour cream, sugar, salt, orange juice and 1 tablespoon pineapple juice. Add cherries and vanilla. Mix in gelatine mixture. Pack into greased mold; chill for several hours until firm. Unmold and garnish with avocado rings, apple slices, bananas, quartered, or orange segments. Serves 10 to 12.   *M. Weinstock*

COTTAGE CHEESE MOLD

1 teaspoon unflavored gelatine

¼ cup cold water

¼ teaspoon salt

1½ cups creamed cottage cheese

2 3-oz. packages soft cream cheese

1 cup seedless grapes

½ cup pecans

2 tablespoons chopped chives

1 cup heavy cream, whipped

Soften gelatine in cold water; dissolve over hot water. Add salt. Combine cottage cheese and cream cheese; mash and blend well. Stir in gelatine mixture. Add grapes, nuts and chives. Fold in whipped cream. Turn into individual molds or 1-qt. mold. Chill in refrigerator until firm. Unmold onto serving plate; arrange fresh fruits around mold; garnish with avocado slices and pistachio nuts. Makes 6 to 8 servings.   *Sylvea Zimmerman*

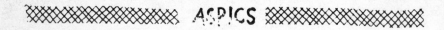

ASPICS

TOMATO ASPIC RING

2 envelopes unflavored gelatine

½ cup water

1 can tomato soup

½ cup mayonnaise

½ cup chili sauce

6 hard-cooked eggs, chopped

Juice of 1 lemon

1 teaspoon granulated sugar

½ teaspoon salt

Dissolve gelatine in water. Bring soup to boiling; add to gelatine with remaining ingredients, stirring to mix well. Pour into ring mold. Chill in refrigerator until firm. Unmold; fill center with sea-food salad, if desired. Serves 12.   *Florence Solomon*

INDIVIDUAL ASPICS WITH CHEESE BALLS

2 cups tomato juice

2 tablespoons vinegar

Pinch salt

1 package lemon-flavored gelatin

1 3-oz. package cream cheese

1 tablespoon onion juice

2 tablespoons chopped nuts

Combine tomato juice, vinegar and salt in saucepan; bring to boiling. Pour over gelatin, stirring until gelatin is dissolved. Cool and pour into individual molds. Chill in refrigerator until partially set. Meanwhile, mix cream cheese, onion juice and nuts. Shape into small balls. Place cheese balls in gelatin. Chill until firm. Makes 6 servings.   *Gerry Freedman*

 ## MOLDED VEGETABLE SALADS

NEW-LOOK PARTY POTATO SALAD

1 envelope unflavored gelatine	8 stuffed green olives, sliced
¼ cup cold water	4 cups diced cooked potatoes
1 cup hot water	1 cup diced celery
¼ cup lemon juice	¼ cup diced green pepper
2 tablespoons granulated sugar	¼ cup chopped onion
1 teaspoon salt	1 cup mayonnaise
2 hard-cooked eggs, sliced	½ cup heavy cream, whipped

Soften gelatine in cold water. Add hot water, lemon juice, sugar and salt, stirring until dissolved. Pour thin layer of gelatine mixture into greased 1½-qt. ring mold. Chill in refrigerator until partially set. Press some hard-cooked egg and olive slices into gelatine in mold. Chill until firm. Chop remaining egg and olive slices. Mix with potatoes, celery, green pepper and onion. Combine mayonnaise and whipped cream. Fold into potato mixture with remaining gelatine. Pour into mold and chill until firm. Unmold onto serving plate. Serves 8.   *Lila Pizer*

CUCUMBER-COTTAGE CHEESE MOLD

1 envelope unflavored gelatine	2 or 3 tablespoons sour cream
¼ cup cold water	1 cup grated cucumber, well drained
½ cup boiling water	2 tablespoons lemon juice
¼ cup granulated sugar	1 tablespoon grated onion or onion juice
1 cup creamed cottage cheese	½ teaspoon salt

Soften gelatine in cold water; dissolve with sugar in hot water; stir. Chill in refrigerator until partially set. Blend together cottage cheese, sour cream, cucumber, lemon juice, onion and salt. Fold into gelatine mixture. Pour into greased mold and chill until firm. Unmold onto serving plate; garnish with cucumber slices, ripe olives and parsley sprigs. Serves 6.   *Poppy Brooks*

CUCUMBER MOLD

1 envelope unflavored gelatine

¼ cup cold water

1 cut clove garlic

2 cups grated cucumber, drained

¼ cup minced onion

¼ cup chopped parsley

1 cup mayonnaise

3 3-oz. packages soft cream cheese

½ teaspoon salt

Few drops green food coloring

Dissolve gelatin in cold water; melt over hot water. Rub mixing bowl with garlic. Place cucumber, onion, parsley, mayonnaise, cream cheese and salt in bowl; mix well. Add gelatine and food coloring. Mix again. Pour into greased mold. Chill in refrigerator overnight. Unmold onto serving plate. Serves 6 to 8. *Beverly Rapper*

MOLDED COLESLAW

1 package lemon-flavored gelatin

1 cup hot water

½ cup cold water

½ cup mayonnaise

2 tablespoons vinegar

¼ teaspoon salt

1½ cups finely shredded cabbage

½ cup diced celery

2 tablespoons diced green pepper

2 green onions, diced, or 1 tablespoon diced onion

Dissolve gelatin in hot water. Blend in cold water, mayonnaise, vinegar and salt. Chill in refrigerator until partially set. Beat until fluffy; add remaining ingredients. Pour into individual molds or 1-qt. ring mold. Chill until firm. Unmold. Makes 6 to 8 servings. *Ruth Landsman*

BEET RING

1 package lemon-flavored gelatin

1 cup boiling water

1 9-oz. can diced beets

2 teaspoons onion juice

3 tablespoons vinegar

½ teaspoon salt

1 tablespoon horse-radish

¾ cup diced celery

Dissolve gelatin in hot water. Drain beets, reserving ¾ cup juice. Add to gelatin the beet juice, onion juice, vinegar, salt, horse-radish, beets and celery in order listed. Mix well. Turn into ring mold. Chill in refrigerator

until firm. Unmold onto serving plate; fill center with sea-food salad.
Serves 6. *Ann Metzger*

GARDEN SALAD MOLD

3 packages lemon-flavored gelatin	1 cup cubed or thinly sliced cucumber
3 cups hot water	½ cup thinly sliced radishes
2 cups cold water	½ cup chopped onion
1 tablespoon vinegar	½ cup chopped celery
1 teaspoon salt	½ cup chopped green pepper

Dissolve gelatin in hot water; add cold water, vinegar and salt, stirring until dissolved. Pour into greased mold. Chill in refrigerator until partially set. Add remaining ingredients and chill until almost set. Remove from refrigerator and stir to distribute vegetables evenly. Chill until firm. Unmold; serve with a sour cream dressing to which celery seed has been added for extra flavor. Serves 16. *Bertha Gross*

SALAD DRESSINGS

SLIMMING "MAYONNAISE" (without egg)

1 teaspoon unflavored gelatine	1 teaspoon salt
¼ cup cold milk	½ teaspoon paprika
½ cup hot milk	¼ teaspoon dry mustard
4 tablespoons lemon juice	Dash cayenne pepper

Soften gelatine in cold milk; add hot milk, stirring until dissolved. Add remaining ingredients; chill in refrigerator until partially set. Whip with wire whisk until fluffy. Chill until almost firm. Whip again and store in refrigerator until ready to serve. Stir vigorously, adding milk or lemon juice if necessary to thin. Makes 1 cup. *Dee Stein*

SLIMMING MAYONNAISE (with egg)

1 egg

¼ cup milk

2 tablespoons vinegar

½ teaspoon salt

¼ teaspoon paprika

¼ teaspoon dry mustard

Pinch cayenne pepper

Combine all ingredients in heavy 6-inch mixing bowl. Place bowl in iron skillet filled with hot water. Bring water to boiling, beating constantly with wire whisk, until mixture thickens (about 4 minutes). Pour immediately into jar. Cover tightly and chill in refrigerator. To vary, use only 1 tablespoon vinegar and 5 tablespoons milk, or substitute 2 tablespoons lemon juice for the vinegar. If desired. whip a little yoghurt into chilled dressing. Makes ½ cup.   *Dee Stein*

CHERRY FRUIT SALAD DRESSING

½ cup salad oil

¼ cup lemon juice

¼ cup maraschino cherry juice

6 maraschino cherries

1 tablespoon granulated sugar

½ teaspoon salt

½ teaspoon paprika

1 3-oz. package cream cheese, or 1 cup heavy cream, whipped

Combine all ingredients in blender container; blend until smooth. If substituting whipped cream for cream cheese, fold in after other ingredients have been blended. Chill in refrigerator. Makes 1⅓ cups.   *Marge Sandberg*

FRUIT SALAD DRESSING

¼ cup pineapple juice

¼ cup lemon juice

¼ cup orange juice

2 eggs

½ cup granulated sugar

Pinch salt

1 cup heavy cream

Combine fruit juices in saucepan; bring to boiling. Beat eggs until light, adding sugar and salt gradually. Add to fruit juices; boil, stirring constantly, until mixture thickens. Cool; chill in refrigerator. Just before serving, whip cream; fold into egg mixture. Makes 2 cups.   *Ruth Friedman*

PARTY PINEAPPLE DRESSING

1 cup mayonnaise

½ cup pineapple juice

½ cup crushed pineapple

Few drops yellow food coloring

Combine all ingredients; mix well. Chill in refrigerator. Makes 2 cups.

Joan Florence

BOILED DRESSING

2 eggs

¼ cup vinegar

2 tablespoons water

½ cup granulated sugar

1 teaspoon dry mustard

½ teaspoon salt

1 cup sour cream

Combine eggs, vinegar, water, sugar, mustard and salt in top of double boiler. Cook over boiling water, stirring constantly, until mixture boils and thickens. Cool. Beat in sour cream. Chill in refrigerator. Makes 2 cups.

Florence Kalish

BASHA'S SOUR CREAM DRESSING

½ cup sour cream

¼ cup mayonnaise

1 teaspoon tarragon-wine vinegar

Lemon juice

½ can anchovies, drained

1½ teaspoons minced parsley

1 green onion and top, finely chopped

1 small clove garlic, mashed

Pinch orégano

Salt and pepper

Combine all ingredients; mix well. Chill in refrigerator. Makes ¾ cup.

Rachel Long

RUSSIAN DELIGHT

1 cup mayonnaise

½ 3-oz. package cream cheese

¼ cup chili sauce

½ 2-oz. jar pimiento

1 cup heavy cream, whipped

Place mayonnaise, cream cheese, chili sauce and pimiento in blender container. Blend until well mixed. Fold into whipped cream. Chill in refrigerator until ready to serve. Makes about 2 cups. *Elaine Gayle*

TOMATO DRESSING

⅔ cup tomato juice

2 teaspoons cornstarch

½ cup lemon juice

3 tablespoons salad oil

2 tablespoons catchup

1 teaspoon Worcestershire sauce

1 teaspoon prepared mustard

1 teaspoon horse-radish

¾ teaspoon granulated sugar

¼ teaspoon paprika

¼ teaspoon garlic salt

¼ teaspoon onion salt

¼ teaspoon celery salt

¼ teaspoon monosodium glutamate

Mix tomato juice with cornstarch in saucepan until smooth. Cook, stirring constantly, until thick. Cool. Combine with remaining ingredients in blender container; blend until creamy. Chill in refrigerator. Makes about 1½ cups.

Marian D. Horwitz

GREEN GODDESS DRESSING

1 cup mayonnaise

½ cup sour cream

3 tablespoons tarragon-wine vinegar

1 tablespoon lemon juice

½ cup finely chopped parsley

3 tablespoons finely chopped onion

3 tablespoons mashed anchovies

1 tablespoon chopped chives

2 teaspoons chopped capers

1 small clove garlic, crushed

½ teaspoon salt

⅛ teaspoon pepper

Combine all ingredients in blender container; blend well. Chill in refrigerator. Serve over crisp greens. Makes 2 cups.

Elnora Weissbuch

CREAMY ROQUEFORT DRESSING

2 cups mayonnaise

1 cup sour cream

½ cup wine vinegar

3 tablespoons anchovy paste (optional)

2 tablespoons lemon juice

2 cloves garlic, mashed

½ pound Roquefort cheese

⅓ cup chopped parsley

⅓ cup chopped green onions and tops

Combine mayonnaise, sour cream, vinegar, anchovy paste, lemon juice and garlic in mixing bowl. Beat on electric mixer until well blended. Crumble cheese into mixture. Mix lightly. Chill in refrigerator. Just before serving, add parsley and onion. Makes about 4 cups.   *Tillie Shafer*

GREEN PIQUANT DRESSING

1 small bunch parsley

3 small green onions

½ clove garlic

2 cups mayonnaise

¼ cup cream

Place parsley, onions and garlic in blender container. Blend at high speed until thoroughly minced. Add mayonnaise and cream; blend at low speed for several minutes. Chill in refrigerator until ready to serve. Excellent over sea-food salads and vegetable salads. Makes 3 cups.   *Florence Kite*

SURPRISE DRESSING

1 clove garlic, cut

2 eggs

1 tablespoon granulated sugar

1 teaspoon salt

½ teaspoon paprika

½ teaspoon dry mustard

½ cup catchup

1 teaspoon Worcestershire sauce

2 cups salad oil

½ cup vinegar

⅔ cup warm water

Rub mixing bowl with cut clove of garlic. Combine in bowl eggs, sugar, salt, paprika, mustard, catchup and Worcestershire sauce. Stir into a smooth paste. Beat on electric mixer, adding oil and vinegar until mixture thickens. Add warm water slowly, beating constantly, until dressing is of desired consistency. Keep in a cool place. Makes 2 pints.   *Sharon Hockman*

HONEY FRENCH DRESSING

½ cup French dressing

1 tablespoon honey

1 teaspoon grated lemon rind

2 teaspoons lemon juice

Combine all ingredients and mix well. Chill in refrigerator. Serve over fruit salads. Makes about ⅔ cup.   *Joan Florence*

FRENCH DRESSING

6 tablespoons vinegar

5 tablespoons olive oil

¼ cup granulated sugar

1 teaspoon salt

1 teaspoon paprika

Pinch cayenne pepper

Combine all ingredients in covered jar and shake well. Chill in refrigerator. Dressing will thicken upon standing. Makes about ⅔ cup. *Jean Finston*

ITALIAN DRESSING

2 tablespoons wine vinegar

2 large cloves garlic, minced

½ teaspoon prepared mustard

1 teaspoon salt

⅛ teaspoon pepper

¾ cup salad oil

Combine vinegar, garlic, mustard, salt and pepper in covered jar or blender container. Shake or blend thoroughly. Add oil; shake or blend again. Store in refrigerator. Keeps well for several weeks. Makes about 1 cup.

Rosalyn Rubin

GARLIC VINEGAR DRESSING (French dressing substitute)

1 clove garlic, crushed

3 tablespoons any herb vinegar

½ teaspoon salt

½ teaspoon paprika

⅛ teaspoon freshly ground black pepper

3 tablespoons juice from pimientos

Marinate garlic in vinegar for 5 minutes. Remove garlic and discard. Add remaining ingredients and mix well. Chill in refrigerator. To vary, add 1 tablespoon minced parsley, pinch each of orégano, basil and thyme. Or add anise seed, caraway seed, dill seed or celery seed to taste. Makes 2 servings.

Dee Stein

VINAIGRETTE DRESSING

½ cup salad oil

5 tablespoons vinegar

3 tablespoons sweet pickle relish

2 tablespoons snipped parsley

1 teaspoon salt

½ teaspoon granulated sugar

Combine all ingredients. Chill in refrigerator. Use as salad dressing for mixed greens, or as marinade for vegetables. *Alice B. Weitzenfeld*

RELISHES AND PRESERVES

"The rule is, jam to-morrow, and jam
yesterday—but never jam *today*."
"It *must* come sometimes to 'jam
to-day'," Alice objected.
"No, it can't," said the Queen. "It's
jam every *other* day: to-day isn't
any *other* day, you know."

Lewis Carroll

EGGPLANT RELISH

1 medium eggplant (about 1 lb.)

1 large green pepper

1 medium onion

2 tablespoons mayonnaise

1 tablespoon sour cream

2 teaspoons vinegar

Salt and pepper

Cook eggplant and green pepper, covered, in small amount of boiling salted water about 10 minutes, or until soft. Pare eggplant; cut top from green pepper. Scoop out seeds from eggplant and green pepper; cut into pieces. Put through food chopper with onion. Add mayonnaise, sour cream, vinegar, salt and pepper. Mix well. Chill in refrigerator.   *Pearl Ginsberg*

TOMATO RELISH

4 large tomatoes, thinly sliced

1 large Bermuda onion, finely chopped

½ cup olive or salad oil

1 teaspoon orégano

½ teaspoon salt

¼ teaspoon freshly ground black pepper

Cut tomato slices in half. Mix tomatoes, onion, oil, orégano, salt and pepper. Chill in refrigerator for 1 hour or longer, tossing gently occasionally to marinate thoroughly. Serve on lettuce cups as salad, or serve as relish with roast meat.   *Elnora Weissbuch*

GREEN PEPPER RELISH

6 green peppers, chopped	1 teaspoon fresh dill (optional)
¼ cup salad oil	3 tablespoons wine vinegar
1 clove garlic, minced	¼ teaspoon salt

Sauté garlic in hot oil until clear. Add peppers and dill; cook until peppers are tender. Remove from heat; add vinegar and salt. Chill in refrigerator.

Marian D. Horwitz

FLOATING ISLAND RELISH

1 cup tarragon or garlic vinegar	Salt and pepper
1 cup cold water	2 tomatoes, sliced
1 tablespoon salad oil	1 large onion, thinly sliced
2 teaspoons orégano	1 green pepper, sliced
1 teaspoon thyme	½ cucumber, sliced

Combine vinegar, water, oil, orégano, thyme, salt and pepper. Place tomatoes, onion, green pepper and cucumber in layers in salad bowl. Pour vinegar mixture over vegetables; chill in refrigerator. Serves 4 to 6.   *Joan Florence*

FRUIT CHILI SAUCE

6 fresh peaches, skinned and pitted	2 cups granulated sugar
6 fresh pears, pared and cored	2 cups vinegar
6 medium white onions	2 teaspoons mixed pickling spices
4 large tomatoes, peeled	2 teaspoons salt
2 large green peppers, tops removed	

Put peaches, pears, onions, tomatoes and green pepper through food chopper. Place in large saucepan. Add sugar, vinegar, spices and salt. Cook for 1½ to 2 hours over low heat. Pour immediately into sterilized jars. Seal tightly. Makes 3 to 4 pints.   *Marian D. Horwitz*

To sterilize jars, place clean jars on rack in large kettle. Pour boiling water over them and boil for 15 minutes, keeping jars covered with water. Remove jars from kettle with tongs and drain on wire rack.

CANDIED BEETS

4 cups shredded beets

4 cups granulated sugar

2 small oranges, in sections

2 small lemons, sliced

¼ cup water

1 teaspoon ground ginger

½ cup Brazil nuts

Combine beets, sugar, orange sections, lemon slices, water and ginger in large saucepan. Cook until mixture is jellied, about 1 hour. Add Brazil nuts. Cool; spoon into jars. Cover and store in cool place away from light. Makes 3 or 4 pints.   *Stella Ellyne*

FRESH PEACH CHUTNEY

2 quarts peeled fresh peach slices

1 cup boiling vinegar

¼ cup cold vinegar

1½ cups granulated sugar

½ cup seedless raisins

½ cup chopped red pepper

⅓ cup chopped onion

2¼ tablespoons whole mustard seed

¾ oz. crystallized ginger

Cook peaches in boiling vinegar until soft, but not mushy. Add cold vinegar, sugar, raisins, red pepper, onion, mustard seed and ginger. Simmer for 1 to 1½ hours, or until thick and clear, stirring occasionally. Immediately fill sterilized jars and seal tightly. Makes 4 to 5 pints.   *Marcella Haskin*

PEAR CHUTNEY

1 No. 2½ can pear or apricot halves

1 No. 2 can tomatoes

1 green pepper, chopped

1 onion, diced

1 cup granulated sugar

1 teaspoon salt

½ teaspoon ground ginger

½ teaspoon dry mustard

⅛ teaspoon cayenne pepper

½ cup vinegar

1 2-oz. can pimiento

Combine all ingredients except pimiento in large saucepan. Bring to boiling; simmer for 1½ hours, stirring occasionally. Add coarsely chopped pimiento. Simmer for 10 minutes longer. Immediately fill sterilized jars and seal tightly. Makes 2 pints.   *Jay Phillips*

CHERRY-CRANBERRY RELISH

1 No. 300 can jellied cranberry sauce

1 No. 1 can pitted Bing cherries, drained

1 tablespoon grated orange rind

Place cranberry sauce in bowl; break up with fork. Add cherries and orange rind; toss gently. Chill in refrigerator.
Gert Liberson

CRANBERRY CONSERVE

4 cups cranberries

1 cup water

1 cup coarsely chopped nuts

1 cup seedless raisins

1 orange, sliced

2½ cups granulated sugar

Cook cranberries in water until skins pop. Force through a sieve; add nuts. Mix well. Add raisins, orange slices and sugar. Simmer for 15 minutes. Chill in refrigerator.
Dolores Streicker

PICKLED PEACHES

1 No. 2½ can cling peach halves

3 tablespoons vinegar

1 teaspoon allspice

1 stick cinnamon

Drain peaches, reserving juice. Combine reserved peach juice, vinegar, allspice and cinnamon stick. Cook over medium heat for 10 minutes. Add peach halves; cook over low heat for 5 minutes. Chill in refrigerator; remove cinnamon stick before serving.
Ruth Knapp

SPICED PEACHES

1 No. 303 can water-packed peaches

¼ cup vinegar

2 teaspoons non-caloric sweetening solution

2 sticks cinnamon

½ teaspoon allspice

7 or 8 cloves

Drain peaches, reserving liquid. Combine reserved liquid with vinegar, sweetening solution, cinnamon, allspice and cloves. Boil for 2 minutes. Add peaches and simmer for 10 minutes. Chill in refrigerator for at least 24 hours. Drain and serve.
Belle D. Guralnik

CAKES AND FROSTINGS

Oh, cakes and friends we
should choose with care,
Not always the fanciest cake
that's there
Is the best to eat! And the
plainest friend
Is sometimes the finest
one in the end!

Margaret E. Sangster

YELLOW CAKES

CHERRY CAKE

1 No. 2 can sour cherries	2 teaspoons baking powder
½ cup granulated sugar	½ teaspoon salt
1 tablespoon cornstarch	TOPPING:
½ cup soft shortening	¼ cup flour
1 cup granulated sugar	¼ cup granulated sugar
2 eggs	2 tablespoons butter
2 cups sifted flour	¼ cup chopped nuts

Combine cherries, ½ cup sugar and cornstarch in saucepan; cook, stirring, until thick and glossy. Cream shortening, 1 cup sugar and egg until light and fluffy. Sift together sifted flour, baking powder and salt. Add to creamed mixture. Spread half of batter in greased 13x9x2-inch pan. Cover carefully with cherry mixture. Spoon remaining batter on top. Mix together ¼ cup flour, ¼ cup sugar and butter until crumbly. Mix in nuts. Sprinkle over batter in pan. Bake at 350° for about 50 minutes.   *Florence M. Mayron*

APPLE CAKE

4 eggs	1 teaspoon baking powder
1 cup granulated sugar	Pinch salt
1 cup melted butter	1 can apple pie filling
2 cups sifted cake flour	Cinnamon-sugar

Beat eggs. Add sugar gradually, beating well. Sift together flour, baking powder and salt. Add melted butter and flour to creamed mixture. Mix well. Pour half of batter into greased 11x7x1½-inch pan. Cover with half of apple filling. Sprinkle with cinnamon-sugar. Repeat with remaining batter and filling. Bake at 325° for about 30 minutes. Cool; cut into squares.

Alice Beegun

MARBLE CAKE

1 cup soft butter or shortening	1 cup sour cream
2 cups granulated sugar	½ teaspoon baking soda
5 egg yolks, beaten	5 egg whites
1 teaspoon vanilla	Few grains salt
2 cups sifted cake flour	¼ cup chocolate syrup
2 teaspoons baking powder	

Cream butter and sugar well; add beaten egg yolks; beat until light and fluffy. Mix in vanilla. Sift together flour and baking powder. Combine sour cream and soda. Add flour alternately with sour cream to creamed mixture, beating well after each addition. Beat egg whites with salt until stiff. Fold into batter. Remove ⅓ of batter to small bowl; mix in chocolate syrup. Spoon light and dark batter alternately into greased 10-inch tube pan. Cut through with knife to give marble effect. Bake at 350° for 1 hour and 15 minutes. Serves 16.

Frieda Endler

MAPLE NUT CAKE

2 cups firmly packed brown sugar	½ cup butter
2 cups sifted flour	½ cup chopped nuts
1 teaspoon baking powder	1 cup soured half-and-half
½ teaspoon baking soda	2 eggs
½ teaspoon salt	¾ teaspoon maple flavoring

Mix together brown sugar, flour, baking powder, soda and salt in large bowl. Crumble butter and cut into flour mixture until mealy. Add chopped nuts. Mix well; reserve 1 cup of mixture for topping. Add soured half-and-half, eggs and maple flavoring to remaining flour mixture. Mix well; pour into greased and floured 11x7x1½-inch pan. Sprinkle reserved crumb mixture over top. Smooth with rubber spatula. Bake at 375° for 35 to 40 minutes.

Emma Oesterreicher

"SPECIAL OCCASION" RAINBOW CAKE

2 cups soft butter

2½ cups granulated sugar

4 large eggs

5 cups sifted cake flour

5 teaspoons baking powder

¼ teaspoon salt

1¼ cups lukewarm milk

1 teaspoon almond extract

Food colorings

Have eggs at room temperature. Cream butter and sugar; add eggs, one at a time, beating well after each. Sift together cake flour, baking powder and salt. Add alternately with milk to egg mixture, beginning and ending with flour. Add almond extract; mix well. Divide batter into 4 parts. Tint one fourth pink, one fourth green and remainder yellow with few drops food coloring. Pour half of yellow batter into greased and floured 9 or 10-inch tube pan. Pour pink batter over yellow; pour green batter over pink; top with remaining yellow batter. Bake at 325° for 1 hour; increase oven temperature to 375° and bake for 15 minutes longer. Allow to stand for 5 minutes after removing from oven. Invert on wire rack and cool. Slice very thin. Serves 30 to 40.

Evelyn Segal

CHOCOLATE CHIP CAKE

2 bars (½ lb.) German's sweet chocolate, grated

2 cups sifted cake flour

2 teaspoons baking powder

1 cup soft unsalted butter

2 cups granulated sugar

6 egg yolks

1 cup half-and-half or cream

2 teaspoon vanilla

6 egg whites, beaten

Mix together grated chocolate, flour and baking powder. Cream butter and sugar; add egg yolks; mix well. Add flour mixture alternately with half-and-half, beginning and ending with flour, beating well after each addition. Mix in vanilla. Fold in beaten egg whites. Pour into greased 13x9x2-inch pan. Bake at 350° for 1 hour.

Gertrude Ludwig

LEMON CAKE WITH FRESH FRUIT

1 cup sifted flour	½ teaspoon vanilla
½ cup granulated sugar	½ teaspoon lemon extract
1½ teaspoons baking powder	3 peaches or plums, sliced
½ teaspoon salt	¼ cup granulated sugar
3 tablespoons soft butter	½ teaspoon cinnamon
1 egg, beaten	3 tablespoons raisins (optional)
½ cup milk	

Sift together flour, ½ cup sugar, baking powder and salt. Mix well with butter. Combine egg, milk, vanilla and lemon extract. Add gradually to flour mixture, beating well after each addition. Pour into greased 8x8x2-inch pan. Cover with peach slices. Mix together ¼ cup sugar and cinnamon. Sprinkle over top. Sprinkle with raisins, if desired. Bake at 350° for 35 minutes.

Gerry Freedman

Sprinkle waxed paper with confectioners' sugar before wrapping a frosted cake— the frosting will stick to the cake, not to the paper.

POPPY SEED CAKE

2 cups sifted cake flour	1 can poppy seed filling
1 teaspoon baking soda	4 egg yolks
½ teaspoon salt	1 cup sour cream
1 cup soft butter	1 teaspoon vanilla
1½ cups granulated sugar	4 egg whites, stiffly beaten

Sift together flour, soda and salt. Cream butter and sugar, beating until light and fluffy. Add poppy seed filling; blend well. Add egg yolks, one at a time, beating well after each. Add sour cream and vanilla; blend well. Add flour mixture gradually, beating well after each addition. Fold in stiffly beaten egg whites. Pour into well-greased 10-inch tube pan, which has been lined with waxed paper on the bottom only. Bake at 350° for about 1 hour, or until cake tester comes out clean. Allow cake to stand in pan 5 minutes. Invert on wire rack to cool. Remove waved paper; dust with confectioners' sugar, or frost as desired.

Mina Siegel

CHOCOLATE CAKES

CHOCOLATE CAKE

2 squares unsweetened chocolate

1 cup milk

¼ cup brown sugar

⅓ cup soft butter

1 cup granulated sugar

2 eggs

1½ cups sifted cake flour

1 teaspoon baking soda

½ teaspoon salt

1 teaspoon vanilla

FROSTING:

3 or 4 squares unsweetened chocolate

3 tablespoons butter

3 cups sifted confectioners' sugar

7 tablespoons milk

1 teaspoon vanilla

Melt 2 squares chocolate in 1 cup milk over low heat. Add brown sugar; set aside. Cream soft butter and granulated sugar; add eggs; mix well. Sift together flour, soda and salt. Add alternately to creamed mixture with chocolate, beating well after each addition. Add vanilla. Pour into greased 12x8x2-inch pan. Bake at 350° for 35 minutes. Meanwhile, melt 3 to 4 squares chocolate with butter. Combine confectioners' sugar, 7 tablespoons milk and vanilla. Add hot chocolate mixture and stir. Spread on cake while thin. If frosting thickens upon standing, thin with a small amount of cream.

Zelda Greenfield

CHOCOLATE BANANA CAKE

2¼ cups sifted cake flour

1 teaspoon baking powder

1 teaspoon salt

¾ teaspoon baking soda

⅔ cup soft butter or margarine

1½ cups granulated sugar

2 eggs

1 teaspoon vanilla

2 squares unsweetened chocolate, melted

1 cup mashed bananas (2 or 3)

½ cup soured milk or buttermilk

Sift together flour, baking powder, salt and soda. Cream shortening and sugar, beating until fluffy. Add eggs and beat thoroughly. Add vanilla and melted chocolate; stir in. Add flour mixture alternately with bananas and soured milk. Beat well. Pour into greased 13x9x2-inch pan. Bake at 350° for 30 to 35 minutes. Frost when cool, if desired.

Dorothy Salkin

FUDGE CAKE

½ cup soft butter

1½ cups granulated sugar

2 eggs

1 teaspoon vanilla

2 cups sifted flour

1 teaspoon vinegar

1 teaspoon baking soda

1 cup sour cream

2 squares unsweetened chocolate, melted

Cream butter and sugar. Add eggs and vanilla; beat well. Sift half of flour into creamed mixture; beat. Combine vinegar and soda; add and beat again. Add remaining flour and sour cream, mixing until well blended. Add melted chocolate; beat well. Pour into greased and floured 9x9x2-inch pan. Bake at 350° for 35 to 40 minutes. Frost in pan; cut into squares. *Sylvia Nieberg*

CHOCOLATE LAYER CAKE

¾ cup cake meal

3 tablespoons cocoa

8 egg yolks

1½ cups granulated sugar

Grated rind of 1 orange

¼ cup orange juice

½ cup sweet wine

8 egg whites

Sift together cake meal and cocoa. Beat egg yolks; add sugar and beat until thick and lemon-colored. Add orange rind and juice and wine; beat thoroughly. Stir in sifted cake meal mixture. Beat egg whites until stiff but not dry; fold into batter. Pour into 2 greased waxed-paper lined 8x8x2-inch pans. Bake at 350° for 35 to 40 minutes. Cool; fill and frost as desired.

Florence M. Mayron

CHOCOLATE YEAST CAKE

1 scant cup soft butter

2 cups granulated sugar

3 eggs, beaten

3 cups sifted flour

1 cup milk

¾ cup grated unsweetened chocolate, melted

¾ cake compressed yeast

¼ cup warm water

1 teaspoon baking soda

¼ cup hot water

FROSTING:

2 cups sifted confectioners' sugar

2 heaping tablespoons cocoa

¼ cup soft butter

Strong coffee

Cream scant cup butter with granulated sugar; add eggs. Add sifted flour alternately with milk to creamed mixture, beating well after each addition. Dissolve yeast in warm water. Add to flour mixture with melted chocolate. Let stand overnight. Next day, dissolve soda in hot water; add to batter. Spoon batter into 3 greased and floured 9-inch round layer pans. Bake at 350° for 35 minutes. Meanwhile, beat together confectioners' sugar, cocoa and ¼ cup butter, adding coffee slowly until of spreading consistency. Cool baked layers on wire rack. Fill and frost.   *Mrs. Julian R. Breakstone*

   CUPCAKES

FUDGE CUPCAKES

2 squares unsweetened chocolate, melted	1½ teaspoons baking powder
1 tablespoon butter	1 egg
1 cup granulated sugar	Cream
1 cup sifted flour	1 teaspoon vanilla

Add butter to melted chocolate, stirring until butter is melted. Add sugar and mix well. Sift together flour and baking powder. Break egg into measuring cup; add enough cream to make 1 cup. Add vanilla. Add flour and egg mixture alternately to chocolate mixture, mixing well after each addition. Pour into muffin cups lined with paper baking cups to about two-thirds full. Bake at 350° for 30 minutes. Frost as desired. Makes 12 cupcakes.

Natalie Caplin

DEVIL'S FOOD CUPCAKES

1 cup sifted cake flour	¼ cup shortening
¾ cup granulated sugar	¼ cup water
¼ cup cocoa	½ teaspoon vanilla
½ teaspoon baking powder	¼ cup plus 2 tablespoons soured milk
½ teaspoon baking soda	1 egg
½ teaspoon salt	1 egg yolk

Sift together flour, sugar, cocoa, baking powder, soda and salt into large bowl. Add shortening; pour in water; add vanilla and 2 tablespoons soured milk. Beat for 2 minutes. Add remaining milk, egg and egg yolk; beat 1 minute longer. Fill greased muffin cups about two-thirds full. Bake at 350° for 25 minutes. Makes 1 dozen.

Ruth Rose

CHIFFON AND SPONGECAKES

SPONGECAKE SUPREME

½ cup sifted matzo cake flour

½ cup sifted potato starch

10 egg whites

1¾ cups granulated sugar

Pinch salt

10 egg yolks

Grated rind of 1 lemon

Juice of 1 lemon

Sift together flour and potato starch 4 times. Beat egg whites until stiff but not dry. Add sugar gradually, beating until stiff peaks form. Add salt. Beat egg yolks until thick and lemon-colored. Add lemon rind and juice. Fold in egg white mixture. Add flour mixture slowly, folding in with rubber spatula, scraping bottom of bowl frequently, until well blended. Turn into ungreased 10-inch tube pan. Place in cold oven; bake at 325° for 70 minutes. *Do not open oven during baking period.* Invert on wire rack and cool in pan.

Rose Gontovnick

ORANGE SPONGECAKE

7 egg yolks

1½ cups granulated sugar

Grated rind of 1 orange

½ cup orange juice

1½ cups sifted cake flour

Pinch salt

7 egg whites

1½ teaspoons baking powder

Beat egg yolks well; add sugar, orange rind and juice, mixing well. Sift together flour and salt. Sift into egg yolk mixture, beating well. Beat egg whites until stiff, adding baking powder. Fold into batter. Turn into ungreased 10-inch tube pan. Bake at 350° for 55 minutes. Sift confectioners' sugar over cooled cake.

Mrs. Samuel J. Gold

WINE CAKE

12 eggs, separated

2 cups granulated sugar

½ cup finely chopped nuts

½ cup sweet wine

1 teaspoon cinnamon

1½ cups cake meal

Beat egg whites until stiff but not dry, gradually adding 1 cup sugar. Beat egg yolks until thick; add nuts, wine, cinnamon and remaining sugar. Add cake meal; blend well. Fold in egg whites. Pour into ungreased 10-inch tube pan. Bake at 350° for 70 minutes. Invert and cool.   *Faye M. Basan*

CUSTARD CHIFFON CAKE

¼ cup plus 2 tablespoons scalded milk

3 egg yolks, slightly beaten

1 cup sifted flour

¾ cup granulated sugar

1½ teaspoons baking powder

½ teaspoon salt

1 cup salad oil

1 teaspoon vanilla

½ cup egg whites (about 4)

¼ teaspoon cream of tartar

Blend together *hot* milk and egg yolks; cool. Sift together flour, sugar, baking powder and salt. Make a well in center of dry ingredients; pour in oil, vanilla and cooled egg yolk mixture. Beat until smooth with spoon (or electric mixer at medium speed) for 1 minute. Beat egg whites and cream of tartar until *very stiff*. Pour batter slowly over beaten egg whites, folding gently just until blended. *Do not stir.* Turn into ungreased 9-inch tube pan. Bake at 325° for 50 to 55 minutes, or until top springs back when lightly touched. Invert on wire rack to cool. Sprinkle with confectioners' sugar or frost as desired.   *Mrs. Reuben Stiglitz*

6-EGG SPONGECAKE

6 large eggs, separated

1½ cups granulated sugar

Pinch salt

½ cup orange juice

1 teaspoon vanilla

1½ cups sifted matzo cake flour

Beat egg whites until stiff but not dry; gradually add ¾ cup sugar and salt, beating until stiff peaks form. Beat egg yolks with remaining sugar, orange juice and sifted flour. Add vanilla; mix well. Fold in egg white mixture. Pour into ungreased 9-inch tube pan. Bake at 325° for 1 hour. Remove from pan; invert and cool for 1 hour before serving.   *Sophie Markovitz*

SUNSHINE FRUIT JUICE CAKE

8 egg yolks

1¼ cups superfine granulated sugar, sifted 3 times

¼ cup pineapple juice

1 tablespoon orange juice

1 tablespoon lemon juice

2 teaspoons vanilla

1 cup cake flour, sifted 3 times

Pinch salt

8 egg whites

1 teaspoon cream of tartar

FRUIT FROSTING:

2 teaspoons soft butter

1¼ cups sifted confectioners' sugar

1 tablespoon orange juice

1 tablespoon lemon juice

1 teaspoon grated orange rind

1 teaspoon grated lemon rind

Beat egg yolks. Add granulated sugar, a teaspoonful at a time, beating constantly (about 15 minutes). Set aside. Mix together pineapple juice, 1 tablespoon orange juice and 1 tablespoon lemon juice with vanilla; set aside Sift together flour and salt. Add flour alternately with juice mixture to creamed mixture, beating well after each addition. Beat egg whites until frothy; add cream of tartar and beat until stiff. Fold into batter. Pour into ungreased 10-inch tube pan. Bake at 325° for 55 minutes; increase oven temperature to 350° and bake for 5 minutes longer. Meanwhile, cream butter and confectioners' sugar. Add 1 tablespoon orange juice, 1 tablespoon lemon juice and grated orange and lemon rinds. Mix well. Invert cake on wire rack to cool. Remove from pan; pour frosting over top and let drip down sides. Do not spread.

Gloria Rosenbloom

STRAWBERRY WHIPPED CREAM CAKE

5 egg yolks

2 tablespoons granulated sugar

2 tablespoons non-caloric sweetening solution

2 tablespoons cold water

1 tablespoon lemon juice

½ cup sifted flour

⅓ cup sifted potato flour

5 egg whites

¼ teaspoon salt

¼ teaspoon cream of tartar

FILLING AND TOPPING:

4 egg whites

2 teaspoons granulated sugar

1 teaspoon vanilla

½ cup heavy cream, whipped

2 cups strawberries, washed and hulled

2 teaspoons non-caloric sweetening solution

Beat egg yolks with 2 tablespoons sugar, 2 tablespoons sweetening solution, water and lemon juice until thick and light. Sift together flour and potato flour. Add to egg yolk mixture; mix well. Beat 5 egg whites with salt and cream of tartar until stiff but not dry. Fold into batter carefully. Pour into ungreased 9-inch tube pan. Bake at 350° for 45 minutes, or until cake springs back when touched. Invert on cake rack to cool. Split cooled cake into 2 layers. Beat 4 egg whites with 1 teaspoon sugar and vanilla. Fold into whipped cream. Sprinkle strawberries with 2 teaspoons sweetening solution. Slice berries, reserving several larger whole berries for top of cake. Spread bottom layer with half of whipped mixture. Cover with sliced berries. Place top layer on berries. Frost with remaining whipped mixture. Garnish with reserved whole berries. Chill in refrigerator until ready to serve. Makes 16 servings.

Separate eggs about 1 hour before using. Eggs separate best when cold, but beat to greater volume at room temperature. This is especially important when making a sponge-type cake.

MOCHA LOG

5 egg yolks

1 cup sifted confectioners' sugar

3 tablespoons cocoa

5 egg whites

MOCHA BUTTER CREAM:

1 cup soft sweet butter

1 cup granulated sugar

1 tablespoon Dutch process cocoa

2 teaspoons double-strength coffee

2 cups heavy cream

½ cup superfine granulated sugar (optional)

¼ cup chopped pistachio nuts

Beat egg yolks until thick and pale. Add confectioners' sugar and cocoa; beat well. Beat egg whites until stiff; fold into egg yolk mixture. Spread batter evenly in greased and floured 17½x11½x2¼-inch (roasting) pan. Bake at 325° for 12 to 15 minutes. Immediately turn out cake onto dampened towel which has been sprinkled with confectioners' sugar. Trim edges; roll cake in towel and set aside to cool. Meanwhile, cream butter with granulated sugar; add Dutch process cocoa and coffee; beat until of spreading consistency. Whip cream with superfine sugar until stiff. Unroll cake; spread with 3 tablespoons creamed mixture. Cover with whipped cream; reroll. Place on serving plate. Frost with remaining mocha cream. Roughen surface with spatula. Decorate with mocha cream forced through pastry tube, if desired. Press chopped pistachio nuts onto ends. Chill until ready to serve. Serves 8 to 10. *Elayne Franklin*

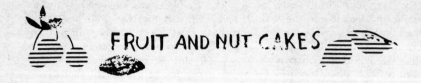

FRUIT AND NUT CAKES

DATE-NUT CAKE

1 package pitted dates	¼ cup soft shortening
1 teaspoon baking soda	1 cup granulated sugar
1 cup hot water	1 egg
1½ cups sifted flour	Whipped cream
½ cup chopped nuts	

Cut dates into thirds. Place in bowl; sprinkle with soda and cover with hot water. Let stand. Sift flour into bowl; mix in chopped nuts. Cream shortening and sugar until light and fluffy. Add egg and mix well. Add nut mixture and date mixture alternately, mixing well after each addition. Pour into greased 8x8x2-inch pan. Bake at 350° for 45 to 50 minutes. When cool, cut into squares. Serve topped with whipped cream, or sprinkle with confectioners' sugar.   *Gwen Spear*

BANANA CAKE

1½ cups sifted flour	3 tablespoons buttermilk or soured milk
1 teaspoon baking soda	1 teaspoon vanilla
½ teaspoon salt	TOPPING:
½ teaspoon nutmeg	1 cup corn flakes, crushed
½ cup soft shortening	¼ cup granulated sugar
1½ cups granulated sugar	1 tablespoon butter
2 eggs, slightly beaten	½ teaspoon cinnamon
1 cup mashed bananas (2 or 3)	¼ cup finely chopped nuts

Sift flour, soda, salt and nutmeg together twice. Cream shortening and 1½ cups sugar; add eggs and beat thoroughly. Combine bananas, buttermilk and vanilla. Add flour and banana mixture alternately to creamed mixture, beating well after each addition. Pour into greased 9x9x2-inch pan. Combine corn flakes, ¼ cup sugar, butter, cinnamon and nuts until crumbly. Sprinkle over batter in pan. Bake at 350° for 45 minutes, or until done. *Frieda Deutsch*

BANANA NUT CAKE

8 large eggs, separated

1½ cups granulated sugar

Grated rind of 1 orange

Juice of 1 orange

1 banana, mashed

¼ cup sweet red wine

1 cup ground nuts

¾ cup cake meal

¼ cup potato starch

Beat egg yolks with sugar, orange rind and juice, banana, wine and nuts. Beat egg whites until stiff but not dry. Fold into egg yolk mixture. Sift together cake meal and potato starch. Fold into batter. Pour into ungreased 10-inch tube pan. Bake at 350° for 1 hour. Invert on wire rack and cool.

Ethel Savin

CHERRY NUT LOAF

1 small bottle maraschino cherries

1 cup soft butter

1 cup granulated sugar

2 eggs, separated

1 cup sour cream

2 cups sifted cake flour

1 teaspoon baking powder

1 scant teaspoon baking soda

½ cup chopped walnuts

Drain cherries, reserving juice. Cream butter and sugar. Add egg yolks, sour cream and reserved cherry juice. Sift together flour, baking powder and soda. Add to creamed mixture; mix well. Beat egg whites until stiff; fold into batter. Add cherries and nuts. Pour into greased 9x5x3-inch pan. Bake at 350° for about 45 minutes, or until cake tester comes out clean. Serve cut into thin slices.

Mrs. Sam Tavalin

WALNUT DATE CAKE

6 eggs, separated

1 cup granulated sugar

1 cup chopped walnuts

1 cup chopped dates

6 heaping tablespoons matzo meal

Juice of 1 lemon

Beat egg yolks with sugar until thick and lemon-colored. Stir walnuts and dates into matzo meal. Fold into egg yolk mixture. Beat egg whites with a little salt until stiff but not dry. Fold into egg yolk mixture. Add lemon juice. Pour into ungreased 8-inch spring-form pan. Bake at 325° for 1 hour or until cake tests done.

Rosabelle Perrye

CHOCOLATE DATE CAKE

½ cup dates, cut into small pieces

1 cup boiling water

1 teaspoon baking soda

1 cup soft butter

1 cup granulated sugar

2 eggs

1¾ cups sifted flour

2 heaping tablespoons cocoa

1 teaspoon vanilla

Semi-sweet chocolate pieces

Chopped nuts

Combine dates with boiling water and soda. Set aside to cool. Cream butter and sugar; add eggs; beat well. Sift together flour and cocoa; add alternately with cooled date mixture to creamed mixture, beginning and ending with flour, beating well after each addition. Mix in vanilla. Pour into greased 9x9x2-inch pan. Sprinkle top with chocolate pieces and nuts. Bake at 350° for 15 minutes; reduce oven temperature to 325° and bake for 20 to 25 minutes longer. *Tillie Shafer*

QUICKY FRUITCAKE

¾ cup sifted flour

½ teaspoon baking soda

1 9-oz. package prepared mincemeat

½ cup water

1 cup chopped walnuts

¾ cup diced mixed candied fruit

1 can sweetened condensed milk

1 egg, beaten

Sift together flour and soda. Break mincemeat into small pieces. Place mincemeat with water in saucepan; heat, stirring, until all lumps are broken. Boil vigorously for 1 minute, stirring constantly; cool. Add walnuts, fruit, milk and egg; mix well. Add flour; mix only until smooth. Turn into greased, waxed-paper lined 9x5x3-inch pan. Bake at 350° for 70 minutes, or until done.

BRAZIL NUT CAKE

¾ cup sifted flour

¾ cup granulated sugar

½ teaspoon baking powder

½ teaspoon salt

3 cups whole Brazil nuts (about 1 lb.)

1 pound pitted dates

1 8-oz. bottle maraschino cherries, drained

3 eggs

1 teaspoon vanilla

Sift together flour, sugar, baking powder and salt. Place nuts, dates and cherries in large bowl. Sift flour mixture over top; mix with hand until well coated. Beat eggs until frothy; add vanilla. Pour over nut mixture. Blend well with fork. (Mixture will not be smooth.) Line 9x5x3-inch pan with waxed paper, grease and flour bottom only. Spread mixture evenly in pan. Bake at 300° for 1 hour and 45 minutes. Cool in pan; chill in refrigerator overnight. Cut into thin slices. Keeps for weeks if wrapped in aluminum foil.

Shirley Goldberg

ORANGE RAISIN CAKE

1 cup firmly packed brown sugar	1 teaspoon baking soda
1 egg	Pinch salt
½ cup soft butter	½ cup raisins
1 cup buttermilk	½ cup nuts
2 cups sifted flour	Grated rind of 1 orange
1 teaspoon baking powder	Juice of 1 orange

Beat together sugar, egg, butter and buttermilk. Sift together flour, baking powder, soda and salt. Add to sugar mixture, beating well. Grind together raisins, nuts and orange rind. Add half of ground mixture to batter. Mix well. Pour into greased 10-inch spring-form pan. Bake at 350° for 40 minutes. Remove cake from oven; pour orange juice over top. Add remaining ground mixture to confectioners' sugar icing. Spread over cooled cake

Lillian Feigenbaum

RAISIN CAKE

1 package seedless raisins	1 teaspoon vanilla
2 cups boiling water	4 cups sifted flour
2 teaspoons baking soda	1 teaspoon ground cloves
4 eggs	Pinch salt
1½ cups granulated sugar	½ cup ground nuts
1 cup salad oil	

Place raisins in boiling water; add soda and simmer for 10 minutes. Drain raisins, reserving liquid. Beat eggs; add sugar, oil and vanilla. Sift together flour, cloves and salt. Add alternately with reserved raisin liquid to egg mixture, beating well after each addition. Add raisins and nuts. Mix well. Pour into greased 13x9x2-inch pan. Bake at 350° for about 45 minutes, or until cake tester comes out clean.

Mina Siegel

LEMONADE CAKE

1 cup soft butter	1 cup chopped raisins or dates
1 cup granulated sugar	¾ cup chopped nuts
2 eggs	Grated rind of 1 orange
1 cup sour cream	Juice of 2 oranges
2 cups sifted flour	Juice of 1 lemon
1 teaspoon baking powder	¼ cup granulated sugar
1 teaspoon baking soda	

Cream butter and 1 cup sugar. Add eggs and sour cream. Sift together flour, baking powder and soda. Mix ½ cup flour with combined raisins and nuts. Add remaining flour gradually to creamed mixture, beating well after each addition. Add orange rind and half of orange juice. Mix well. Pour into greased 9-inch tube pan. Bake at 375° for about 1 hour. Mix together remaining orange juice, lemon juice and ¼ cup sugar. Pour over hot cake.

Caryl Loevy

To keep fruit and nuts suspended in cake, mix them with a small amount of flour mixture before adding them to the cake batter.

LEKACH (Traditional Honey Cake)

6 eggs	¼ teaspoon ground cloves
1 cup granulated sugar	¼ teaspoon allspice
1 cup honey	¼ teaspoon cinnamon
2 tablespoons salad oil or melted shortening	½ cup raisins
	½ cup chopped nuts
3½ cups sifted flour	½ cup finely cut citron
1½ teaspoons baking powder	2 tablespoons brandy
1 teaspoon baking soda	

Beat eggs; add sugar gradually, beating until light and fluffy. Stir in honey and shortening. Sift together flour, baking powder, soda, cloves, allspice and cinnamon. Add raisins, nuts and citron to flour mixture. Combine with honey mixture, blending well. Add brandy. Turn into greased waxed-paper-lined 12x8x2-inch pan. Bake at 310° for 1 hour. Invert cake and allow to cool before removing from pan. When ready to serve, cut into squares or diamonds.

Jean Berk

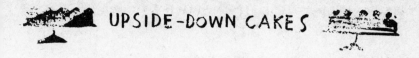

UPSIDE-DOWN CAKES

CARAMEL WALNUT UPSIDE-DOWN CAKE

⅓ cup melted butter	2 teaspoons baking powder
½ cup firmly packed brown sugar	½ teaspoon salt
1 teaspoon light corn syrup	½ cup soft shortening
1 cup chopped walnuts	⅔ cup milk
1½ cups sifted flour	1 teaspoon vanilla
1 cup granulated sugar	2 eggs

Combine butter, brown sugar and corn syrup in saucepan; bring to boiling. Pour into ungreased 8x8x2 or 9x9x2-inch pan. Arrange chopped walnuts over mixture. Sift together flour, granulated sugar, baking powder and salt. Add shortening, then add milk and vanilla all at once. Beat for 2 minutes on medium speed of electric mixer. Add eggs and beat for 2 minutes longer. Pour batter into pan. Bake at 350° for 35 to 40 minutes. Invert onto serving plate and allow caramel to drain over cake for 1 minute. Remove pan. Serve warm. Or cool, freezer-wrap and freeze. *Mrs. J. Sklansky*

PINEAPPLE UPSIDE-DOWN CAKE

¼ cup soft butter	½ cup milk
1 cup granulated sugar	2 egg whites
2 egg yolks	2 tablespoons butter
½ teaspoon vanilla	1 cup firmly packed brown sugar
1½ cups sifted flour	1 No. 2½ can pineapple slices
2 teaspoons baking powder	

Cream soft butter with granulated sugar. Add egg yolks and vanilla; mix well. Sift together flour and baking powder 3 times. Add alternately with milk to creamed mixture, beating well after each addition. Beat egg whites until stiff. Fold into batter. Melt 2 tablespoons butter; add brown sugar and stir until blended. Arrange pineapple slices in greased 8x8x2-inch pan. Pour brown sugar mixture over pineapple; cover with batter. Bake at 350° for 25 to 30 minutes. Turn cake out onto serving plate immediately. *Dianne Kraus*

MELT-IN-YOUR-MOUTH POUND CAKE

1 cup soft butter	2 teaspoons baking powder
1 pound sifted confectioners' sugar	Pinch salt
6 egg yolks, beaten	¾ cup milk
3 cups sifted cake flour	1 teaspoon vanilla

Cream butter; add sugar, a little at a time, beating constantly. Add egg yolks. Sift together flour, baking powder and salt. Add to creamed mixture alternately with milk, beating well after each addition. Add vanilla. Beat egg whites until stiff. Fold into batter *by hand.* Pour into greased 10x5x3-inch pan. Bake at 350° for about 1 hour.   *Eunice Kaplan*

VELVET MOCHA POUND CAKE

⅔ cup soft shortening (or part butter, part shortening)	½ teaspoon cream of tartar
2 cups sifted cake flour	½ cup water
1¼ cups granulated sugar	1 teaspoon vanilla
1 tablespoon instant coffee powder	3 eggs
1 teaspoon salt	2 squares unsweetened chocolate, melted
¼ teaspoon baking soda	Confectioners' sugar

Cream shortening. Sift together flour, sugar, instant coffee, salt, soda and cream of tartar. Sift into shortening. Add water and vanilla; mix until dry ingredients are moistened. Beat vigorously for 2 minutes. Add eggs and melted chocolate; beat 1 minute longer. Pour into waxed-paper-lined 9x5x3-inch pan. Bake at 325° for 65 to 70 minutes. Cool; sift confectioners' sugar over top.   *Esther Weiner*

Pound cake "the way that Mother used to make it" was a pound each of sugar, butter, flour and eggs. There was little if any leavening, and no liquid. Today's pound cakes are lighter and tastier, though not quite so authentic.

✳✳✳✳✳✳✳✳✳ FROSTINGS ✳✳✳✳✳✳✳✳✳

SEVEN-MINUTE FROSTING

2 egg whites

1½ cups granulated sugar

⅓ to ½ cup water

1 tablespoon light corn syrup

½ teaspoon salt

1 teaspoon vanilla

Combine all ingredients except vanilla in top of double boiler. With electric mixer at high speed, beat for about 1 minute. Place over rapidly boiling water and beat for 7 minutes, or until peaks form. Remove from heat; add vanilla and continue beating until of spreading consistency. Fills and frosts 8 or 9-inch 2-layer or 10-inch tube cake.

BUTTER CREAM FROSTING

⅓ cup flour

⅔ cup granulated sugar

2 tablespoons cornstarch

2¼ cups cold milk

3 egg yolks, slightly beaten

2 teaspoons vanilla

¾ cup butter, well creamed

Combine flour, sugar and cornstarch in saucepan. Blend in milk and cook until thick, stirring constantly. Blend a little of hot mixture into egg yolks, then add yolks to hot mixture. Cook, over low heat, stirring, constantly, for 2 minutes. Add vanilla; cover and cool to lukewarm. Add to butter; mix well and cool completely. Fills and frosts 8 or 9-inch 2-layer cake.

MARSHMALLOW FUDGE FROSTING

16 large marshmallows

3 squares unsweetened chocolate

½ cup water

2 tablespoons shortening

⅛ teaspoon salt

1 teaspoon vanilla

3 cups sifted confectioners' sugar

Combine marshmallows, chocolate, water, shortening and salt in saucepan; stir over low heat until well blended. Cool. Add vanilla. Gradually add confectioners' sugar, beating until of spreading consistency. Fills and frosts 8 or 9-inch 3-layer cake.   *Dee Kamins*

WHIPPED CHOCOLATE FROSTING

1 cup heavy cream

2 tablespoons Dutch process cocoa

2 tablespoons confectioners' sugar

1 teaspoon vanilla

Pour cream into chilled bowl. Sift in cocoa and sugar. Add vanilla; mix. Chill in refrigerator for 2 hours. Whip until stiff. Fills and frosts 8 or 9-inch 2-layer cake. *Mrs. I. Olex*

NEVER-FAIL CHOCOLATE FROSTING

1 cup sugar

1 square unsweetened chocolate

1 egg

¼ cup cream

1 tablespoon butter

1 teaspoon vanilla

Combine sugar, chocolate, egg, cream and butter in saucepan. Mix well. Cook, stirring constantly, until thick. Add vanilla. Cool; beat until of spreading consistency. Should be glossy. Fills and frosts 8-inch 2-layer cake. *Mrs. Harold Collen*

OLD-FASHIONED FROSTING

1 egg

¾ cup granulated sugar

¼ cup melted butter

1 cup heavy cream, whipped

1 teaspoon vanilla or rum extract

Nutmeg

Beat egg; add sugar and beat well. Add butter; mix in. Slowly add whipped cream and vanilla. Chill until ready to use. Serve over warm gingerbread or chocolate cake squares. Sprinkle nutmeg over top. *Jeanie Greene*

HOLIDAY CAKE TOPPING

1 cup chopped pecans or almonds

½ cup granulated sugar

1 teaspoon cinnamon

½ cup melted butter

Combine nuts, sugar and cinnamon. After cake has baked for 15 minutes, remove from oven; quickly sprinkle nut mixture over top. Drizzle with melted butter and return to oven for remaining baking period. Covers top of 12x8 or 13x9-inch cake (spice, yellow or white). *Helen Rock*

PIES AND PASTRY

An apple-pie without
some cheese
Is like a kiss without
a squeeze.

Old English Rhyme

PASTRY

PASTRY FOR 8 OR 9-INCH 2-CRUST PIE

1½ cups sifted flour

1 tablespoon granulated sugar

½ teaspoon baking powder

⅛ teaspoon salt

½ cup butter

3 tablespoons shortening

Ice water

Sift together flour, sugar, baking powder and salt. Cut butter and shortening into flour mixture with pastry blender or 2 knives until mixture resembles coarse meal. Add ice water, a little at a time, mixing with a fork, until dough can be formed into a ball. Chill in refrigerator for at least 2 hours. Roll out half of dough on lightly floured surface; fit into 8 or 9-inch pie plate. Fill as desired. Bake as directed in pie recipe. Roll out remaining dough for top crust. FOR PIE SHELL: Roll out half of dough (refrigerate remainder); fit into pie plate. Fold edges under; flute as desired. Prick generously. Bake at 425° for 12 to 15 minutes.

Selma Melvoin

❖❖❖❖❖❖❖❖❖❖❖❖❖❖❖❖❖❖❖❖❖❖❖❖❖❖❖❖❖❖❖❖❖❖❖

To keep pie shell from shrinking during baking, line unbaked shell with waxed paper and fill with uncooked rice.

DE LUXE PASTRY FOR 9-INCH 2-CRUST PIE

2 cups sifted flour

¾ teaspoon salt

½ teaspoon baking soda

¾ cup butter or margarine

6 to 8 tablespoons cold milk

Sift together flour, salt and baking soda. Using pastry blender or 2 knives, cut in butter until mixture resembles small peas. With fork, mix in milk, 1 tablespoon at a time. Knead 3 times on lightly floured surface. Roll out half of dough. Fit into 9-inch pie plate. Fill as desired. Roll out remaining dough for top crust. Place over filling; seal, trim and flute. Bake as directed in pie recipe.   *Mrs. Reuben Stiglitz*

TART SHELLS

2 cups sifted flour

½ cup sifted confectioners' sugar

1 teaspoon salt

½ cup butter

1 egg, slightly beaten

2 tablespoons milk

Sift together flour, sugar and salt. Cut in butter with pastry blender or 2 knives. Add egg and enough milk to form medium dough, mixing with a fork. Knead gently a few seconds. Wrap dough in waxed paper and chill in refrigerator about 30 minutes. (Do not allow dough to become too hard to roll easily.) Roll out on lightly floured surface; cut into 8 rounds. Fit over inverted lightly greased tart pans; prick generously with fork. Bake at 350° for 30 minutes, or until slightly browned. Cool on wire rack. Fill as desired. Makes 8 tart shells.   *Rosabelle Perrye*

BUTTER CRUNCH TART SHELLS

1⅓ cups sifted flour

¾ cup butter

3 tablespoons cold water

1 cup crushed corn flakes

Fruit filling

Whipped cream

Sift flour into mixing bowl; cut in butter with pastry blender or 2 knives until mixture resembles coarse meal. Add water and mix with fork until dough clings together. Mix in corn flakes. Roll out on lightly floured surface. Cut into 12 rounds and pat into muffin cups. Prick with fork. Bake at 450° for 10 to 12 minutes, or until lightly browned. Cool slightly, then remove from pans. Fill with favorite fruit filling and top with whipped cream. Makes 12 tart shells.   *Rose Krichiver*

DRIED APPLE PIE

Pastry for 8 or 9-inch 2-crust pie

½ pound dried apples

2 cups water

1 cup granulated sugar

¼ teaspoon lemon juice

1 tablespoon lemon rind

1 teaspoon cinnamon

½ teaspoon nutmeg

Pinch salt

Line 8 or 9-inch pie plate with bottom crust. Simmer apples in water, covered, until apples are soft. Drain. Add lemon juice and rind, cinnamon, nutmeg and salt to apples. Toss gently. Pour into pie plate. Roll out top crust; make 2 long slits. Place over filling; trim, seal and flute. Bake at 400° for 45 minutes.

LATTICE APPLE PIE

Pastry for 9-inch 2-crust pie

¾ cup brown sugar

3 tablespoons flour

½ teaspoon cinnamon

¼ teaspoon nutmeg (optional)

⅛ teaspoon salt

6 to 8 cups pared tart apple slices

2 tablespoons butter

¾ cup heavy cream

1 cup grated Cheddar cheese

Line 9-inch pie plate with bottom crust. Roll out remaining dough; cut into strips and weave for lattice top. Place on 9-inch round of aluminum foil. Set aside. Combine brown sugar, flour, cinnamon, nutmeg and salt. Fill pie plate with alternating layers of sugar mixture and apples, starting and ending with sugar. Dot with butter. Bake at 450° for 10 minutes. Reduce oven temperature to 350° and bake 30 to 35 minutes longer. Place foil with lattice top on filling for last 20 minutes of baking time. When pie is done, remove from oven and cool. Whip cream; fold in grated cheese. Lift off foil and lattice top; spoon cream mixture onto apples. Remove lattice top from foil *carefully* and place on whipped cream.

APPLE-PINEAPPLE PIE

Pastry for 9-inch 2-crust pie

1 cup granulated sugar

2 tablespoons flour or quick-cooking tapioca

½ teaspoon salt

3 cups thinly sliced peeled tart apples

1 cup crushed pineapple

1 tablespoon lemon juice

2 tablespoons butter

½ teaspoon cinnamon

Line 9-inch pie plate with bottom crust. Combine sugar, flour and salt; add apples, pineapple and lemon juice. Toss lightly to mix. Turn into pie plate. Dot with butter; sprinkle with cinnamon. Moisten edge of crust. Roll out top crust, making slits with knife. Lay over filling. Seal; trim and finish with favorite edging. Bake at 400° for 40 minutes.   *Florence M. Mayron*

BRANDIED APRICOT PIE

1 baked 9-inch graham cracker crust

1 No. 2½ can peeled apricot halves

½ cup granulated sugar

1 package orange-flavored gelatin

Boiling water

¾ cup brandy

1 cup heavy cream

Drain apricot halves thoroughly, reserving juice. Cover with sugar. Let stand 20 minutes. Dissolve gelatin in reserved apricot juice and enough boiling water to make 1½ cups liquid. Pour over apricot halves; add brandy. Mix carefully. When mixture begins to thicken, pour into baked crust. Chill in refrigerator for 2 hours. Whip cream; add brandy to taste; spread over pie.   *Lois Senescu*

GLAZED STRAWBERRY PIE

1 baked 9-inch pie shell

4 cups strawberries, washed and hulled

1 cup water

1 cup granulated sugar

3 tablespoons cornstarch

⅓ cup water

1 cup heavy cream

1 tablespoon confectioners' sugar

Mix 1 cup strawberries, 1 cup water and granulated sugar. Bring to boiling quickly; reduce heat and simmer for 15 minutes. Mix cornstarch and ⅓ cup water to a paste. Add to cooked strawberries. Cook over low heat, stirring constantly, until thick and clear. Strain and cool. Beat cream until stiff;

gently stir in confectioners' sugar. Spread half of whipped cream in bottom of baked pie shell. Place 3 cups whole strawberries over cream. Pour strawberry glaze over top. Chill in refrigerator for at least 3 hours. Just before serving, spoon remaining whipped cream over glazed strawberries.

CRANBERRY NUT PIE

Pastry for 8 or 9-inch 2-crust pie

½ cup soft butter or margarine

1½ cups granulated sugar

3 eggs, separated

2 cups fresh cranberries

1 cup chopped pecans or walnuts

Line 8 or 9-inch pie plate with bottom crust. Fold edge under and flute as desired. Cream butter; slowly add sugar, creaming until light and fluffy. Add egg yolks; blend well. Stir in cranberries and nuts. Beat egg whites until stiff; fold into cranberry mixture. Pour into pie plate. Cut remaining pastry into strips; place on top of filling crisscross fashion. Seal ends of strips to bottom crust. Bake on lower oven rack at 375° for 40 minutes.

Edith Lirtzman

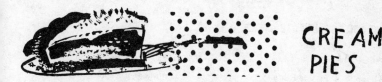

CREAM PIES

EXTRA-ORDINARY CHOCOLATE PIE

21 chocolate wafers, crushed

3 tablespoons melted butter

FILLING:

2 6-oz. packages semi-sweet chocolate pieces

4 eggs, separated

4 tablespoons instant coffee powder

2 cups heavy cream, whipped

TOPPING:

1 cup heavy cream

Shaved chocolate

Combine chocolate wafer crumbs and melted butter thoroughly. Press into 8 or 9-inch pie plate. Bake at 350° for 8 minutes. Melt chocolate pieces in top of double boiler over hot, *not boiling,* water. Cool slightly. Beat egg yolks; add to cooled chocolate. Add instant coffee. Beat egg whites until stiff; fold into chocolate mixture. Fold in 2 cups cream, whipped. Pour into baked crust. Chill in refrigerator for 2 hours. Just before serving, whip 1 cup cream; spread over pie and garnish with shaved chocolate.

Rona Shapiro

CHOCOLATE MINT PIE

30 vanilla wafers, finely crushed

⅓ cup melted butter

FILLING:

½ cup soft butter

1 cup sifted confectioners' sugar

2 squares unsweetened chocolate, melted

2 eggs

1 teaspoon vanilla

⅛ teaspoon peppermint extract

1 cup heavy cream, whipped

Shaved chocolate

Combine vanilla wafer crumbs and melted butter; mix thoroughly. Press mixture firmly over bottom and sides of 8 or 9-inch pie plate or spring-form pan. Chill in refrigerator for at least 1 hour. Meanwhile, cream soft butter; add sugar gradually, creaming until light and fluffy. Gradually add cooled chocolate. Add eggs, one at a time, beating well after each. Stir in vanilla and peppermint extract. Spread mixture in chilled pie shell. Chill in refrigerator for 4 to 6 hours. Top with whipped cream and shaved chocolate just before serving.

Audrey Cooper

CHERRY CHEESE PIE DE LUXE

1½ cups sifted flour

1 tablespoon granulated sugar

1 teaspoon baking powder

1 teaspoon salt

½ cup shortening

1 egg, slightly beaten

FILLING:

½ cup granulated sugar

2 tablespoons cornstarch

1 No. 2 can pitted sour cherries

Few drops red food coloring

4 3-oz. packages cream cheese

½ cup granulated sugar

3 eggs

1 teaspoon vanilla

TOPPING:

1 cup sour cream

2 tablespoons granulated sugar

1 teaspoon vanilla

Sift together flour, 1 tablespoon sugar, baking powder and salt into a bowl. Cut in shortening with pastry blender or 2 knives until mixture resembles coarse meal. Add beaten egg; stir with fork, then with hands press dough together. Spread in 12x8x2-inch pan, pressing about ½ inch up sides. Combine ½ cup sugar and cornstarch. Drain cherries, reserving juice; add enough water to make 1 cup liquid. Stir in cornstarch mixture and cook, stirring, until thick and glossy. Add cherries and food coloring. Spread over crust. Cream cheese with ½ cup sugar; add eggs and vanilla. Blend well and pour over cherries. Bake at 400° for 30 minutes. Meanwhile, combine sour cream, 2 tablespoons sugar and 1 teaspoon vanilla. Remove pie from oven; spread sour cream mixture over top. Bake for 5 minutes longer. Cool; chill thoroughly before serving. Cover with aluminum foil while chilling so topping will not discolor.   *Florence M. Mayron*

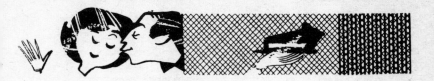

MEMPHIS LEMON PIE

1 baked 9-inch pie shell or graham cracker crust

½ cup lemon juice

1 14-oz. can sweetened condensed milk

5 egg whites

2 tablespoons granulated sugar

1 tablespoon grated lemon rind

Add lemon juice to milk, stirring until thick and smooth. Beat egg whites until frothy. Add sugar, a tablespoon at a time, beating until stiff peaks form. Fold in lemon-milk mixture. Sprinkle lemon rind on bottom of pie shell. Pour filling into shell; chill until set. NOTE: Pie may be frozen.

Grayce Dorf

DEEP LEMON PIE

1 baked 8-inch pie shell

2 cups water

Grated rind of 1 lemon

1 cup granulated sugar

2 tablespoons cornstarch

3 eggs

½ cup lemon juice

2 tablespoons butter

MERINGUE:

3 egg whites

3 tablespoons granulated sugar

⅛ teaspoon cream of tartar

1 tablespoon crushed lemon drops

Combine water and lemon rind; heat. Stir in sugar and cornstarch. Beat eggs with lemon juice and butter. Add to sugar mixture; cook, stirring, until thick and smooth. Pour into baked pie shell. Beat egg whites stiff but not dry. Add sugar gradually with cream of tartar; beat until stiff peaks form. Fold in crushed lemon drops. Spread over filling in pie shell. Bake at 350° for 10 to 12 minutes.

Clara Blum

LEMON MERINGUE PIE

½ cup soft butter or shortening

1 cup matzo meal

2 tablespoons granulated sugar

¼ teaspoon cinnamon

¼ teaspoon salt

FILLING:

1 cup granulated sugar

¼ cup potato starch

¼ teaspoon salt

2 cups water

3 egg yolks

2 tablespoons butter or shortening

5 tablespoons lemon juice

1 tablespoon grated lemon rind

MERINGUE:

3 egg whites

6 tablespoons sugar

Pinch salt

Combine soft butter with matzo meal, 2 tablespoons sugar, cinnamon and ¼ teaspoon salt. Blend well. Press into 9-inch pie plate. Bake at 375° for 10 to 15 minutes, or until lightly browned. Set aside to cool. Mix together potato starch, ½ cup sugar, and ¼ teaspoon salt in top of double boiler; add water. Cook, stirring constantly, until thick. Cover, cook, stirring occasionally, for 10 minutes. Combine egg yolks with remaining ½ cup sugar. Spoon a little of hot mixture over egg yolk mixture. Stir rapidly until smooth. Pour egg yolk mixture into top of double boiler; cook, stirring constantly, for 2 minutes. Remove from heat; stir in butter, lemon juice and rind. Set aside to cool. Pour into cooled baked crust. Beat egg whites with 6 tablespoons sugar and pinch salt until stiff and glossy. Cover filling in crust, spreading meringue to very edge. Bake at 325° for 15 minutes, or until lightly browned. Chill in refrigerator until ready to serve.   *Florence M. Mayron*

KEY LIME PIE

1 baked 8-inch pie shell or graham cracker crust

1 14-oz. can sweetened condensed milk

3 egg yolks

½ cup lime juice

Few drops red food coloring

TOPPING:

1 cup heavy cream, whipped

¼ cup chopped pecans

Mix milk, egg yolks, lime juice and food coloring in a bowl; beat 2 to 3 minutes, or until thick. Pour into baked pie shell. Top with whipped cream; sprinkle with pecans. Chill in refrigerator until firm.   *Mrs. Lewis Abrams*

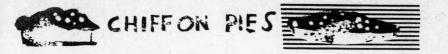

CHIFFON PIES

CHILLY CHERRY PIE

1 baked 9-inch pie shell

1 envelope unflavored gelatine

¼ cup cold water

1 No. 2 can pie cherries

½ cup granulated sugar

⅛ teaspoon salt

1 tablespoon lemon juice

½ cup heavy cream, whipped

GLAZE:

1 No. 2 can pie cherries

½ cup granulated sugar

2 tablespoons cornstarch

Whipped cream

Dissolve gelatine in cold water. Drain 1 can cherries, reserving juice. Heat cherries with ½ cup sugar and ¾ cup reserved cherry juice. Add softened gelatine and salt; mix well. Add lemon juice. Chill in refrigerator. When mixture begins to thicken, fold in whipped cream. Pour into baked pie shell. Chill in refrigerator until set. Meanwhile, drain 1 can cherries, reserving juice. Combine ½ cup sugar, cornstarch and 1 cup reserved cherry juice. Cook until thick and clear. Add drained cherries and cool. Spoon glaze over filling in pie shell. Top with whipped cream. Chill again before serving.   *Robin Crystal*

LEMON CHIFFON PIE

1 baked 8 or 9-inch pie shell

4 egg yolks, slightly beaten

½ cup granulated sugar

Grated rind of 1 lemon

Juice of 1 lemon

Pinch salt

1 envelope unflavored gelatine

¼ cup cold water

4 egg whites

½ cup granulated sugar

1 cup heavy cream

Combine egg yolks, ½ cup sugar, lemon rind, lemon juice and salt in top of double boiler. Cook, stirring often, until thickened. Dissolve gelatine in cold water. Add to egg mixture; cool. Beat egg whites until stiff but not dry. Add sugar gradually, beating until stiff peaks form. Fold in cooled custard. Pour into baked pie shell; chill in refrigerator for 3 hours. Just before serving, whip cream; spread over pie.   *Jeanie Greene*

PINEAPPLE CHIFFON PIE

1 baked 9 or 10-inch pie shell

2 envelopes unflavored gelatine

2 tablespoons cold water

1 No. 2 can crushed pineapple

½ cup granulated sugar

4 egg yolks, slightly beaten

4 egg whites

½ cup granulated sugar

1 cup heavy cream, whipped

Dissolve gelatine in cold water. Drain pineapple, reserving juice; set aside. Combine ½ cup reserved pineapple juice, ½ cup sugar and egg yolks. Cook over very low heat, stirring constantly, until sugar is dissolved and mixture coats spoon. Add gelatine and continue cooking until gelatine is completely melted. Strain crushed pineapple; add to custard mixture; blend thoroughly. Beat egg whites just until they cling to sides of bowl. Add ½ cup sugar and beat until just blended. Pour egg whites all at once into hot custard mixture and fold until well blended. Pour into baked pie shell. Chill in refrigerator for several hours. Serve topped with whipped cream.

Mrs. Sidney Mussman

Perfect pie garnish—chocolate curls. Let square of unsweetened chocolate stand at room temperature. With sharp knife or vegetable parer, cut off thin shavings from back of square. Chocolate curls as you shave it.

RUM CHIFFON PIE

1½ cups zweiback crumbs

½ cup brown sugar

½ cup melted butter

6 egg yolks

1 scant cup granulated sugar

1 envelope unflavored gelatine

½ cup cold water

2 cups heavy cream, whipped

½ cup dark rum

Shaved chocolate

Whipped cream (optional)

Mix together zweiback crumbs, brown sugar and melted butter. Press mixture firmly into 10-inch pie plate. Chill in refrigerator for about 20 minutes. Beat egg yolks until light; add granulated sugar and mix well. Dissolve gelatine in cold water. Place over low heat and bring to boiling. Pour over egg-yolk mixture, stirring rapidly. Cool slightly. Fold in whipped cream and rum. Cool until mixture begins to thicken; pour into pie shell. Chill in refrigerator until firm. Sprinkle with shaved chocolate; garnish with whipped cream, if desired. Serve cold.

CHERRY ALMOND ICE CREAM PIE

1 baked 10 or 11-inch graham cracker crust (with ½ cup chopped nuts added)

1 package cherry-flavored gelatin

1 cup hot water

½ pint vanilla ice cream

½ pint strawberry ice cream

1 teaspoon cherry liqueur

1 teaspoon almond extract

1 No. 303 can pitted Bing cherries, drained

1 cup heavy cream

Dissolve gelatin in hot water. Add vanilla and strawberry ice creams; melt slightly, then whip thoroughly. Add cherry liqueur and almond extract; whip again. When mixture begins to thicken, fold in cherries. Pour into baked crust. Chill in refrigerator. Just before serving, whip cream; spread over chilled pie. *Judith Simon*

MYSTERY PIE

3 egg whites

½ teaspoon baking powder

Pinch salt

1 cup granulated sugar

½ cup coarsely chopped nuts

18 scalloped round crackers, coarsely crushed

CREME DE COCOA FILLING:

1 envelope unflavored gelatine

¼ cup cold very strong coffee

¼ cup granulated sugar

1¼ cups hot strong coffee

2 eggs, separated

¼ cup granulated sugar

⅛ teaspoon salt

¼ cup creme de cocoa

2 cups heavy cream, whipped

Shaved chocolate

Beat egg whites until frothy. Add baking powder and pinch salt; beat until stiff but not dry. Add 1 cup sugar gradually, beating until very stiff peaks form. Fold in nuts and cracker crumbs. Spread in greased 10-inch pie plate (oven-glass preferred). Heat oven to 350°. Place crust in oven; reduce temperature to 325°. Bake for 35 to 40 minutes. Meanwhile, dissolve gelatine in cold coffee. Dissolve ¼ cup sugar in hot coffee; add to gelatine mixture. Beat egg yolks; pour coffee mixture slowly over yolks and mix well. Chill in refrigerator. Beat egg whites; add ¼ cup sugar and ⅛ teaspoon salt gradually, beating until stiff. When coffee mixture is beginning to set, fold in egg yolks, then fold in half of whipped cream (refrigerate remainder) and creme de cocoa. Pour into baked crust and chill in refrigerator for 3 to 4 hours. Spread remaining whipped cream over pie and garnish with shaved chocolate. *Emma Oesterreicher*

BANANA CREAM PIE

1 baked 9 or 10-inch graham cracker
crust

1 envelope unflavored gelatine

¼ cup cold water

1 package vanilla pudding mix

1⅔ cups milk

1 pint vanilla ice cream

3 bananas, sliced

Whipped cream

Dissolve gelatine in cold water. Cook vanilla pudding mix with milk, stirring, until thick and smooth. Blend in gelatine and vanilla ice cream. Beat thoroughly. Alternate layers of sliced bananas and pudding mixture in baked crust. Top with whipped cream. Chill in refrigerator.   *Gloria Wechter*

FROZEN PIES

CHOCOLATE CRUNCH-CRUST PIE

1 6-oz. package semi-sweet chocolate
pieces

3 tablespoons butter

2 cups crisp rice cereal

1 quart green mint ice cream, slightly
softened

1 square unsweetened chocolate, shaved

Melt chocolate pieces and butter in top of double boiler over hot, *not boiling,* water, stirring to blend. Add rice cereal; mix well. Press into 9-inch pie plate. Chill in refrigerator until firm. Fill with alternating layers of ice cream and shaved chocolate. Freezer-wrap and freeze. Thaw at room temperature for 10 minutes before serving.   *Edith Weiser*

DATE AND NUT PIE

1 4¾-oz. package vanilla wafers, crushed

⅓ cup melted butter

1 tablespoon confectioners' sugar

FILLING:

1 7¼-oz. package pitted dates, quartered

½ cup granulated sugar

½ cup water

1 tablespoon lemon juice

1 envelope unflavored gelatine

½ cup cold water

¼ cup chopped pecans

2 pints vanilla ice cream, softened

Mix vanilla wafer crumbs with melted butter and confectioners' sugar. Press firmly into bottom and sides of 9-inch pie plate. Chill in refrigerator. Combine dates, ½ cup sugar, ½ cup water and lemon juice in small saucepan. Cover and cook until dates are soft (about 5 minutes). Remove from heat. Dissolve gelatine in cold water. Add gelatine to date mixture. Mix in nuts; cool. Spread 1 pint ice cream over crust. Top with cooled date-nut mixture, then spread remaining ice cream over top. Freezer-wrap and freeze. Allow to thaw about 5 minutes before serving for easier cutting. *Selma Abramson*

ICE CREAM PIE

16 graham crackers, crushed

½ cup granulated sugar

2 tablespoons melted butter

1 teaspoon cinnamon

2 quarts Neopolitan ice cream, slightly softened

MERINGUE:

6 egg whites

½ cup granulated sugar

Combine graham cracker crumbs, ½ cup sugar, melted butter and cinnamon. Press mixture firmly into sides and bottom of 9-inch pie plate. Bake at 350° for 10 minutes. Cool. Spread softened ice cream in cooled crust. Place in freezer for 24 hours. Beat egg whites until stiff, gradually adding ½ cup sugar. Cover top of pie, spreading meringue to very edge of crust. Bake at 450° for 8 to 12 minutes or until meringue is lightly browned. Freezer-wrap and freeze. Allow to thaw 20 to 30 minutes before serving. *Estelle Wolf*

FROZEN LEMON PIE

14 graham crackers, crushed

½ cup melted butter

4 eggs, separated

½ cup granulated sugar

Grated rind of 1 lemon

4 tablespoons lemon juice

Pinch salt

1 cup heavy cream, whipped

Combine graham cracker crumbs and melted butter. Reserve 1 tablespoon for topping. Spread remainder in 9-inch pie plate. *Do not press down.* Set crust aside. Beat egg yolks until light. Add sugar, reserving 1 tablespoon; add lemon rind and juice. Cook in top of double boiler, stirring, until thick and smooth. Chill in refrigerator. Meanwhile, beat egg whites with salt and reserved 1 tablespoon sugar until stiff peaks form. Fold gently into *cold* custard mixture with whipped cream. Pour into crust. Sprinkle reserved crumbs over top. Freezer-wrap and freeze. Allow to thaw 10 minutes before serving. *Gloria Davis*

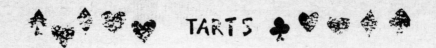

CHERRY TARTS

6 to 8 baked tart shells

1 No. 303 can pie cherries

⅔ to ¾ cup granulated sugar

⅛ teaspoon salt

1 tablespoon cornstarch

1 tablespoon butter

¼ teaspoon almond extract

Drain cherries, reserving juice. Combine cherries, sugar and salt in saucepan. Combine ¼ cup reserved cherry juice with cornstarch; mix to a paste. Add to cherries, stirring well. Cook over medium heat, stirring constantly, until thick and smooth. Remove from heat; add butter and almond extract. Cool; pour into baked tart shells.

PEACH TARTS

6 to 8 baked tart shells

2 cups sliced fresh or frozen peaches

⅔ to ¾ cup granulated sugar*

⅛ teaspoon salt

¼ cup peach juice or water

1 tablespoon cornstarch

1 tablespoon butter

Combine peaches, sugar* and salt in saucepan. Combine peach juice and cornstarch to make a paste. Add to peaches and stir well. Cook over medium heat, stirring constantly, until thick and smooth. Remove from heat and add butter. Cool; pour into baked tart shells.
*If using frozen peaches, omit sugar.

BLUEBERRY TARTS

6 to 8 baked tart shells

2 cups fresh blueberries (or 1 No. 303 can water-packed blueberries, drained)

1 tablespoon lemon juice

⅔ to ¾ cup granulated sugar

⅛ teaspoon salt

¼ cup cold water

1 tablespoon cornstarch

1 tablespoon butter

Combine blueberries, lemon juice, sugar and salt in saucepan. Combine water and cornstarch; mix to a paste. Add to blueberries, stirring well. Cook over medium heat, stirring constantly, until thick and smooth. Remove from heat; add butter. Cool; pour into baked tart shells.

STRAWBERRY TARTS

6 to 8 baked tart shells

2 cups hulled, washed strawberries, sliced

⅔ to ¾ cup granulated sugar

⅛ teaspoon salt

¼ cup water

1 tablespoon cornstarch

1 tablespoon butter

Combine strawberries, sugar and salt in saucepan. Combine water and cornstarch; mix to make a paste. Add to strawberries. Cook over medium heat, stirring constantly, until thick. Remove from heat; add butter. Cool; pour into baked tart shells.

VANILLA CREAM TARTS WITH FRUIT JUICE GLAZE

6 to 8 baked tart shells

¼ cup flour

¼ cup granulated sugar

1 tablespoon cornstarch

Pinch salt

1 egg yolk

¼ cup cold milk

1¼ cups warm milk

1 teaspoon butter

1 teaspoon vanilla

Fruit

GLAZE:

1 cup strained fruit juice

½ cup granulated sugar

2 tablespoons cornstarch

¼ cup cold water

Combine flour, ¼ cup sugar, 1 tablespoon cornstarch and salt; mix thoroughly. Add egg yolk and cold milk, stirring to form a paste. Pour warm milk slowly over paste; cook, stirring, until thick. Continue cooking for several minutes, then add butter. Cool; stir in vanilla. Chill in refrigerator for at least 2 hours. Meanwhile, blend fruit juice with ½ cup sugar and 2 tablespoons cornstarch dissolved in cold water. Cook, stirring constantly, until thick and clear (about 8 minutes). Let stand until lukewarm. Fill tart shells with cream mixture (if filling has thickened upon standing, add a little cool milk and beat well). Top with favorite fruit. Place wire rack over baking sheet or waxed paper. Place tart shells on rack. With teaspoon carefully spoon lukewarm glaze over fruit. Any drippings may be reheated. Makes 6 to 8 tarts.   *Rosabelle Perrye*

DESSERTS AND DESSERT SAUCES

The proof
of the pudding
is in the
eating.

Miguel de Cervantes in Don Quixote

FRUIT DESSERTS

STUFFED BAKED APPLES

½ cup seedless raisins

6 large baking apples

1 cup granulated sugar

½ cup cooked rice

¼ cup melted butter

1½ teaspoons cinnamon

2 cups water

Soak raisins in hot water for 10 minutes. Cut 1-inch slice from top of each apple, reserving tops. Scoop out centers of apples, being careful not to break skin. Sprinkle 1 teaspoon sugar in each. Drain raisins. Combine with rice, butter and ¼ cup sugar. Stuff apples with rice mixture; sprinkle with cinnamon. Replace tops. Place apples in greased oven-glass baking dish. Sprinkle remaining sugar over and around apples. Add water. Bake at 325° for 45 minutes, basting frequently. Serve hot or cold as dessert, or as garnish for roast meat or poultry. Serves 6.   *Sandra Kaufman*

HONEYDEW PARFAIT

Honeydew melon

Vanilla ice cream

Mint jelly

Place scoops of melon alternately with scoops of ice cream in tall glass or parfait glass ending with ice cream. Top with dab of mint jelly.   *Ceil Luke*

APPLE-CRUNCH CASSEROLE

2½ cups canned apple slices, drained

2 tablespoons honey

1 tablespoon flour

¼ teaspoon salt

½ cup biscuit mix

¼ cup liquified nonfat dry milk

2 tablespoons granulated sugar

¼ teaspoon cinnamon

Toss apples, honey, flour and salt together in a 1-quart casserole. Combine biscuit mix with milk and 1 tablespoon sugar; drop by spoonfuls onto apples. Mix remaining sugar with cinnamon; sprinkle over biscuit mix. Bake at 425° for 40 minutes, or until crisp and nicely browned. Serve warm. Makes 4 servings.

HEAVENLY BANANAS

¼ cup butter

6 firm bananas, sliced lengthwise

½ 8-oz. package soft cream cheese

4 tablespoons granulated sugar

1 teaspoon cinnamon

1 cup heavy cream

Melt butter in skillet; brown bananas quickly in butter over high heat. Place half of banana slices in greased pie plate. Blend cream cheese with sugar and cinnamon, creaming until light and smooth. Spread half of cream cheese mixture over bananas. Repeat with remaining banana slices and cream cheese. Pour cream over top. Bake at 375° for 20 minutes, or until most of cream is absorbed and top is lightly browned. Serve hot, topped with whipped cream, if desired. Serves 6.   *Sandra Kaufman*

FRUIT COMPOTE

1 No. 2 can pitted Bing cherries

1 No. 2 can sliced peaches

1 package (1 lb.) dried apricots

Grated rind of 1 lemon

Juice of 1 lemon

Grated rind of 1 orange

Juice of 1 orange

1¼ cups firmly packed brown sugar

Drain cherries and peaches, reserving juices. Mix apricots with reserved juices, lemon and orange rinds, lemon and orange juices and sugar. Stir until sugar is dissolved. Add cherries and peaches. Pour into 2-quart casserole. Bake at 350° for 2 hours. Serve lukewarm, topped with sour cream, if desired. May also be served as accompaniment for meat. Makes 12 servings.   *Florence Collen*

FRUIT COMPOTE SUPREME

2 pounds mixed dried fruit	Pinch salt
¼ cup granulated sugar	16 to 18 macaroons
1 tablespoon lemon juice	Scant ½ cup bourbon or brandy

Combine fruit, sugar, lemon juice and salt in saucepan. Add enough water to barely cover. Cook, covered, until fruit begins to soften. Drain, reserving liquid. Arrange fruit in 2-quart casserole; cover with macaroons. Pour reserved liquid over fruit; add bourbon. Bake at 300° for 20 to 30 minutes. Serve warm or cold. Or make in advance and freeze until ready to serve. Makes 12 servings.   *Ruth Ostreicher*

FRUIT PUDDING DELIGHT

2 pounds fresh peaches or apples, pared and sliced	Grated rind of 1 lemon
½ cup granulated sugar	1 teaspoon lemon juice
1 teaspoon cinnamon	1 teaspoon vanilla
TOPPING:	1 cup sifted flour
½ cup granulated sugar	1 teaspoon baking powder
2 tablespoons soft butter	Pinch salt
1 egg	½ cup milk
	Clear Lemon Sauce, Page 270

Place fruit in greased 2-qt. casserole. Sprinkle with ½ cup sugar and cinnamon. Combine in bowl ½ cup sugar, butter and egg. Add lemon rind, lemon juice and vanilla. Mix well. Sift together flour, baking powder and salt. Add alternately with milk to egg mixture, mixing well after each addition. Pour over fruit in casserole. Bake at 350° for about 1 hour. Serve warm with clear Lemon Sauce.   *Jenny Frost*

PINEAPPLE AND GRAPES IN KIRSCH

1 pineapple, peeled and cored	1 pound seedless grapes
½ to ¾ cup granulated sugar	Kirsch

Dice pineapple; sprinkle with sugar to taste. Combine with grapes. Sprinkle with Kirsch and chill in refrigerator for 3 hours. Serve in sherbet glasses. Serves 6 to 8.

FRUITY TOOT

1 No. 2 can Bartlett pears

1 No. 2 can peaches

1 No. 2 can Bing cherries

2 bananas, sliced

¼ cup blanched almonds

¼ cup brown sugar

1 tablespoon melted butter

¼ cup brandy

¼ cup Cointreau

Drain pears, peaches and cherries, reserving juice. Place layers of fruit and almonds in oven-glass baking dish. Heat reserved fruit juices with brown sugar and melted butter. Pour over fruit. Bake at 325° for 25 minutes. Just before serving, pour brandy and Cointreau over fruit. Serve hot. Makes 6 servings.   *Rosalind Lowe*

STRAWBERRIES ROMANOFF

1 pint vanilla ice cream, slightly softened

1 cup heavy cream, whipped

6 tablespoons Triple Sec or Cointreau

2 quarts chilled sweetened strawberries

Beat ice cream slightly. Fold in whipped cream. Add liqueur and pour over berries. Serve immediately. Makes 6 servings.   *Maxine Lennon*

GELATINE DESSERTS

JELLIED CREAM MOLD

1 cup sweet cream

¾ cup granulated sugar

2 teaspoons unflavored gelatine

½ cup cold water

1 cup sour cream, slightly beaten

¼ teaspoon salt

½ teaspoon vanilla

Fresh sweetened berries or fruit

Heat sweet cream with sugar in top of double boiler. Soften gelatine in cold water for 5 minutes; add to hot cream. Stir until dissolved, then chill in refrigerator until partially set. Fold in sour cream, salt and vanilla. Pour into greased ring mold and chill until firm. Unmold onto serving plate; fill center with berries and syrup. Serves 6.   *Gladys Shutan*

RUM MOLD

2 envelopes unflavored gelatine	4 teaspoons rum flavoring
¼ cup granulated sugar	¼ to ½ cup rum
1 quart chilled egg nog	1 cup heavy cream, whipped
¼ teaspoon nutmeg	Maraschino cherries

Combine gelatine and sugar in top of double boiler; stir in 1 cup cold egg nog. Cook over boiling water, stirring until gelatine and sugar are dissolved. Remove from heat and add remaining egg nog. Add nutmeg, rum flavoring and rum. Chill in refrigerator until partially set. Fold in whipped cream. Place maraschino cherries in bottom of 1½-qt. mold. Pour in gelatine mixture. Chill in refrigerator until set. Unmold onto serving plate. Makes 6 to 8 servings.   *Fera Goldberg*

MOCHA SPONGE

1 envelope unflavored gelatine	2 teaspoons non-caloric sweetening solution
¼ cup cold skim milk	
¾ cup hot skim milk	2 teaspoons Dutch process cocoa
1 tablespoon granulated sugar	1 teaspoon instant coffee
	2 egg whites

Dissolve gelatine in cold milk. Combine with hot milk, sugar, sweetening solution, cocoa and coffee. Stir until well blended. Beat egg whites until stiff but not dry; fold into gelatine mixture. Rinse a 1-quart ring mold or 4 individual molds with cold water. Pour mixture into mold. Chill in refrigerator until firm. Unmold. Serves 4.

BISCUIT TORTONI

¾ cup granulated sugar	½ teaspoon vanilla
½ cup water	½ teaspoon lemon extract
3 egg whites	½ teaspoon almond extract
6 egg yolks	½ teaspoon salt
2 teaspoons unflavored gelatine	¾ cup cake or vanilla wafer crumbs
¼ cup cold water	½ cup chopped blanched almonds
1½ cups heavy cream, whipped	½ cup toasted coconut

Cook sugar and ½ cup water to thread stage (225° on candy thermometer). Beat egg whites until soft peaks form; pour half of syrup over egg whites, beating until fluffy. Beat egg yolks until light; add remaining syrup gradually, beating constantly. Dissolve gelatine in ¼ cup water over hot water. Add to egg yolk mixture. Fold egg whites into egg yolk mixture; fold in whipped cream. Add vanilla, lemon and almond extracts, salt, crumbs, almonds and coconut. Fill paper baking cups three-fourths full. Place in freezing compartment of refrigerator to harden. Makes 8 to 10 servings.

Alice B. Weitzenfeld

CHOCOLATE TOSS-IN CAKE

1 envelope unflavored gelatine	2 squares unsweetened chocolate, melted
¼ cup cold water	1 10-inch angel food cake
Boiling water	1 cup heavy cream
4 eggs, separated	¾ cup confectioners' sugar
1 cup granulated sugar	3 tablespoons cocoa

Dissolve gelatine in cold water; add enough boiling water to make 1 cup. Beat egg yolks; add granulated sugar and melted chocolate. Add gelatine; stir to blend. Cool for 5 minutes. Beat egg whites until stiff but not dry; fold into chocolate mixture. Break angel food cake into 1-inch pieces; add to chocolate mixture, tossing gently. Turn into spring-form pan; chill in refrigerator for several hours or overnight. Unmold onto serving plate. Whip cream with confectioners' sugar and cocoa until thick. Frost top and sides of cake. Serves 8 to 10.

Lois Melvoin

CHOCOLATE MOUSSE

1 package low-calorie chocolate pudding mix	½ cup cold water
2 tablespoons instant cocoa	1½ cups liquified nonfat dry milk, whipped
1 tablespoon instant coffee	2 egg whites, beaten
2½ cups hot water	1 tablespoon grated sweet chocolate
1 tablespoon unflavored gelatine	

Combine pudding mix, cocoa and coffee with hot water; bring to boiling, stirring constantly. Remove from heat. Dissolve gelatine in cold water. Add to pudding mixture; stir and cool. Add whipped dry milk. Fold in beaten egg whites. Turn into mold. Chill in refrigerator for 4 hours. Serve garnished with grated chocolate. Makes 6 to 8 servings.

Clara Blum

CREAMY REFRIGERATOR CAKE

1 envelope unflavored gelatine

½ cup granulated sugar

¼ teaspoon salt

2 teaspoons grated orange rind

⅔ cup orange juice

3 egg yolks, slightly beaten

½ cup sherry

1 tablespoon lemon juice

3 egg whites, stiffly beaten

1 cup heavy cream, whipped

Ladyfingers or thin slices angel food cake

1 10-oz. package thawed frozen raspberries

Combine gelatine, sugar, salt and orange rind in top of double boiler; add orange juice and egg yolks. Stir. Cook over hot, not boiling, water, stirring constantly, until thickened. Remove from heat; stir in sherry and lemon juice. Cool until mixture thickens. Fold in egg whites and whipped cream. Line spring-form pan with split ladyfingers; pour in gelatine mixture. Chill in refrigerator for at least 3 hours, or until firm. Unmold onto serving plate; pour raspberries over top. Serves 8 to 10. *Sara Hirsch*

Add 7 drops of lemon juice to a pint of heavy cream—it will whip up in half the time.

CHOCOLATE CHIFFON PIE

½ teaspoon salad oil

½ cup shredded coconut

1 envelope unflavored gelatine

⅓ cup cold water

2 tablespoons non-caloric sweetening solution

1 teaspoon vanilla

½ teaspoon salt

1 square unsweetened chocolate

¼ cup boiling water

2 egg yolks

½ cup nonfat dry milk powder

½ cup iced water

⅛ teaspoon cream of tartar

Brush 8-inch pie plate with oil; coat sides and bottom with coconut; set aside. Dissolve gelatine in cold water; add sweetening solution, vanilla and salt. Set aside. Melt chocolate in top of double boiler; add boiling water; cook, stirring, until smooth. Remove from heat. Add egg yolks and stir until well blended. Add gelatine mixture; stir until smooth. In chilled bowl, beat dry milk with ice water and cream of tartar at high speed of electric mixer until stiff peaks form. Add chocolate mixture slowly, beating constantly on low speed. Pour into pie plate. Chill until set. Serves 6.

MOCHA CHIFFON SOUFFLÉ

¾ teaspoon unflavored gelatine	½ teaspoon instant coffee powder
1 teaspoon cold water	3 egg whites, stiffly beaten
3 egg yolks, beaten	½ cup heavy cream
¾ cup granulated sugar	1 tablespoon granulated sugar
⅓ cup boiling water	1½ teaspoons brandy
2 squares unsweetened chocolate, melted	¼ cup ground nuts

Dissolve gelatine in cold water. Add ¾ cup sugar to beaten egg yolks; beat until sugar is dissolved. Pour boiling water over gelatine. Stir into egg yolk mixture; stir until dissolved. Add chocolate and coffee. Fold in beaten egg whites. Beat 10 strokes. Turn into small parfait glasses; chill in refrigerator until set. Whip cream with 1 tablespoon sugar and brandy until stiff. Top mocha mixture with whipped cream; sprinkle with nuts. Makes 6 servings.

Alice B. Weitzenfeld

STRAWBERRY-COCONUT MOLD

2 packages strawberry-flavored gelatin	2 ripe bananas, mashed
1 cup hot water	1 3-oz. package soft cream cheese
1 pint vanilla ice cream	1 4-oz. can flaked coconut
1 16-oz. package thawed frozen strawberries	

Dissolve gelatin in hot water; stir and cool. Add ice cream, strawberries and bananas; whip until frothy. Pour into ring mold. Chill in refrigerator until firm. Unmold; frost with cream cheese; sprinkle with coconut. Serves 8.

Peggy Osterbach

RASPBERRY ICE CREAM MOLD

2 packages raspberry-flavored gelatin	1 banana, sliced
3 cups hot water	1 pint vanilla ice cream, slightly softened
1 10-oz. package thawed frozen raspberries	

Dissolve gelatin in hot water. Stir and cool. Add raspberries and banana slices; blend on electric mixer. Blend in ice cream with mixer at low speed. Pour into 1½-qt. ring mold. Chill in refrigerator until firm. Unmold. Makes 6 to 8 servings.

Fagele Holtzman

CHERRY CROWN

1 package cherry-flavored gelatin	1 No. 303 can pitted black cherries
2 tablespoons granulated sugar	1 tablespoon lemon juice
Pinch salt	¼ cup heavy cream, whipped
1 cup hot water	1 cup miniature marshmallows (or 10 large marshmallows, cut into pieces)

Dissolve gelatin, sugar and salt in hot water. Drain cherries, reserving juice. Add enough water to reserved cherry juice to make 1 cup liquid. Add to gelatin mixture with lemon juice. Pour 1 cup mixture into bowl and set aside to thicken. Fold halved cherries into remaining mixture; pour into ring or other mold. Place bowl over ice water and beat until thick and fluffy. Fold in whipped cream alternately with marshmallows. Spoon into mold. Chill in refrigerator until firm. Unmold and serve with additional whipped cream or marshmallow sauce, if desired. Serves 6 to 8.   *Edith Dratler*

FRUIT CREME MOLD

¾ cup evaporated milk	3 tablespoons lemon juice
1 envelope unflavored gelatine	2 egg whites
¼ cup cold water	½ cup granulated sugar
1 No. 2½ can sliced peaches	Pinch salt
½ teaspoon grated lemon rind	½ cup macaroon crumbs

Chill milk in freezing compartment of refrigerator until ice cold. Dissolve gelatine in cold water. Drain peaches, reserving juice. Dice peaches and set aside. Stir heated peach juice into gelatine. Blend in lemon rind and juice. Cool until thickened. Beat egg whites with sugar and salt until stiff peaks form. Fold into gelatine mixture. Beat ice cold milk until fluffy; fold in crumbs and diced peaches. Blend into egg white mixture slowly by hand. Turn into 2-qt. mold; chill in refrigerator until set. Serve with whipped cream, if desired. Makes 8 servings.   *Bea Winchell*

DELMONICO PUDDING

2 envelopes unflavored gelatine	1 9-oz. can sliced pineapple, drained
3 cups milk	1 bottle maraschino cherries, drained
2 cups granulated sugar	½ cup chopped pecans
4 eggs, separated	Whipped cream

Soak gelatine in milk for 1½ hours. Heat, stirring constantly, until mixture begins to thicken. (Do not stop stirring, as mixture scorches easily.) Cream sugar and egg yolks; add to milk mixture, stirring constantly, just until boiling. Remove from heat. Let stand for 5 minutes. Meanwhile, beat egg whites until stiff but not dry. Fold into egg yolk mixture. Cut up pineapple and cherries; arrange in mold with pecans. Pour gelatine mixture over top. Cool; chill in refrigerator until set. Top with whipped cream. Serves 8.

Mayron Apten

LEMON MARSHMALLOW SQUARES

1 envelope unflavored gelatine	½ teaspoon grated lemon rind
½ cup cold water	½ cup lemon juice
3 egg yolks, slightly beaten	1 cup marshmallow creme
½ cup granulated sugar	3 egg whites
½ teaspoon salt	¼ cup granulated sugar

Dissolve gelatine in cold water. Combine egg yolks, ½ cup sugar, salt, lemon rind and juice in top of double boiler. Cook over simmering water, stirring constantly, until thick. Remove from heat; add gelatine, stirring until dissolved. Add marshmallow creme; cook. Beat egg whites until stiff but not dry, adding ¼ cup sugar gradually. Fold into gelatine mixture. Pour into 8x8x2-inch pan. Chill in refrigerator until set. To serve, spread with sweetened whipped cream and sprinkle with chopped nuts. Serves 6 to 8.

Ruth Geller

LEMON REFRIGERATOR CAKE

1 envelope unflavored gelatine	¾ cup lemon juice
¼ cup cold water	6 egg whites
6 egg yolks, slightly beaten	1 10-inch angel food cake
¾ cup granulated sugar	1 cup heavy cream, whipped
1½ teaspoons grated lemon rind	

Dissolve gelatine in cold water. Set aside. Combine egg yolks, sugar, lemon rind and juice in top of double boiler; cook over hot, not boiling, water until mixture coats spoon. Remove from heat; add gelatine and stir until dissolved. Beat egg whites until stiff, gradually adding sugar. Fold into custard mixture. Break angel food cake into small pieces; arrange in layer on bottom of well-greased 10-inch tube pan. Pour custard over cake; repeat layering until all is used. Chill in refrigerator until set. Unmold; frost with whipped cream. Makes 8 to 10 servings.

Ione Comess

MILE-HIGH LEMON CHIFFON TORTE

2 cups graham cracker crumbs	7 egg yolks, beaten
½ cup granulated sugar	1 cup granulated sugar
½ cup soft butter	Juice of 2½ lemons
FILLING:	7 egg whites
1 envelope unflavored gelatine	½ cup granulated sugar
2 tablespoons cold water	

Combine crumbs, ½ cup sugar and butter. Line 7 or 8-inch spring-form pan with crumb mixture, reserving 2 tablespoons for topping. Chill in refrigerator for 1 hour. Dissolve gelatine in cold water. Add 1 cup sugar to beaten egg yolks; beat until thick. Combine egg yolk mixture and lemon juice in top of double boiler; cook over hot water, stirring, until thick. Remove from heat; add gelatine and stir until dissolved. Beat egg whites with ½ cup sugar until stiff. Fold into gelatine mixture. Pour into crumb-lined pan. Sprinkle reserved crumbs over top. Chill in refrigerator overnight. Makes 8 to 10 servings.

Gertrude Pokorny

LIME CHOCOLATE DELICIOUS

1 13-oz. can evaporated milk	2 teaspoons lemon juice
2 cups chocolate wafer crumbs	1 cup granulated sugar
⅓ cup melted butter	Green food coloring
1 package lime-flavored gelatin	Maraschino cherries, walnut halves or shaved chocolate
1¾ cups hot water	
¼ cup lime juice	

Chill evaporated milk in freezing compartment of refrigerator until ice cold. Combine crumbs and melted butter; press into bottom and sides of 13x9x2-inch pan. Chill. Dissolve gelatin in hot water. Chill in refrigerator until partially set; whip until fluffy. Stir in lime juice, lemon juice and sugar. Whip chilled milk; fold into gelatin. Pour into crumb-lined pan. Drizzle green food coloring over top and swirl with spoon for decorative effect. Chill for at least 24 hours. (Flavor improves with longer chilling.) Cut into squares; top each with maraschino cherry, walnut half or shaved chocolate. Makes 12 to 16 servings.

Marian Peterman

PINEAPPLE SPONGE REFRIGERATOR CAKE

1 cup granulated sugar	⅔ cup cold water
Grated rind of 2 lemons	1 No. 2 can crushed pineapple, drained
Juice of 2 lemons	1 cup heavy cream, whipped
6 egg yolks, slightly beaten	6 egg whites, stiffly beaten
2 envelopes unflavored gelatine	1½ packages ladyfingers

Combine sugar, lemon rind, lemon juice and egg yolks in top of double
boiler; cook over boiling water, stirring constantly, until thick. Remove from
heat. Dissolve gelatine in cold water; add to egg yolk mixture; stir. Chill
in refrigerator. Add pineapple. Fold in whipped cream and egg whites.
Break ladyfingers into 1-inch pieces; line bottom of spring-form pan, reserving some of ladyfingers for filling. Pour pineapple mixture into pan. Poke
reserved ladyfingers into filling in desired pattern. Chill in refrigerator for
several hours until firm. Serves 8 to 10. *Serene Flax*

STRAWBERRY CHARLOTTE RUSSE

2 envelopes unflavored gelatine	3 egg whites, stiffly beaten
⅓ cup cold water	1 cup heavy cream, whipped
⅓ cup boiling water	18 ladyfingers, split
¼ cup granulated sugar	Whipped cream
1 10-oz. package thawed frozen straw-berries	Whole fresh strawberries
3 tablespoons lemon juice	

Dissolve gelatine in cold water; add boiling water and stir. Add sugar; cool.
Add thawed frozen strawberries and lemon juice. Whip until frothy, then
fold in beaten egg whites and whipped cream. Line spring-form pan with
split ladyfingers. Turn mixture into pan. Chill in refrigerator for several
hours. Unmold onto serving plate. Spread whipped cream over top and
decorate with whole strawberries. Serves 10. *Rose Ostrof*

*Dessert idea! Remove the core and pulp from halved grapefruit.
Sugar the shells and fill with grapefruit and orange sections.
Sprinkle with finely chopped crystalized ginger.*

CHOCOLATE REFRIGERATOR TORTE

1½ cups vanilla wafer crumbs	½ cup granulated sugar
1 tablespoon confectioners' sugar	½ cup milk
6 tablespoons melted butter	¾ cup soft butter
2 4-oz. bars German's sweet chocolate	1 cup sifted confectioners' sugar
5 egg yolks	5 egg whites, stiffly beaten

Set aside ¼ cup vanilla wafer crumbs for topping. Combine remaining crumbs, 1 tablespoon confectioners' sugar and melted butter. Press onto bottom and sides of spring-form pan. Melt chocolate in top of double boiler. Beat egg yolks with granulated sugar until light. Add milk; add to chocolate and cook until very thick. Cool. Cream soft butter with 1 cup confectioners' sugar; add to chocolate mixture. Fold in beaten egg whites. Pour into crumb-lined pan. Top with reserved crumbs. Chill in refrigerator until firm. Unmold; garnish with whipped cream, if desired. Serves 10.

Marian Jenkins

CHOCOLATE MARSHMALLOW DESSERT

35 vanilla wafers, crushed	2 cups heavy cream
⅓ cup melted butter	Pinch salt
FILLING:	1 teaspoon vanilla
2 cups milk	TOPPING:
1 pound large marshmallows	½ cup heavy cream, whipped
3 squares unsweetened chocolate, grated	Shaved chocolate

Combine vanilla wafer crumbs and melted butter. Press into bottom of 9-inch spring-form pan. Set aside. Scald milk; drop in marshmallows. Add grated chocolate. Stir to mix well; set aside to cool. Whip 2 cups cream with salt and vanilla. Fold into chocolate mixture. Pour into crumb-lined pan. Chill in refrigerator until firm. Unmold; spread whipped cream on top and sprinkle with shaved chocolate. Makes 8 servings. *Polly Cohen*

HAWAIIAN REFRIGERATOR CAKE

1 15½-oz. can sweetened condensed
milk

¼ cup lemon juice

10 large marshmallows, quartered

10 maraschino cherries, quartered

½ cup crushed pineapple, drained

½ cup heavy cream, whipped

Ladyfingers

Whipped cream

Combine milk and lemon juice; stir until thickened. Add marshmallows, cherries, pineapple and whipped cream. Line 9-inch tube pan with split ladyfingers. Pour mixture into pan; cover with ladyfingers. Chill in refrigerator for 6 hours or longer. Unmold onto serving plate. Garnish with whipped cream. Serves 10. *Lois Eichengreen*

MOCHA REFRIGERATOR LOAF

2 tablespoons instant coffee powder

¼ cup boiling water

½ cup granulated sugar

½ cup cold water

½ cup soft butter or margarine

4 egg yolks

1¼ cups sifted confectioners' sugar

1 teaspoon almond extract

½ pound (2 pkgs.) ladyfingers

¼ cup chopped toasted blanched almonds

Dissolve coffee in boiling water. Add granulated sugar, stirring until dissolved. Add cold water; pour into pie plate to cool. Cream butter; add egg yolks and confectioners' sugar alternately, creaming well after each addition. Add almond extract and 2 tablespoons coffee mixture. Dip split ladyfingers lightly in remaining coffee mixture. Arrange some of ladyfingers in double row on serving plate; spread with thin layer of filling. Repeat layering until all are used. Frost top and sides with any remaining filling. Sprinkle with almonds. Chill in refrigerator for 3 to 4 hours. Makes 6 generous servings. *Raye Korshak*

HEAVENLY HASH

2 cups sour cream

14 large marshmallows, quartered

1 No. 2 can crushed pineapple, drained

1 4-oz. can coconut

Mix all ingredients together well. Turn into mold. Chill in refrigerator overnight. Unmold onto serving plate. Garnish with sweetened whipped cream, if desired. Serves 4 or 5. *Mrs. Stuart Sokolsky*

PINEAPPLE REFRIGERATOR CAKE

½ pound vanilla wafers or butter
cookies, finely crushed

½ cup soft butter

1½ cups sifted confectioners' sugar

2 eggs

1 9-oz. can crushed pineapple, drained

1 cup heavy cream, whipped

Sprinkle half of vanilla wafer crumbs evenly over bottom of 12x8x2-inch pan. Cream butter and sugar. Add eggs, one at a time, beating well after each. Beat until smooth and creamy. Pour over crumbs. Fold pineapple into whipped cream. Turn onto creamed mixture. Sprinkle remaining crumbs evenly over top. Chill in refrigerator overnight. Cut into squares. Serves 12.

Carolyn Shepard

PINEAPPLE FLUFF

5½ cups milk

½ cup sifted flour

1 cup granulated sugar

¼ teaspoon salt

4 egg yolks, beaten

1 teaspoon vanilla

4 egg whites

½ cup granulated sugar

1 No. 1 can crushed pineapple, drained

Scald milk in top of double boiler. Sift together flour, ½ cup sugar and salt. Stir into warm milk; cook over hot water for 20 to 25 minutes, or until thick. Beat egg yolks; add some of hot mixture to yolks; add to hot mixture. Cook for 3 to 5 minutes longer. Cool. Add vanilla. Beat egg whites until frothy; add ½ cup sugar gradually, beating until stiff. Fold into egg yolk mixture; fold in pineapple. Divide mixture into 3 parts. With food colorings, tint one-third delicate green and one third delicate pink; leave remaining third yellow. Fill tall parfait glasses with alternating colored mixtures. Garnish each serving with maraschino cherry and sprig of mint, or top with whipped cream. Chill until ready to serve. Makes 10 to 12 servings.

Alice B. Weitzenfeld

LADYFINGER CHOCOLATE CAKE

4 dozen ladyfingers

½ pound milk chocolate

3 tablespoons granulated sugar

3 tablespoons water

4 eggs, separated

1 cup heavy cream, whipped

Line sides and bottom of spring-form pan with ladyfingers. Melt chocolate in top of double boiler; add sugar. Beat egg yolks until fluffy. Add to chocolate mixture with water. Cook slowly over hot water until smooth and thick. Cool. Beat egg whites until stiff but not dry. Fold into chocolate mixture. Pour part of mixture into pan; cover with layer of ladyfingers. Repeat until all are used. Chill in refrigerator for 12 hours. Unmold onto serving plate; top with whipped cream. Makes 8 to 10 servings.   *Eileen Cole*

ANGEL FREEZE

1 10-inch angel food cake

2 pints colored ice cream (chocolate, strawberry, mint, pistachio, etc.)

1 cup heavy cream, whipped

2 pints vanilla ice cream

Place cake on serving plate or tray. With sharp knife, cut out center of cake, leaving ½-inch shell on bottom and sides. Place scoops of colored ice cream in cake; fill spaces with whipped cream. Freeze until firm. Spread cake on all sides with softened vanilla ice cream. Decorate with maraschino cherries or tinted coconut. Freeze until ready to serve. Serves 10 to 12.

Poppy Brooks

RAINBOW SNOWBALL CAKE

1 quart strawberry ice cream

1 quart orange sherbet

1 quart lime sherbet

3 quarts vanilla ice cream, slightly softened

2 cups heavy cream

1 teaspoon vanilla

Chill 10-inch tube pan with removable bottom in refrigerator. With small scoop, make balls of strawberry ice cream, orange and lime sherbets. Place on baking sheet; freeze until firm. Whip vanilla ice cream until fluffy. Drop layer of balls into tube pan; add whipped ice cream to fill spaces; repeat until pan is filled. Freeze for several hours. Whip cream with vanilla until stiff. Unmold ice cream onto serving plate. Frost with whipped cream. Or cover pan with aluminum foil and freeze for several days or until ready to serve; then frost. Makes 16 servings.   *Alice B. Weitzenfeld*

GEORGE WASHINGTON ICE CREAM ROLL

1½ cups heavy cream

2 tablespoons cocoa

¼ cup granulated sugar

½ teaspoon vanilla

2 1-qt. round containers ice cream,
very firm

Stir cream, cocoa, sugar and vanilla together; chill in refrigerator for at least 2 hours. Whip very stiff. Remove ice cream from cartons in rolls; place end to end on serving plate. Spread whipped cream mixture on sides; *do not frost ends.* Draw tines of fork over cream to simulate bark. Decorate with cherries and leaves. Freeze until ready to serve. Serves 14 to 16.

Mrs. Marshall Paskind

CONTINENTAL CREAM PUFFS

Pastry for Eclairs, page 264

Vanilla ice cream

2 6-oz. packages semi-sweet chocolate
pieces

½ pound milk chocolate, broken in
pieces

1 jar marshmallow creme

½ cup double-strength coffee

Drop dough by tablespoonfuls onto greased baking sheets. Bake as directed. Cool; cut off tops and fill with vanilla ice cream; replace tops. Wrap individually in waxed paper. Freeze until ready to serve. Melt chocolate pieces and milk chocolate in top of double boiler over hot, *not boiling,* water. Add marshmallow creme and stir until well blended. Add coffee; mix well. Keep hot in chafing dish. Spoon over frozen puffs just before serving. Makes 1 dozen.

Sis Bloomberg

BANANA FREEZE

½ cup granulated sugar (or equivalent
in non-caloric sweetener)

1 cup water

1 large ripe banana, mashed

¼ cup orange juice

¼ cup lemon juice

Pinch salt

1 egg white

⅓ cup nonfat dry milk

⅓ cup water

Combine sugar and 1' cup water in saucepan; cook until sugar is dissolved. Remove from heat; stir in banana, orange juice, lemon juice and salt. Pour into 2 ice-cube trays and freeze until mushy (about 1 hour). Beat egg white with dry milk and ⅓ cup water until stiff on high speed of electric mixer. Fold gently, but thoroughly, into partially-frozen banana mixture. Freeze until firm. Top each serving with a maraschino cherry or banana slice. Makes 10 servings.

CHOCOLATE-CRUNCH ICE CREAM

7 chocolate sandwich cookies,
coarsely crushed

1 quart vanilla ice cream, slightly
softened

Spoon cookie crumbs into 1-qt. ice-cube tray. Chill in refrigerator. Fold chilled crumbs into softened ice cream. Pour into tray and freeze until ready to serve. Makes 8 servings. *Sandy Ornstein*

COCONUT ICE CREAM

20 large marshmallows

1 cup milk

1 teaspoon vanilla

1 cup heavy cream, whipped

2 cups toasted flaked coconut

Combine marshmallows and milk in saucepan; cook over low heat just until marshmallows begin to melt. Cool; stir in vanilla. Pour into ice-cube tray and freeze until almost firm. Turn into bowl; beat until fluffy. Fold in whipped cream and coconut. Return to tray and freeze until firm. Makes 6 servings. *Sandy Ornstein*

CREME DE MENTHE PARFAITS

½ cup water

½ cup granulated sugar

2 egg yolks

¼ teaspoon salt

2 teaspoons unflavored gelatine

3 tablespoons cold water

½ cup chocolate syrup

2 tablespoons creme de menthe

½ cup heavy cream, whipped

Cook water and sugar until syrup spins a thread (230° to 235° on candy thermometer). Beat egg yolks with salt. Pour hot syrup over egg yolks gradually. Dissolve gelatine in cold water. Add to egg yolk mixture. Cool slightly. Add chocolate syrup and creme de menthe. Chill in refrigerator. Fold in whipped cream; turn into ice-cube tray and freeze until firm without stirring. Serve in sherbet glasses; garnish with sprigs of fresh mint. Serves 6. *Alice B. Weitzenfeld*

LEMON SHERBET

2½ cups cold water

1 cup granulated sugar

Grated rind of 1 lemon

⅓ cup lemon juice

¼ cup Cointreau or Benedictine

½ cup milk

Combine water and sugar in saucepan; boil for 20 minutes. Cool. Soak lemon rind in lemon juice. Add to sugar syrup. Add Cointreau and milk; stir. Pour into 1-qt. ice-cube tray and freeze until firm around edges. Stir; return to freezer until almost firm. Stir again, thoroughly. Freeze until ready to serve. Serve in sherbet glasses; garnish with crushed lemon drops, if desired. Serves 4. *Eve Scheff*

FROZEN CHOCOLATE MOUSSE

1½ teaspoons unflavored gelatine

3 tablespoons cold water

2 squares unsweetened chocolate

¼ cup confectioners' sugar

¾ cup milk

⅔ cup granulated sugar

½ teaspoon vanilla

1½ cups heavy cream, whipped

Rum-flavored whipped cream

Dissolve gelatine in cold water. Melt chocolate in top of double boiler; add confectioners' sugar and milk. Cook until smooth, stirring constantly. Add gelatine, granulated sugar and vanilla. Chill in refrigerator, stirring frequently. Fold in whipped cream. Pour into individual molds or ice-cube tray. Freeze. Allow to thaw several minutes before unmolding. Serve garnished with rum-flavored whipped cream. Serves 6 to 8. *Esther Bass*

GRAPEFRUIT BAKED ALASKA

2 grapefruit

1 pint vanilla ice cream

3 egg whites

6 tablespoons granulated sugar

Green tinted sugar

Halve grapefruit; carefully scoop out and reserve 16 grapefruit sections. Place 4 sections in each grapefruit shell. Fill to within ¼ inch of top with ice cream. Freeze until serving time. Beat egg whites with sugar until stiff peaks form. Spread generously over ice cream to very edges of grapefruit shells. Bake at 450° until meringue is delicately browned. Sprinkle with green tinted sugar. Serves 4. *Esther Bass*

FROZEN LEMON DESSERT

24 vanilla wafers, crushed

3 egg yolks

½ cup granulated sugar

Juice of 1 lemon

1 cup heavy cream, whipped

3 egg whites, stiffly beaten

Line ice-cube tray or 9x5x3-inch pan with vanilla wafer crumbs. Beat egg yolks with sugar and lemon juice. Add to whipped cream. Fold in egg whites. Pour into crumb-lined tray. Freeze for several hours. Slice and serve. Makes 4 to 6 servings.   *Helen Ettinger*

ORANGE MERINGUES

6 large oranges

Orange sherbet

2 egg whites

4 tablespoons honey

Sugar

Shredded coconut

With sharp knife, cut tops from oranges; remove orange sections and pulp. (Reserve orange sections for use in other food preparation.) Fill orange shells with orange sherbet. Beat egg whites with honey until stiff peaks form. Spread generously on top of sherbet. Sprinkle with sugar and shredded coconut. Place oranges on wooden board. Bake at 450° until meringue is delicately browned. Makes 6 servings.

✳ TORTES

CHOCOLATE TORTE

9 egg yolks

1½ cups granulated sugar

1 cup sifted potato starch

½ cup plus 1 tablespoon grated nuts

Grated rind of 1 lemon

Juice of 1 lemon

1 ounce double-strength coffee or sweet wine

1 square unsweetened chocolate, grated

9 egg whites, stiffly beaten

Beat egg yolks, gradually adding sugar and potato starch. Beat in nuts, lemon rind and juice, coffee and chocolate. Fold in stiffly beaten egg whites. Turn into ungreased 9-inch tube pan. Bake at 350° for 45 minutes. Serves 12 to 16.   *Doris Rudman*

CHOCOLATE NUT TORTE

1 6-oz. package semi-sweet chocolate pieces

12 eggs, separated

1½ cups granulated sugar

3 cups finely ground walnuts

1 teaspoon vanilla

1 teaspoon almond extract

1 teaspoon lemon or orange extract

Melt chocolate in top of double boiler over hot, *not boiling,* water. Beat egg yolks until frothy, gradually adding 1 cup sugar. Add melted chocolate and nuts. Beat egg whites until stiff, gradually adding remaining sugar. Add vanilla, almond and lemon extracts. Fold into egg yolk mixture. Pour into ungreased 10-inch tube pan. Bake at 325° for 1 hour and 15 minutes.

Matilda Dubow

DATE AND NUT TORTE

½ cup soft butter

1 cup granulated sugar

1 egg

1 cup boiling water

¾ teaspoon baking soda

1 package pitted dates, cut up

2 ounces walnuts, cut up

1½ cups sifted flour

Cream butter, sugar and egg well. Combine boiling water and soda; pour over dates and nuts. Add alternately to creamed mixture with flour, mixing well after each addition. Pour into greased 12x8x2-inch pan. Bake at 350° for 25 to 30 minutes. Cool in pan; cut into squares. Makes 12 to 16 servings.

Bernice Levee

NUT TORTE

4 eggs, beaten

2 cups firmly packed light brown sugar

2 cups sifted flour

2 teaspoons baking powder

1 teaspoon cinnamon

1½ cups ground walnuts

ICING:

1 cup superfine granulated sugar

Grated rind of 1 lemon

Juice of 1 lemon

Combine eggs and brown sugar; beat until smooth and light. Sift together flour, baking powder and cinnamon; add to sugar mixture. Add nuts; mix well. Pour into ungreased 15½x10½x1-inch (jelly roll) pan. Bake at 375° for 25 minutes. Meanwhile, combine granulated sugar, lemon rind and juice. Remove cake from oven; spread immediately with icing. Cool; cut into bars or squares. Serves 12 to 16.

Esther Goldenberg

COFFEE CHOCOLATE TORTE

1½ cups sifted cake flour

½ teaspoon baking powder

¼ teaspoon salt

1 cup soft butter

2 cups granulated sugar

4 eggs, beaten

4 squares unsweetened chocolate, melted

1 teaspoon vanilla

1 cup chopped nuts

COFFEE FILLING:

6 tablespoons granulated sugar

3 tablespoons cornstarch

½ teaspoon ground cloves

1 cup strong coffee

2 cups heavy cream, whipped

Lightly grease 4 9-inch pie plates. Line bottoms with waxed paper; grease paper. Set aside. Sift together flour, baking powder and salt. Cream butter and 2 cups sugar until light and fluffy. Stir in eggs, cooled chocolate and vanilla. Add flour and mix well. Stir in nuts. Pour batter into pie plates to about ¼-inch depth. Bake at 350° for about 12 minutes, or until edges are crisp and brown. Remove from pans; cool on wire rack. Wash pans; repeat greasing and lining with waxed paper. Bake 4 more layers. Meanwhile, combine 6 tablespoons sugar, cornstarch and cloves in saucepan; blend well. Stir in coffee and cook over medium heat, stirring constantly, until very thick and glossy. Let stand for 1 hour before spreading on cake. Spread each layer with coffee mixture; cover with whipped cream. Stack layers; chill in refrigerator until ready to serve. Makes 10 to 12 servings.

Rosabelle Perrye

BOHEMIAN TORTE

2 hard-cooked egg yolks, chopped or grated

3 egg yolks

¾ cup granulated sugar

¾ cup soft butter

2 to 2½ cups sifted flour

1 teaspoon baking powder

Pinch salt

Grated rind of 1 lemon

Juice of ¼ lemon

Thick tart jam

Chopped nuts

Mix together hard-cooked egg yolks, egg yolks, sugar, butter, flour, baking powder, salt, lemon rind and juice. Beat for 2 minutes. Pat out two-thirds of dough into ungreased 13x9x2-inch pan. Make slight depression in top. Fill with jam and nuts. Roll out remaining dough and prepare lattice top; place over jam. Bake on lower oven rack at 325° for 15 minutes, then on upper rack for 5 minutes longer. Serves 16.

Mrs. Lewis Abrams

VIENNA SACHER TORTE

½ cup soft sweet butter

4 egg yolks

1 cup granulated sugar

4 ounces German's sweet chocolate, melted

1 cup sifted flour

4 egg whites

¼ cup soft jam

ICING:

4 ounces German's sweet chocolate

2 tablespoons shortening

Cream butter on electric mixer. Add egg yolks, one at a time, beating well after each. Add sugar gradually, beating until light and fluffy. Add melted chocolate and flour; beat until well blended. Beat egg whites until stiff; fold into batter. Pour into greased and floured 8-inch spring-form pan. Bake at 350° for 1 hour. Cool in pan. Invert onto serving plate. Spread thin layer of jam over top. Melt chocolate and shortening over hot water. Blend well; spread over jam. Frost sides with chocolate mixture. Chill in refrigerator until ready to serve. Serve garnished with whipped cream.   *Jo Goldberg*

BLUEBERRY TORTE

½ cup soft butter

½ cup granulated sugar

Grated rind of ½ lemon

Juice of ½ lemon

1½ cups sifted cake flour

1 teaspoon baking powder

2 egg yolks

2 tablespoons cold water

FILLING:

2 No. 2 cans blueberries

½ cup granulated sugar

Juice of 1 lemon

2 tablespoons cornstarch

MERINGUE:

2 egg whites

½ cup granulated sugar

½ teaspoon baking powder

Cream butter with ½ cup sugar. Add lemon rind and juice of ½ lemon. Mix well. Sift together flour and 1 teaspoon baking powder. Add egg yolks, water and flour to creamed mixture. Pour into greased 9-inch spring-form pan. Bake at 350° for 30 minutes. Meanwhile, drain blueberries, reserving juice. Combine reserved juice, ½ cup sugar, juice of 1 lemon and cornstarch in saucepan. Cook, stirring, until mixture thickens. Add blueberries; cool. Beat egg whites until stiff, gradually adding ½ cup sugar and ½ teaspoon baking powder. Spoon cooled blueberry mixture onto cake. Cover with egg white mixture. Bake at 300° for 30 minutes. Cool in pan. Refrigerate until ready to serve.   *Lillian Lewis*

DOBOS TORTE

7 egg yolks	1¼ teaspoons confectioners' sugar
½ cup granulated sugar	3 squares unsweetened chocolate, melted
1 cup sifted cake flour	¼ cup cold strong coffee
7 egg whites	1 tablespoon rum
CHOCOLATE FILLING AND FROSTING:	1 egg
1 cup soft butter	

Beat egg yolks until thick and lemon-colored. Add granulated sugar gradually, beating well. Slowly add sifted flour; mix until batter is smooth. Beat egg whites until stiff but not dry. Carefully fold into batter. Pour small amount into 2 lightly-greased 9-inch round layer pans which have been lined in bottoms only with lightly-greased waxed paper. Batter should not be deeper than ¼ inch. Bake at 350° for 7 or 8 minutes, or until done. Remove from pans; cool on wire rack. Wash pans; repeat greasing and lining with waxed paper. Bake 2 or more layers. Repeat until all batter is used. (There will be 6 or 7 layers in all.) Cool layers. Meanwhile, cream butter with confectioners' sugar. Add melted chocolate, coffee, rum and egg. Blend thoroughly till of spreading consistency. Spread on cooled layers; stack layers and frost entire cake with remaining frosting. Chill in refrigerator until ready to serve. *Mildred Weinstock*

MOCHA TORTE

1 cup ground coffee	4 egg whites, stiffly beaten
2 cups water	FILLING AND FROSTING:
4 egg yolks, well beaten	2 cups heavy cream
1 cup granulated sugar	⅓ cup granulated sugar
1 cup sifted cake flour	1 teaspoon vanilla
1 teaspoon baking powder	¼ cup chopped nuts

Combine coffee and water in saucepan; bring to boiling. Boil down to ½ cup liquid; strain and set aside to cool. Mix egg yolks, 1 cup sugar and ¼ cup coffee liquid. Sift together flour and baking powder. Add to egg yolk mixture; fold in beaten egg whites. Pour into 2 greased 8-inch round layer pans which have been lined in bottoms with waxed paper. Bake at 325° for 25 minutes. Cool on wire rack. Meanwhile, beat cream until stiff, gradually adding ⅓ cup sugar, remaining coffee liquid and vanilla. Spread on cooled layers; stack. Frost top and sides; sprinkle with nuts. Chill in refrigerator for at least 1 hour before serving. *Erika Brodsky*

FILBERT TORTE

½ cup filberts, toasted and finely ground	1½ teaspoons vanilla
½ cup sifted cake flour	9 egg whites
¼ teaspoon salt	FILBERT FILLING AND FROSTING:
9 egg yolks	2 cups heavy cream
1 cup granulated sugar	½ cup granulated sugar
1 tablespoon lemon juice	1 cup chopped toasted filberts

Mix together filberts, flour and salt. Beat egg yolks, gradually adding 1 cup sugar; continue beating until all graininess disappears and mixture is light and lemon-colored (about 15 minutes on electric mixer). Add lemon juice and vanilla. Spoon nut mixture over egg yolks. Beat egg whites until stiff and dry. Spoon over nut mixture. Fold all together gently but thoroughly. *Do not beat.* Spoon batter into lightly-greased and floured 9-inch round pan with straight sides. Bake at 325° for about 1 hour, or until cake tester comes out clean. Cool slightly and place in refrigerator to chill. Remove from pan; let stand for at least 3 hours. About 1 hour before serving, split cake into 3 layers. Whip cream, beating in ½ cup sugar. Add chopped filberts. Fill and frost layers; garnish with chopped or sliced filberts, if desired. Serves 12.

Alice B. Weitzenfeld

DANISH LAYER CAKE

6 egg yolks	FILLING AND FROSTING:
1 cup granulated sugar	Raspberry jam
6 egg whites	Vanilla pudding
½ cup potato starch	Sweetened whipped cream
1 teaspoon baking powder	

Beat egg yolks with sugar until frothy. Beat egg whites until stiff. Sift together potato starch and baking powder. Add to egg yolk mixture, mixing well. Fold in beaten egg whites. Pour into 3 ungreased 9-inch round layer pans. Bake at 400° for 10 to 15 minutes. Cool; spread bottom layer with raspberry jam; second layer with vanilla pudding. Top with third layer and frost entire cake with sweetened whipped cream. Chill until ready to serve.

Lillian Lewis

❖❖❖❖❖❖❖❖❖❖❖❖❖❖❖❖❖❖❖❖❖❖❖❖❖❖❖❖❖❖❖❖❖❖❖❖

To keep fillings and frostings from soaking into cake layers, sprinkle the layers with confectioners' sugar before spreading with filling or frosting.

SCHAUM TORTE

6 egg whites	2 cups granulated sugar
½ teaspoon baking powder	2 teaspoons vanilla
⅛ teaspoon salt	Sweetened berries or other fruit
2 teaspoons vinegar	1 cup heavy cream
2 teaspoons water	½ teaspoon vanilla

Beat egg whites with baking powder and salt until stiff. Combine vinegar
and water. Add sugar, ½ teaspoonful at a time, to beaten egg whites alternately with vinegar mixture, beating constantly. Add 2 teaspoons vanilla;
beat for several minutes longer. Pour into 2 greased and lightly floured
10-inch spring-form pans. Bake at 275° for 1½ hours. Cool. Whip cream
with ½ teaspoon vanilla until stiff. Fill cake with sweetened berries. Frost
top with whipped cream. Chill in refrigerator until ready to serve.

Rosabelle Perrye

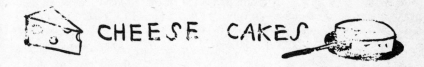

CHEESE CAKES

CHOCOLATE CHEESE CAKE

18 graham crackers, crushed	¾ cup firmly packed light brown sugar
¼ cup light brown sugar	⅛ teaspoon salt
⅛ teaspoon nutmeg	2 eggs, separated
⅓ cup melted butter	1 cup heavy cream, whipped
1 6-oz. package semi-sweet chocolate pieces	1 teaspoon vanilla
1 8-oz. package cream cheese	

Combine graham cracker crumbs, ¼ cup sugar, nutmeg and melted butter.
Reserve 2 tablespoons of mixture for topping. Press remainder onto bottom
and sides of 9-inch pie plate. Chill in refrigerator. Melt chocolate pieces in
top of double boiler over hot, not boiling, water. Cool for about 10 minutes.
Blend together cream cheese, ½ cup sugar and salt. Add egg yolks; beat
thoroughly; stir in cooled chocolate. Beat egg whites until stiff but not dry;
gradually beat in remaining ¼ cup sugar. Fold into chocolate mixture. Fold
in whipped cream and vanilla. Pour into chilled crust; sprinkle reserved
crumb mixture over top. Chill in refrigerator for several hours or overnight.
Makes 8 servings.

Bertha Pinsky

SOUR CREAM CHEESE CAKE

15 graham crackers, crushed	1 cup sour cream
¼ cup melted butter	2 tablespoons cornstarch
1 cup dry cottage cheese	1 cup milk
1 cup creamed cottage cheese	1 teaspoon vanilla
1 8-oz. package cream cheese	5 egg whites
1 cup granulated sugar	1 teaspoon cream of tartar
5 egg yolks	

Mix graham cracker crumbs with melted butter. Press in bottom only of 10-inch spring-form or tube pan. Bake at 350° for 5 minutes. Blend cheeses together well (an electric mixer is fine for this). Add sugar, egg yolks and sour cream. Mix well. Combine cornstarch and milk; add to cheese mixture. Then add vanilla. Beat egg whites until stiff, adding cream of tartar. Fold into cheese mixture. Pour into cooled graham cracker crust. Bake at 325° for 1¼ hours, or until a silver knife inserted in center comes out clean. Cool cake in pan on wire rack away from drafts. Makes 14 to 16 servings.

Lee Bateman

CHEESE CAKE

1½ cups zwieback crumbs	4 egg yolks
6 tablespoons ground almonds	Scant ¼ cup flour
1 tablespoon granulated sugar	Pinch salt
3 tablespoons melted butter	1 cup milk
2 8-oz. packages plus 1 3-oz. package cream cheese	1 teaspoon vanilla
	4 egg whites
⅔ cup granulated sugar	

Mix crumbs, almonds and 1 tablespoon sugar with melted butter. Reserve ½ cup for topping. Press remaining crumb mixture onto sides and bottom of 13x9x2-inch pan. Chill in refrigerator. Have cream cheese at room temperature. Blend with sugar, egg yolks, flour, salt, milk and vanilla until smooth and creamy. Beat egg whites until stiff. Fold into cheese mixture. Turn into crumb-lined pan. Sprinkle reserved crumb mixture over top. Bake at 325° for 50 minutes. Serves 15 to 18.

Rose Sebring

EASY CREAM CHEESE CAKE

1¼ cups graham cracker crumbs	1 egg
3 tablespoons sugar	¾ cup granulated sugar
⅓ cup melted butter	½ teaspoon vanilla
2 8-oz. packages cream cheese	Canned pie filling

Mix graham cracker crumbs and 3 tablespoons sugar with melted butter. Press onto bottom and sides of 9-inch round layer cake pan. Chill in refrigerator. Mix together cream cheese, egg, ¾ cup sugar and vanilla. Beat for 20 minutes on electric mixer. Turn into chilled crust. Bake at 350° for 20 minutes. Top with favorite canned pie filling. Serves 8. *Esther Blustein*

 PIE-LIKE DESSERTS

CHOCOLATE FUDGE PIE

1 cup granulated sugar	⅔ cup sifted flour
½ cup melted butter	1 square unsweetened chocolate, melted
2 eggs	1 teaspoon vanilla

Beat sugar and butter together well; add eggs. Beat until thoroughly mixed. Add flour and blend well. Add chocolate and vanilla. Pour into greased 9-inch oven-glass pie plate. Bake at 325° for 25 minutes. Serve with vanilla ice cream. Makes 8 servings. *Minnie Landers*

RAISIN-COCONUT PIE

½ cup raisins	½ cup flaked coconut
4 egg whites	1 teaspoon vanilla
½ teaspoon salt	1 teaspoon rum extract
1 cup granulated sugar	1 cup heavy cream
1 cup graham cracker crumbs	1 tablespoon confectioners' sugar

Chop raisins; set aside. Beat egg whites with salt until stiff. Gradually add granulated sugar, beating until stiff peaks form. Fold in crumbs, coconut and raisins. Add vanilla and rum extract. Turn into greased 9-inch round layer pan with removable bottom. Bake at 350° for 30 minutes. Cool. Whip cream with confectioners' sugar until stiff. Serve over wedges of pie. Serves 8.

PASTRY
DESSERTS

MANDEL BREAD

3 eggs

1 cup granulated sugar

½ cup salad oil

2¾ cups cake meal

1 tablespoon potato starch

1 cup chopped nuts

Cinnamon-sugar

Combine eggs, sugar, oil, cake meal, potato starch and nuts. Mix well. Divide mixture into 4 parts. Shape into rolls; place on greased baking sheet. Bake at 375° for 25 to 30 minutes. Cool for about 15 minutes on baking sheet. Cut into slices; sprinkle with cinnamon-sugar. Return to oven to brown for about 5 minutes. Makes about 4 dozen. *Faye Witz*

FESTIVE FRUIT STRUDEL

3 cups sifted flour

2 tablespoons granulated sugar

1 teaspoon baking powder

1 teaspoon salt

⅔ cup salad oil

1 egg

FILLING:

2 pounds white raisins

1 pound sweetened prunes

1 cup crushed pineapple, drained

½ cup chopped walnuts

½ cup vanilla wafer crumbs

1 teaspoon grated orange rind

1 teaspoon grated lemon rind

2 tablespoons jam

Cinnamon-sugar

Sift together flour, sugar, baking powder and salt. Make a well in center of dry ingredients; add oil and egg. Add warm water, a little at a time, mixing until dough is soft and pliable. Brush top with oil; cover and set aside. Soften raisins and prunes in a little hot water; drain. Combine with remaining ingredients; grind all and mix well. Divide dough into 5 or 6 parts. On well floured surface, roll out each part paper thin; brush with oil; sprinkle with cinnamon-sugar. Sprinkle with chopped nuts, if desired. Place filling in strip down center of dough; roll as for jelly roll, turning ends under. Cut through slightly to mark slices. Sprinkle top with cinnamon-sugar. Place on well greased baking sheets. Bake at 350° for 1 hour. Makes 4 dozen slices.

Sue Weissman

CREAM CHEESE KOLACKY

1 cup soft butter	2 teaspoons baking powder
3 3-oz. packages soft cream cheese	¼ teaspoon salt
2 cups sifted flour	2 eggs, well beaten
2 tablespoons granulated sugar	1 cup preserves, cottage cheese or any canned filling

Cream butter and cheese until well blended. Sift together flour, sugar, baking powder and salt. Cut into creamed mixture with pastry blender or 2 knives. Add egg yolks and beat until mixture forms stiff dough. Chill in refrigerator for 2 hours. Roll out to ¼-inch thickness. Cut with floured biscuit cutter Place 1 teaspoon preserves on each round. Pinch opposite edges together to seal. Place on ungreased baking sheet. Bake at 375° for 15 to 18 minutes, or until lightly browned. Sprinkle with confectioners' sugar. Makes 4 dozen.

Lee Rosenmutter

APRICOT STRUDEL

1 cup soft butter or margarine	1 cup chopped nuts
1 8-oz. package soft cream cheese	1 15-oz. package white raisins
2 cups sifted flour	1 4-oz. package shredded coconut
2 cups apricot preserves	

Cream butter and cream cheese together thoroughly; blend in flour, mixing until dough forms ball. Chill in refrigerator for 3 to 4 hours. Divide dough into 4 parts. Roll out each part on floured surface to 14x16-inch rectangle. Spread preserves over dough carefully with back of spoon. Do not tear dough. Sprinkle with nuts, raisins and coconut. Roll as for jelly roll; turn ends under. Place on ungreased baking sheet; flatten slightly to even roll. Bake at 350° for 45 minutes. Cool; place in refrigerator for several hours. Or freezer-wrap and freeze. Allow to thaw for 15 minutes before slicing. Sprinkle slices with confectioners' sugar. Makes 5 dozen. *Lillian Minkus*

ECLAIRS

½ cup shortening	1 egg yolk
1 cup hot water	½ cup cold milk
1 cup sifted flour	2 cups warm milk
4 eggs	2 teaspoons rum extract
FILLING:	CHOCOLATE ICING:
½ cup granulated sugar	3 tablespoons milk
¼ cup flour	2 tablespoons butter
2 tablespoons cornstarch	2 squares unsweetened chocolate
Pinch salt	2 cups sifted confectioners' sugar

Heat shortening and water to boiling in saucepan; add flour. Stir with wooden spoon until mixture leaves sides of pan. Remove from heat; cool slightly. Add eggs, one at a time, beating well after each. (Dough should be soft but not runny.) Shape dough with spoon or pastry tube into oblongs; place on greased baking sheet. Bake at 400° for about 30 minutes, or until golden brown. Meanwhile, combine granulated sugar, flour, cornstarch and salt. Beat egg yolk; add cold milk. Stir into sugar mixture. Add warm milk; cook, stirring constantly, until thick. Cook for 5 minutes longer. Cool; add rum extract. Fill cooled split eclairs. Heat together 3 tablespoons milk, butter and chocolate. Stir to mix; remove from heat. Add confectioners' sugar and beat until of spreading consistency. Spread on filled eclairs. Chill in refrigerator until ready to serve. Makes 1 dozen.

** * DESSERT PANCAKES AND FRITTERS

CHOCOLATE CHIP DESSERT PANCAKES

½ cup pancake mix	½ cup milk
⅓ cup semi-sweet chocolate pieces	1 egg, slightly beaten
1 tablespoon granulated sugar	Vanilla ice cream or whipped cream

Combine pancake mix, chocolate pieces and sugar. Stir in milk and egg. Drop by tablespoonfuls onto hot griddle or skillet. Cook until bubbly; turn and cook until browned. Spread each pancake with softened ice cream; stack and cut into wedges. Serve with chocolate sauce, if desired. Serves 2.

GERMAN PANCAKES

2 eggs	1 pound apples, peeled and thinly sliced
½ cup milk	¼ cup melted butter
½ cup sifted flour	¼ cup granulated sugar
¼ teaspoon salt	⅛ teaspoon nutmeg
1 tablespoon butter	⅛ teaspoon cinnamon

Combine eggs, milk, flour and salt. Beat 2 or 3 minutes on electric mixer. Melt butter in 9-inch skillet. When very hot, pour batter into skillet. Bake at 450° for 15 minutes; reduce oven temperature to 350° and bake 10 minutes longer, or until golden brown and crisp. (If pancake puffs in center while baking, prick with fork.) Meanwhile, sauté apple slices in melted butter. Add granulated sugar and cook for 7 or 8 minutes, turning frequently. Season with nutmeg and cinnamon. Apples should be crisply tender. Cool to lukewarm. Remove pancake from skillet to large serving platter. Place apple mixture in center; fold each side toward center and sprinkle with confectioners' sugar. Cut into wedges. Makes 4 servings.   *Rochelle Spitz*

APPLE FRITTERS

3 apples, cut into ¼-inch slices	1 tablespoon melted butter
Cinnamon-sugar	1 tablespoon brandy
Lemon juice	1 cup sifted flour
2 egg yolks, beaten	½ teaspoon salt
⅔ cup milk	2 egg whites, stiffly beaten

Sprinkle apple slices with cinnamon-sugar and lemon juice. Let stand about 1 hour, turning frequently until all juice is absorbed. Meanwhile, combine beaten egg yolks, milk and butter. Add brandy and blend well. Sift together flour and salt; add to egg yolk mixture, stirring just until blended. Fold in beaten egg whites. Dip apple slices in batter. Fry, a few at a time, in hot deep fat (370°) until golden brown. (Or fry slowly in a little hot butter in heavy skillet.) Drain on absorbent paper. Sprinkle with confectioners' sugar or top with whipped cream. Makes 4 servings.
GLAZED APPLE SLICES: Omit batter. Arrange apple slices in buttered shallow baking pan sprinkled with sugar on the bottom. Sprinkle apple slices with more sugar. Place under broiler for several minutes until they glaze. Serve with whipped cream flavored with a little brandy.

CUSTARDS AND PUDDINGS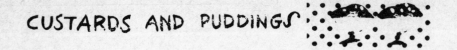

APPLE RICE

1 cup dried apple slices	1½ cups firmly packed brown sugar
1¼ cups uncooked rice	1 tablespoon cinnamon
¼ cup soft butter	1½ teaspoons salt
1 peeled lemon, diced	3 cups hot water

Simmer dried apples in water to cover until they are doubled in size. Drain. Combine rice, butter, lemon, brown sugar, cinnamon, salt and apples in greased 2-qt. casserole. Mix gently; pour 3 cups water over all. Bake at 325° for about 2 hours, or until rice is tender. Or cook rice in water in top of double boiler; add remaining ingredients and cook over low heat for 1½ hours longer, stirring once every 30 minutes. Serves 6 to 8.

Geraldine Kaplan

ROSE'S RICE PUDDING

2 cups scalded milk	1 tablespoon butter
1 cup cooked rice	¼ teaspoon salt
⅓ cup granulated sugar	2 eggs, beaten
⅓ cup raisins	1 teaspoon vanilla

Add rice, sugar, raisins, butter and salt to *hot* scalded milk. Remove from heat. Stir in eggs and vanilla. Pour into 1-qt. casserole. Set in pan of hot water. Bake at 325° for about 1 hour, or until set. Cool; serve topped with whipped cream and garnished with a maraschino cherry. Serves 4.

Rose Fishman

RICE PUDDING

2½ cups milk	¼ teaspoon salt
⅓ cup uncooked rice	1 teaspoon vanillla
2 egg yolks	Raisins (optional)
⅓ cup granulated sugar	3 egg whites

Combine milk and rice in top of double boiler. Cover and cook over boiling water about 45 minutes, or until rice is tender. Remove from heat. Beat egg yolk with ⅓ cup sugar and salt. Slowly add to hot rice mixture. Mix thoroughly; set pan over hot water and cook for 2 minutes, stirring constantly. Remove from heat; add vanilla; cool. Boil raisins in a little water for 3 minutes. Add to rice mixture. Beat egg whites until stiff but not dry, adding remaining sugar gradually. Fold into rice mixture. Chill in refrigerator. Serves 4 to 5. *Jean Kowitt*

LEMON CUPS

2 cups granulated sugar

6 tablespoons flour

¼ teaspoon salt

4 tablespoons melted butter

Grated rind of 1 lemon

Scant ⅔ cup lemon juice

6 egg yolks

3 cups milk

6 egg whites, stiffly beaten

Blend together sugar, flour, salt, butter, lemon rind and juice. Beat egg yolks until thick and lemon-colored. Add milk; mix well. Add sugar mixture gradually, beating well. Fold in beaten egg whites. Pour into greased oven-glass custard cups. Bake in pan of hot water at 350° for 45 minutes. Serves 6 to 8. *Zelma Kay*

UPSIDE-DOWN KUGEL

1 pound medium noodles, cooked

1 cup sour cream

½ cup granulated sugar

Pinch salt

4 eggs, beaten

1 cup creamed cottage cheese

1 teaspoon vanilla

Cinnamon to taste

½ cup raisins

GLAZE:

¼ cup butter

1 cup firmly packed brown sugar

1 cup whole pecans

Rinse noodles with cold water; drain. Add sour cream, granulated sugar, salt, eggs, cottage cheese, vanilla, cinnamon and raisins in order listed; mix well. Melt butter in 13x9x2-inch pan. Sprinkle brown sugar evenly over butter; press pecans into brown sugar. Pour in noodle mixture. Bake at 350° for 1 hour, or until done. Cool in pan for 10 minutes. Run knife around edges and invert onto serving plate. Allow to cool for 10 minutes before removing pan. Makes 12 servings. *Ferne Kron*

NOODLE PUDDING

1 pound broad noodles, cooked

4 eggs, separated

¼ cup granulated sugar

1 No. 2 can crushed pineapple, drained

½ cup melted butter

1 cup cottage cheese

3 tablespoons sour cream

TOPPING:

1 cup sugar-coated corn flakes

½ cup melted butter

Rinse noodles with cold water; drain. Beat egg yolks with sugar; add pineapple, ½ cup melted butter, cottage cheese and sour cream. Blend well. Beat egg whites until stiff but not dry. Fold egg yolk mixture and egg whites alternately into noodles. Pour into lightly greased ring mold. Combine corn flakes with ½ cup melted butter. Pour over batter in mold. Bake at 350° for 40 minutes. Serves 6 to 8.   *Rose Lustbader*

NOODLE KUGEL

1 pound medium noodles, cooked

2 tablespoons melted butter

6 eggs

1 15-oz. can applesauce

½ cup granulated sugar

¼ cup milk

White raisins

Cinnamon-sugar

Rinse noodles with cold water; toss with melted butter. Beat eggs; add applesauce, sugar, milk and raisins. Add noodles; mix well. Sprinkle with cinnamon-sugar. Turn into greased 2-quart casserole. Bake at 375° for 1 hour. Makes 16 servings.   *Gloria Wechter*

BLUEBERRY PUDDING WITH SHERRY HARD SAUCE

⅔ cup light molasses

⅓ cup milk

2 cups plus 2 tablespoons sifted flour

⅔ teaspoon baking soda

1 tablespoon hot water

1 pint blueberries

SHERRY HARD SAUCE:

½ cup soft butter or margarine

1½ cups sifted confectioners' sugar

2 tablespoons sherry

1 tablespoon light cream

Combine molasses and milk. Add flour and mix well. Dissolve soda in hot water; add to flour mixture. Fold in blueberries. Pour into greased and floured 1½-qt. mold. Cover tightly. Place on rack in deep kettle. Pour boiling water in kettle and steam for 3 hours. Keep water boiling during steaming process. Add more water as necessary. Meanwhile, cream butter and confectioners' sugar well. Blend in wine. Add cream and beat until mixture is fluffy. Chill in refrigerator until cold but not hard. Sprinkle with nutmeg. Serve with unmolded pudding. Makes 8 to 10 servings.   *Allene Jastromb*

FRUIT FARFEL

½ pound matzo farfel

1 No. 2 can apple slices, drained, or 4 large cooking apples, sliced

1 No. 2 can sour cherries, drained

1 No. 2 can sweet Bing cherries, drained

1 13-oz. can pineapple tidbits

4 eggs, separated

Brown sugar

Cinnamon

Grated lemon rind

Slivered almonds

Rinse farfel with hot water; drain well. Add apples, cherries and pineapple. Beat egg yolks with a little brown sugar until thick. Fold into fruit mixture. Beat egg whites until stiff but not dry. Fold into egg yolk mixture with cinnamon, lemon rind and slivered almonds, if desired. Turn into greased deep oven-glass baking dish. Bake at 350° for about 1 hour.

Sylvea Zimmerman

BEST-EVER STEAMED CHOCOLATE PUDDING

8 squares unsweetened chocolate

4 cups milk

1 cup granulated sugar

1 teaspoon cinnamon

1 cup dry bread crumbs

5 tablespoons melted butter

12 eggs, separated

1 tablespoon granulated sugar

1 cup heavy cream, whipped

Melt chocolate in milk. Simmer for 2 minutes. Add 1 cup sugar, cinnamon, bread crumbs and butter. Cook for 2 minutes longer. Set aside for several hours to cool. Add egg yolks, one at a time, mixing after each. Beat egg whites until frothy; fold into chocolate mixture. Sprinkle 2 tablespoons sugar in greased 2-qt. mold. Pour in pudding; cover tightly. Place on rack in deep kettle; pour boiling water into kettle and steam for 1¼ hours. Keep water boiling during steaming process. Add more water as necessary. Unmold; serve hot or cold with whipped cream. Makes 8 to 10 servings. *Ann Metzger*

CLEAR LEMON SAUCE

2 tablespoons granulated sugar

2 tablespoons flour

Pinch salt

1 tablespoon soft butter

1 tablespoon water

1½ cups boiling water

½ teaspoon lemon juice

½ teaspoon vanilla

Combine sugar, flour, salt and butter; add water and mix. Add to boiling water and stir for 5 minutes. Add lemon juice and vanilla. Serve hot over pudding.

Jenny Frost

CHOCOLATE SAUCE

3 squares unsweetened chocolate

¼ cup butter

1½ cups sifted confectioners' sugar

1 6-oz. can evaporated milk

½ teaspoon vanilla

Combine all ingredients in top of double boiler. Cook over hot water, stirring occasionally, for 30 minutes. Makes about 1½ pints.

Muriel Kahn

HOT FUDGE SAUCE

2 cups granulated sugar

⅔ cup cocoa

¼ cup flour

¼ teaspoon salt

2 cups water

2 tablespoons butter

1 teaspoon vanilla

Mix sugar, cocoa, flour and salt in heavy saucepan; add water and butter. Bring to boiling. Reduce heat and cook for about 8 minutes, stirring constantly. Cool. Stir in vanilla. Serve over angel food cake, ice cream, etc. Keeps well in refrigerator.

Eve Scheff

COOKIES

BAR COOKIES

COOKIE CRUNCH

1 cup butter

1 cup granulated sugar

1 egg, separated

2 cups sifted flour

½ teaspoon cinnamon

¼ cup chopped nuts

Cream butter with pastry blender. Blend in sugar and egg yolk. Sift together flour and cinnamon; cut into butter mixture until mixture resembles coarse crumbs. Press into 15½x10½x1-inch pan. Spread with unbeaten egg white; sprinkle with nuts. Bake at 350° for 30 minutes. Cut into squares while hot. Makes about 3 dozen.   *Alice Ellis*

LILLIAN'S BROWNIES

½ cup soft butter

2 cups granulated sugar

4 eggs

2 teaspoons vanilla

2 cups cake flour

½ teaspoon baking powder

½ cup milk

3 squares unsweetened chocolate, melted

Cream butter and sugar. Add eggs, one at a time, creaming well after each. Add vanilla. Sift together flour and baking powder. Add alternately with milk to creamed mixture. Mix in *cooled* chocolate. Spread in 15½x10½-1 inch (jelly roll) pan. Bake at 350° for about 20 minutes. Cool. Cut into bars. Makes about 3 dozen.   *Lillian Preis*

COOKIE CAKE BARS

¾ cup soft shortening

1 cup sugar

2 eggs, beaten

1¾ cups sifted flour

1 teaspoon salt

¼ teaspoon baking soda

⅓ cup milk

1 teaspoon vanilla

1 square unsweetened chocolate, melted

½ cup chopped nuts

½ pound graham crackers

¾ cup semi-sweet chocolate pieces

Cream shortening and sugar; add eggs. Sift together flour, salt and baking soda. Add flour mixture alternately with milk to creamed mixture. Add vanilla. Pour slightly less than half of mixture into a second bowl. To this, add melted chocolate and nuts. Spread evenly in greased 12x8x2-inch pan. Cover with layer of graham crackers. Add chocolate pieces to remaining batter. Pour over graham crackers. Bake at 350° for 25 minutes. Cool; cut into squares. Makes 2 dozen.   *Gus Dobrofsky*

CHOCOLATE BROWNIES

1 6-oz. package semi-sweet chocolate pieces

¼ cup butter

2 eggs

½ cup granulated sugar

1 teaspoon vanilla

½ cup sifted flour

½ teaspoon baking powder

½ cup chopped nuts

Melt chocolate pieces and butter in top of double boiler over hot, *not boiling,* water. Set aside. Beat eggs slightly; add sugar and vanilla, mixing well. Sift together flour and baking powder; add to sugar mixture. Add to chocolate and mix thoroughly. Add nuts. Pour into greased 9x9x2-inch pan. Bake at 350° for 25 minutes. Cool; cut into squares. Makes 3 dozen.
Mrs. Leo Levee

BROWNIE DELIGHT

2 eggs

1 cup granulated sugar

½ cup semi-sweet chocolates pieces

2 squares unsweetened chocolate

½ cup butter

1 teaspoon vanilla

½ cup sifted flour

1 cup miniature marshmallows

½ cup broken walnuts

Beat eggs until thick and lemon-colored. Add sugar gradually, continuing to beat. Melt chocolate, chocolate pieces and butter in top of double boiler over hot, *not boiling,* water; add to sugar mixture. Add vanilla. Fold in flour. Add marshmallows and walnuts. Pour into greased 8x8x2-inch pan. Bake at 350° for about 30 minutes. Cool slightly; cut into squares. Makes 1 dozen.   *Clare Palmer*

DATE BARS

¼ cup soft butter	1 teaspoon baking powder
1 cup granulated sugar	1 cup dates, cut
2 eggs, beaten	1 cup chopped walnuts
1 cup sifted flour	

Cream butter and sugar; add eggs and beat well. Sift together flour and baking powder. Mix some flour mixture with dates and nuts. Then add to creamed mixture. Add remaining flour and mix well. Spread in greased and floured 8x8x2-inch pan. Bake at 350° for 45 minutes. Cut into squares while still warm. Remove from pan and dust with confectioners' sugar. Makes 16 bars.   *Sylvia Abrams*

CRANBERRY FROSTS

1¾ cups sifted flour	½ teaspoon vanilla
⅓ cup confectioners' sugar	1 No. 303 can whole cranberry sauce
½ teaspoon salt	SUGAR GLAZE:
½ cup soft margarine or butter	½ cup sifted confectioners' sugar
½ cup soft shortening	2 tablespoons warm water
¼ cup evaporated milk	3 squares unsweetened chocolate, melted

Sift together flour, ½ cup sugar and salt. With electric mixer at medium speed, cream margarine and shortening. Gradually add flour mixture and milk alternately, beating just until mixed. Add vanilla. Divide dough into 2 parts. Pat one part firmly into bottom of greased 8x8x2-inch pan. Bake at 375° for 10 minutes. Cool; spread cranberry sauce over top. Turn remaining dough onto floured waxed paper. Pat into 8-inch square; invert over cranberry sauce. Bake at 375° for 30 to 35 minutes. Cut into 2-inch squares; cool on wire rack. Combine ½ cup sugar with warm water. Frost squares; drizzle melted chocolate on top; draw wooden pick across chocolate for zigzag effect. Makes 16 bars.   *Dee Kamins*

MARSHMALLOW FUDGE BARS

½ cup soft shortening

¾ cup granulated sugar

2 eggs

¾ cup sifted flour

2 tablespoons cocoa

¼ teaspoon baking powder

¼ teaspoon salt

1 teaspoon vanilla

½ cup chopped pecans

50 to 60 miniature marshmallows (or ½ jar marshmallow creme)

FROSTING:

½ cup firmly packed brown sugar

¼ cup water

2 squares unsweetened chocolate

3 tablespoons butter

1 teaspoon vanilla

1½ cups sifted confectioners' sugar

Cream shortening and granulated sugar until light and fluffy. Blend in eggs, one at a time, beating well after each. Sift together flour, cocoa, baking powder and salt. Add to creamed mixture, mixing well. Blend in 1 teaspoon vanilla. Add pecans. Spread in greased and floured 12x8x2-inch pan. Bake at 350° for 25 to 30 minutes. Remove from oven; top with marshmallows; return to oven for 3 minutes or until marshmallows are soft enough to spread evenly. Cool. Combine brown sugar, water and chocolate in saucepan. Bring to boiling and cook 3 minutes, or until chocolate is melted. Add butter and 1 teaspoon vanilla. Cool. Mix in confectioners' sugar and beat to spreading consistency. Thin with a little cream, if necessary. Frost cooled cookies. Cut into 2x1-inch bars. Makes 4 dozen. *Alice B. Weitzenfeld*

COCONUT MERINGUE BARS

1½ cups sifted flour

½ cup instant nonfat dry milk powder

½ cup firmly packed brown sugar

½ teaspoon baking powder

½ cup butter

1 cup coconut

2 egg yolks, beaten

2 egg whites

1 cup firmly packed brown sugar

Sift together flour, dry milk powder, ½ cup brown sugar and baking powder into a bowl. Cut in butter with pastry blender or 2 knives until mixture is crumbly. Add coconut; stir in egg yolks. Pack firmly into greased 9x9x2-inch baking dish. Beat egg whites until stiff but not dry. Gradually add 1 cup brown sugar; continue beating until glossy (about 3 minutes). Spread over coconut mixture and swirl with knife to make desired pattern. Bake at 325° for about 30 minutes, or until meringue is firm and lightly browned. Cool in baking dish. Cut into bars. Makes 18 bars. *Alice B. Weitzenfeld*

CHOCOLATE CINNAMON BARS

2 cups sifted flour	1 egg
1 cup granulated sugar	1 egg, separated
1 tablespoon cinnamon	⅓ cup granulated sugar
1 teaspoon baking powder	1 teaspoon cinnamon
½ cup soft butter or margarine	1 6-oz. package semi-sweet chocolate pieces
½ cup soft shortening	½ cup chopped nuts

Sift together flour, 1 cup sugar, 1 tablespoon cinnamon and baking powder. Add butter, shortening, egg and egg yolk. Blend well with wooden spoon or on low speed of electric mixer. Turn into lightly greased 15½x10½x1-inch (jelly roll) pan; spread evenly with spatula. Beat egg white slightly; brush over mixture in pan. Combine ⅓ cup sugar, 1 teaspoon cinnamon, chocolate pieces and nuts; sprinkle over top. Bake at 325° for 25 minutes. Cool; cut into bars. Makes about 3 bars.   *Alice B. Weitzenfeld*

MERINGUE COOKIES

2 cups sifted flour	1 teaspoon vanilla
¾ cup fine graham cracker crumbs	Marmalade
½ cup granulated sugar	**MERINGUE:**
1 teaspoon baking powder	4 egg whites
Pinch salt	¾ cup granulated sugar
1 cup unsalted butter	½ teaspoon vanilla
4 egg yolks	1 cup chopped nuts
1 tablespoon milk	

Sift together flour, crumbs, ½ cup sugar, baking powder and salt into a large mixing bowl. Cut butter into flour mixture with pastry blender or 2 knives. Add egg yolks, milk and 1 teaspoon vanilla. Mix well. Spread in greased 15½x10½x1-inch (jelly roll) pan. Spread favorite marmalade evenly over top. Beat egg whites; gradually add sugar, beating until stiff peaks form. Add vanilla. Fold in nuts. Spread on top of marmalade. Bake at 325° for 1 hour. Cool; cut into squares. Makes 4 dozen.   *Eve Gurvey*

MAPELINE BARS

1 cup soft butter	2 teaspoons maple flavoring
2 cups firmly packed brown sugar	Pinch salt
2 egg yolks	2 bars (½-lb.) German's sweet chocolate
2 cups sifted flour	½ cup finely chopped nuts

Cream butter and sugar. Add egg yolks and flour, creaming well. Mix in maple flavoring and salt. Pat mixture into 12x8x2-inch pan. Bake at 350° for 20 minutes. Melt chocolate in top of double boiler; spread over baked mixture. Sprinkle with nuts. Cut into 2x1-inch bars. Makes 4 dozen.

Gerry Freedman

BUTTERSCOTCH BROWNIES

¼ cup butter or shortening	1 teaspoon baking powder
1 cup firmly packed light brown sugar	½ teaspoon salt
1 egg	½ teaspoon vanilla
¾ cup sifted flour	½ cup chopped nuts

Melt butter. Remove from heat and blend in sugar; cool. Stir in egg. Sift together flour, baking powder and salt. Add to sugar mixture. Add vanilla and nuts. Spread in greased 8x8x2-inch pan. Bake at 350° for 25 minutes. Do not overbake. Cool in pan on wire rack. Cut into bars. Makes 16 bars.

Helen Ettinger

LINZER CHERUBS

1½ cups sifted flour	1 egg
½ cup firmly packed brown sugar	½ cup granulated sugar
½ teaspoon salt	Pinch salt
½ cup butter	1 cup filberts, finely chopped
¾ to 1 cup raspberry jam	

Sift together flour, brown sugar and ½ teaspoon salt. Cut flour mixture into butter with pastry blender. Pack evenly into lightly greased 12x8x2-inch pan. Spread evenly with jam. Bake at 350° for about 8 minutes, or long enough to set jam. Meanwhile, beat egg. Add granulated sugar and pinch salt; beat well. Add nuts. Spread evenly over partially-baked layer. Bake 20 minutes longer. Cut into small strips and remove from pan while still warm. Makes about 7 dozen. *Dorothy Rothenberg*

TOFFEE BARS

½ cup soft butter

¾ cup firmly packed brown sugar

¼ cup granulated sugar

1 egg yolk

½ cup quick-cooking rolled oats

½ cup sifted flour

½ teaspoon vanilla

½ cup chopped nuts

½ cup semi-sweet chocolate pieces

Combine all ingredients except chocolate pieces. Mix well. Press into greased 9x9x2-inch pan. Bake at 350° for 15 to 20 minutes. Let stand a few minutes, then scatter chocolate pieces over top. Allow chocolate to melt; spread evenly with back of spoon. Cool; cut into bars. Makes 12 to 16 bars.

Mrs. Herman Shaffer

DROP COOKIES

CHOCOLATE CHIP OATMEAL COOKIES

½ cup soft shortening

6 tablespoons brown sugar

6 tablespoons granulated sugar

1 egg

¾ cup sifted flour

½ teaspoon baking powder

½ teaspoon salt

½ cup chopped nuts

1 6-oz. package semi-sweet chocolate pieces

1 cup quick-cooking rolled oats

½ teaspoon vanilla

Hot water

Cream shortening and sugars; add egg and beat until very light and fluffy. Sift together flour, baking powder and salt. Blend into creamed mixture with nuts, chocolate pieces, rolled oats, vanilla and enough water to make a very stiff dough, *just until* mixed. Drop by rounded teaspoonfuls, 2 inches apart, onto greased baking sheet. Bake at 375° for 12 minutes, or until golden brown. Makes about 3½ dozen.

Mrs. Jerome Don

COFFEE CRUNCHIES

½ cup soft butter

1 cup granulated sugar

1 egg

3 cups sifted flour

1½ teaspoons baking powder

1 teaspoon ginger

1 teaspoon cinnamon

¼ teaspoon ground cloves

¼ teaspoon salt

1 cup cold strong coffee

1 teaspoon vinegar

2 cups broken walnuts

Cream butter and sugar thoroughly. Add egg; beat well. Sift together flour, baking powder, ginger, cinnamon, cloves and salt. Combine coffee and vinegar. Add flour and coffee mixtures alternately to creamed mixture, beginning and ending with flour, beating well after each addition. Add walnuts. Drop by teaspoonful onto baking sheets covered with waxed paper. Bake at 350° for about 20 minutes, or until lightly browned. When cool, frost with a coffee icing, if desired. Makes about 30 3-inch cookies.

Rosabelle Perrye

CHOCOLATE MACAROONS

2 egg whites

½ cup granulated sugar

6 ounces German's sweet chocolate, melted

½ teaspoon vanilla

¾ cup chopped nuts

Beat egg whites until stiff, gradually adding sugar. Add melted chocolate, vanilla and nuts. Drop by teaspoonfuls onto baking sheet which has been lined with aluminum foil. Bake at 350° for 10 minutes. Makes about 2 dozen.

Libby Strauss

CHOCOLATE MERINGUE COOKIES

1 6-oz. package semi-sweet chocolate pieces

2 egg whites

Pinch salt

½ cup granulated sugar

½ teaspoon vanilla

½ teaspoon vinegar

¾ cup chopped walnuts

Melt chocolate in top of double boiler over hot, *not boiling,* water. Set aside to cool. Beat egg whites with salt until frothy but not stiff. Add sugar gradually, beating until stiff peaks form. Add vanilla and vinegar. Fold in melted chocolate and walnuts. Drop by ½ teaspoonfuls, 3 inches apart, onto well greased baking sheet. Bake at 350° for 10 minutes. (Cookies should be dull when done.) Remove immediately from baking sheet *very carefully* with spatula. Cool on wire rack. Makes about 3 dozen.   *Janice Tatz*

CRISP CHOCOLATE COOKIES

1 cup soft butter or margarine	1 cup sifted flour
1 cup firmly packed brown sugar	¼ cup cocoa
1 egg	½ teaspoon baking soda
1 tablespoon milk	1 cup crisp rice cereal
1 teaspoon vanilla	

Cream butter and sugar until light and fluffy. Add egg, milk and vanilla; beat thoroughly. Sift together flour, cocoa and soda. Add to creamed mixture with cereal; beat well. Drop by teaspoonfuls onto ungreased baking sheets. Bake at 350° for 8 to 10 minutes. Makes 5 dozen.   *Esther Weiner*

To avoid hard-to-wash patches on your baking sheets, grease only the spots where dough is to be dropped, allowing room for cookies to spread during baking.

FRUIT AND NUT DROPS

5 eggs	1 teaspoon ground cloves
2¼ cups plus 2 tablespoons granulated sugar	1 tablespoon brandy
	FROSTING:
1 pound filberts, toasted and ground	1 egg white
½ pound almonds	1 cup sifted confectioners' sugar
8 oz. glazed fruits, chopped	Juice of ½ lemon
2 teaspoons cinnamon	1 teaspoon rum or brandy

Cream eggs and granulated sugar thoroughly. Add nuts, fruits, cinnamon, cloves and 1 teaspoon brandy. Mix well. Drop by teaspoonfuls onto *waxed* baking sheets. (Or shape into balls; have hands wet.) Bake at 325° for 20 minutes. Mix all frosting ingredients together; beat until very stiff (about 2 minutes). Cool cookies and frost. Makes about 65 cookies.   *Edith Eis*

MACAROONS

3 egg whites, stiffly beaten   ½ pound shredded or flaked coconut

1 cup granulated sugar   Lemon or almond extract

Mix together all ingredients. If desired, add few drops food coloring. Drop by teaspoonfuls onto greased baking sheet. Bake at 400° for 7 to 10 minutes, or until brown. Makes about 1 dozen.   *Lorraine Pohn*

MOLDED COOKIES

PEANUT BUTTER COOKIES

½ cup soft butter   1 teaspoon vanilla

½ cup firmly packed brown sugar 1½ cups sifted flour

½ cup peanut butter   1 teaspoon baking soda

1 egg, beaten   ½ teaspoon salt

Cream butter; add sugar, peanut butter, egg and vanilla. Sift together flour, baking soda and salt. Add to sugar mixture. Mix well. Shape into round balls. Place on greased baking sheet; flatten with floured fork. Bake at 375° for 12 minutes. Makes about 3 dozen.   *Shirley Brosilow*

BROWN SUGAR COOKIES

1 cup soft shortening   1 teaspoon vanilla

1 cup firmly packed brown sugar ½ teaspoon maple flavoring

1 egg, beaten   2 cups sifted flour

Cream together shortening, sugar, egg, vanilla and maple flavoring. Add flour and mix well. Shape into small balls. Place on ungreased baking sheet; flatten with sugared glass or floured fork. Top each cookie with a semi-sweet chocolate piece, if desired. Bake at 375° for 10 to 15 minutes. Makes 3½ dozen.   *Annette Swidler*

PECAN TASSIES

½ cup soft butter

½ cup margarine

1 3-oz. package cream cheese

1½ cups sifted flour

FILLING:

1 egg

¾ cup firmly packed light brown sugar

1 tablespoon melted butter

Pinch salt

Few drops vanilla

½ cup pecans, coarsely cut

Cream soft butter, margarine and cheese until smooth and creamy. Add flour gradually and blend in thoroughly. Chill dough in refrigerator overnight. Line *miniature* muffin cups with paper baking cups. Press dough against bottom and sides. Beat egg, gradually adding sugar and melted butter. Add salt and vanilla. Mix thoroughly. Sprinkle some of pecans over dough in muffin cups. Spoon filling over nuts; top with remaining nuts. Bake at 350° for 15 to 17 minutes. Reduce oven temperature to 250° and bake for 12 minutes longer. Makes about 4 dozen.   *Elnora Weissbuch*

CHANUKAH COOKIES

2 cups soft butter

2 tablespoons brown sugar

2 tablespoons granulated sugar

1 teaspoon vanilla

1 cup sifted flour

½ cup finely chopped toasted almonds

½ cup finely chopped semi-sweet chocolate pieces

½ cup sifted confectioners' sugar

Cream butter and sugars. Add vanilla. Add flour; mix well. Fold in almonds and chocolate pieces. Chill in refrigerator for 20 to 30 minutes. Shape into 1-inch balls. Place on ungreased baking sheet. Bake at 350° for 15 minutes. Cool. Roll in confectioners' sugar. Makes 4 to 5 dozen.   *Gladys Sabath*

PUDDIN' COOKIES

¾ cup biscuit mix

1 package instant pudding mix

1 egg

¼ cup salad oil

Mix all ingredients together. Shape into small balls. Place on ungreased baking sheet; flatten with sugared glass or floured fork. Bake at 350° for 8 minutes. Makes about 3 dozen.   *Dee Stein*

PECAN BALLS

1 cup soft butter

¼ cup granulated sugar

2 teaspoons vanilla

2 cups sifted flour

2 cups finely chopped pecans

Cream butter and sugar. Add vanilla, flour and pecans. Mix well. Chill in refrigerator for 2 hours. With teaspoon measure dough and shape into small balls. Place on ungreased baking sheet. Bake at 300° for 20 minutes. Remove from oven and roll in confectioners' sugar. Cool; roll in confectioners' sugar again. Makes 4 to 5 dozen. *Marie Dube*

DATE AND NUT MELTAWAYS

4 egg whites

1 cup granulated sugar

2 to 4 tablespoons cake meal (or sifted matzo meal)

6 tablespoons cake meal

1 pound dates, cut up

1 pound walnuts, chopped

Beat egg whites; add sugar and beat until stiff. Fold in 2 to 4 tablespoons cake meal. Combine 6 tablespoons cake meal, dates and walnuts. Drop egg-white mixture, a teaspoonful at a time, into date-nut mixture. Roll to coat well; place on ungreased baking sheet. Bake at 350° or until lightly browned. Makes about 2 dozen. *Mrs. Lewis Abrams*

CROWN JEWELS

2 cups soft butter or margarine

¾ cup firmly packed brown sugar

¾ cup granulated sugar

2 eggs, separated

5 cups sifted flour

1 tablespoon baking powder

Pinch salt

Chopped nuts

Candied cherries

Cream butter and sugars. Add egg yolks. Sift together flour, baking powder and salt. Add to sugar mixture, mixing well. Chill dough in refrigerator. Beat egg whites slightly. Shape dough into bite-size balls; dip in egg whites, then in chopped nuts. Place on lightly greased baking sheets. Bake at 350° for 5 minutes. Remove from oven and make small indention in each ball. Place cherry in each indention. Return to oven and bake 10 minutes, or until golden brown. Makes about 9½ dozen. *Dorothy Rothenberg*

FINIKIA (Spice Bits)

2 cups salad oil

½ cup granulated sugar

2 teaspoons cinnamon

¼ teaspoon nutmeg

½ cup orange juice

7 cups sifted flour

2 cups finely chopped nuts

SYRUP:

2 cups honey

1 cup water

Blend together oil, sugar, cinnamon and nutmeg. Add orange juice. Add flour gradually until a smooth dough is formed. Knead gently; then add nuts. Pinch off small pieces of dough; shape into small oblong rolls. Place on greased baking sheet. Bake at 375° for 35 minutes, or until well browned. Mix together and heat honey and water. Dip warm cookies into syrup. (Do this quickly so they will not become soggy.) Place on platter and allow to cool. Keep syrup warm during dipping. Makes 6 to 7 dozen. *Lois Polales*

TEIGLACH (Honey Kisses)

3 eggs

2 tablespoons salad oil

2 cups unsifted flour

1 teaspoon baking powder

Pinch salt

2 cups honey

⅔ cup granulated or firmly packed brown sugar

2 teaspoons ground ginger

¾ cup coarsely chopped nuts

Beat eggs and oil together. Mix together flour, baking powder and salt. Gradually add to egg mixture, mixing well. Turn out on lightly floured surface and knead until smooth. Divide dough into 4 parts. Shape each part into ½-inch thick roll; cut rolls into ½-inch pieces. Combine honey, sugar and ginger. Bring to boiling over medium heat. Drop pieces of dough into honey mixture, a few at a time, so that honey continues to boil. When all pieces have been added, cover and cook over low heat for 20 minutes. Stir then cook for 5 minutes longer, or until pieces are golden brown. Stir in chopped nuts. Turn out onto *wet* board to cool, separating pieces with fork. Store in tightly covered container. Makes about 4 dozen. *Roz Weissman*

WALNUT DELIGHTS

1 cup soft butter

1 cup sifted confectioners' sugar

1 teaspoon vanilla

2¼ to 2¾ cups sifted flour

1 pound walnuts (or pecans), chopped medium fine

Cream butter thoroughly; gradually add sugar. Add vanilla; blend well. Add flour alternately with walnuts, beating well after each addition. Shape into crescents, rounds, ovals, etc. Place on very lightly greased baking sheet. Bake at 350° for 25 minutes. Cool. Roll in confectioners' sugar. Store in tight container. Makes 5 dozen. *Gloria Charash*

HAMENTASCHEN

4 cups sifted flour

½ cup granulated sugar

2 teaspoons baking powder

1 teaspoon grated orange rind

½ teaspoon salt

4 eggs

½ cup salad oil

¼ cup orange juice

FILLING:

1 pound prunes, chopped fine

½ cup crushed pineapple, drained

2 tablespoons apricot jam

½ cup granulated sugar

1 teaspoon cinnamon

1 teaspoon grated orange rind

½ cup finely chopped nuts

Sift together flour, sugar, baking powder, orange rind and salt. Make a well in center of dry ingredients; break eggs into well. Add oil and mix well. Gradually add orange juice, stirring until all is absorbed. Knead dough until mooth and shiny. Shape into balls about 1¼ inches in diameter. Roll out on well floured surface to ⅛-inch thickness. Cut into small rounds. Mix together ingredients for filling. Place small amount of filling on each round. Pinch edges together over filling. Place on greased baking sheet. Bake at 350° for about 30 minutes, or until nicely browned. Makes 5 to 6 dozen. *Sue Weissman*

FROSTY DATE BALLS

½ cup soft butter

⅓ cup sifted confectioners' sugar

1 tablespoon water

1 teaspoon vanilla

1¼ cups sifted flour

Pinch salt

⅔ cup dates, chopped

½ cup nuts, chopped

Cream butter and sugar. Stir in water and vanilla. Sift together flour and salt. Add to creamed mixture. blending well. Stir in dates and nuts. Shape into small balls. Place on greased baking sheet. Bake at 300° for 20 minutes. *Do not brown.* Cool; roll in confectioners' sugar. Makes 3 to 4 dozen.

Esther Weiner

FUDGE BALLS

1 cup soft butter	3 cups sifted flour
1 cup granulated sugar	½ cup cocoa
1 egg	1 egg white
1 teaspoon vanilla	1 cup ground nuts
¼ teaspoon salt	

Cream butter and sugar; add egg, vanilla and salt. Sift together flour and cocoa. Add to creamed mixture, mixing well. Shape into small balls; dip into egg white, then roll in nuts. Place on ungreased baking sheet. Bake at 350° for 12 to 15 minutes. Makes about 6 dozen. *Shirley Crane*

ROLLED COOKIES

MOCHA JUMBLES

4 tablespoons soft butter	2 squares unsweetened chocolate, melted
1 cup granulated sugar	1¾ cups sifted flour
1 egg, beaten	2 teaspoons baking powder
2 tablespoons cold strong coffee	½ teaspoon cinnamon

Cream butter; add sugar gradually. Add egg and coffee. Blend in chocolate. Mix well. Sift together flour, baking powder and cinnamon; add to chocolate mixture. Roll out on floured surface to ⅓-inch thickness. Cut with doughnut cutter; sprinkle with granulated sugar. Place on greased baking sheet. Bake at 350° for 10 to 12 minutes. Makes 2 dozen. *Robin Crystal*

SUGAR COOKIES

½ cup soft butter

½ cup granulated sugar

1 egg, beaten

2 tablespoons milk

1½ cups sifted flour

1 teaspoon baking powder

¼ teaspoon baking soda

Pinch salt

¼ cup granulated sugar

1 teaspoon cinnamon

Cream butter and ½ cup sugar. Add egg to milk. Sift together flour, baking powder, soda and salt. Add flour and milk mixtures alternately to sugar mixture; mix until smooth. Roll out on floured surface; cut with biscuit cutter. Sprinkle with combined ¼ cup sugar and cinnamon. Place on lightly greased baking sheets. Bake at 375° for 10 minutes. Makes about 4 dozen.   *Idelle Weisbrod*

APRICOT-PECAN STICKS

¾ cup soft butter

1 cup granulated sugar

2 eggs

1 teaspoon vanilla

3 cups sifted flour

Apricot preserves or jam

2 egg whites

Pinch salt

1 cup granulated sugar

1 tablespoon flour

1 cup pecan halves

Cream butter; add 1 cup sugar and eggs; beat until light. Add vanilla. Blend in 3 cups flour and mix well. Place on greased baking sheet; cover with waxed paper and roll out to ¼-inch thickness. Remove paper; spread dough with thin layer of preserves. Bake at 375° for 6 minutes. Beat egg white with salt until stiff; gradually add 1 cup sugar and 1 tablespoon flour. Fold in pecans. Spread on top of partially-baked dough. Return to oven and bake 15 minutes longer. Cool. Cut into sticks. Makes about 4 dozen.
Lenore Brittan

SOUR CREAM HORNS

1 cup soft butter

2 cups sifted flour

1 ice cold egg, separated

¾ cup sour cream

½ cup granulated sugar

½ teaspoon vanilla

¾ cup nuts, ground or finely chopped

Cream butter; cut in flour with pastry blender, a little at a time, until mixture resembles small peas. Add beaten egg yolk and sour cream. Blend into dough. Divide dough into 4 parts. Roll out each part into a round. Cut into wedges. Beat egg white until stiff, adding sugar gradually. Add vanilla. Spread meringue on wedges; sprinkle with nuts. Roll up wedges into horns and place on greased baking sheet. Bake at 350° for 15 minutes, or until lightly browned. Makes about 3 dozen.   *Mrs. A. Pearlman*

POPPY SEED COOKIES

⅓ cup margarine	½ cup sour cream
¼ cup salad oil	Juice of ½ orange
1 cup granulated sugar	4 cups sifted flour
2 eggs	3 teaspoons baking powder
1 cup poppy seeds	

Cream margarine, oil and sugar. Mix in eggs, poppy seeds, sour cream and orange juice. Sift together flour and baking powder. Add enough flour to creamed mixture to make dough easy to handle but not stiff. Roll out on floured surface to ¼-inch thickness and cut with cookie cutter. Place on greased baking sheets. Bake at 375° for 10 minutes. Makes about 6 dozen.
Dee Stein

❖❖❖

Most cookie doughs freeze well. Pack dough in freezer containers; freeze. When ready to use, transfer dough to refrigerator until it becomes easy to handle—roll out and bake as usual.

❖❖❖

POPPY SEED PASTRIES

½ cup butter	1 cup sour cream
½ cup margarine	1 can poppy seed filling
2 cups sifted flour	

Cut butter and margarine into flour with pastry blender. Add sour cream. Shape pastry into a ball and chill in refrigerator for 1 hour. Divide pastry into 4 parts. Roll out each part into thin circle on floured surface. Cut each circle into 12 wedges. Place 1 teaspoon poppy seed filling on each wedge and roll to points. Place on ungreased baking sheet. Bake at 375° for 25 minutes. Makes 4 dozen.   *Rose Krichiver*

BUTTER DIPS

⅓ cup butter

2¼ cups sifted flour

3½ teaspoons baking powder

1 tablespoon granulated sugar

1½ teaspoons salt

1 cup milk

Heat oven to 450°. Place butter in 13x9x2-inch pan. Melt in oven. Sift together flour, baking powder, sugar and salt into large mixing bowl. Add milk. Stir slowly with fork just until dough clings together. Turn out on floured surface. Knead lightly 10 times; roll out to 12x8-inch rectangle ½ inch thick. Cut dough in half lengthwise, then crosswise into 16 to 18 strips. Dip each strip into melted butter. Place close together in two rows in pan. Bake at 450° for 15 to 20 minutes, or until golden brown. Makes 32 strips.

Dolores J. Bandalin

MANDEL BRATE

3 eggs

¾ cup granulated sugar

¾ cup melted shortening

1 teaspoon vanilla

½ teaspoon salt

1½ teaspoons baking powder

½ cup slivered almonds

½ cup raisins (optional)

2½ cups sifted flour

¼ cup granulated sugar

2 teaspoons cinnamon

Mix together all ingredients, except ¼ cup sugar and cinnamon, in order listed with electric mixer or by hand. Blend to make a thick, smooth dough. Roll out on floured surface into long strips. Place on greased baking sheet. Combine ¼ cup sugar and cinnamon; sprinkle over dough. Bake at 350° for 25 to 30 minutes, or until light brown. Remove, cut into slices and return to oven for 5 minutes. Makes 4 to 5 dozen.

Lill Reizner

PINK ICEBERGS

½ cup soft butter

½ cup plus 2 tablespoons granulated sugar

1 egg yolk

1 cup sifted flour

½ teaspoon baking powder

TOPPING:

1 cup ground pecans or walnuts

4 to 5 tablespoons raspberry jam

ICING:

2 cups sifted confectioners' sugar

3 tablespoons lemon juice

Cream butter, granulated sugar and egg yolk until light and fluffy. Sift together flour and baking powder; add to sugar mixture; beat until blended. Turn out on waxed paper and press into a ball. Chill slightly. Roll out on floured surface to about ¼-inch thickness. Cut into rounds about ¾-inch in diameter, or use small fancy cutters. Place on ungreased baking sheets. Bake at 350° for about 10 minutes, or until delicately browned. Cool. Mix nuts and jam. Place small mound of mixture on each cookie. Mix confectioners' sugar and lemon juice. Tint delicate pink with red food coloring. Drizzle icing over jam. Makes about 3 dozen. *Alice B. Weitzenfeld*

REFRIGERATOR COOKIES

CHOCOLATE SHOT COOKIES

1 cup soft butter	½ teaspoon baking soda
1 cup sifted confectioners' sugar	1 cup quick-cooking rolled oats
2 teaspoons vanilla	2 bottles chocolate shot (about ½ cup)
1½ cups sifted flour	

Cream butter; add sugar gradually, creaming until fluffy. Add vanilla. Sift together flour and baking soda; mix in rolled oats. Add to creamed mixture, mixing thoroughly. Chill dough in refrigerator for several hours. Shape dough into rolls about 1½ inches in diameter. Pour chocolate shot onto waxed paper. Coat rolls in chocolate shot and cut into slices ⅜-inch thick. Place on ungreased baking sheet. Bake at 325° for 25 to 30 minutes. Makes 3 to 4 dozen. *Mabel Raffay*

CHEESE COOKIES

1 8-oz. package cream cheese	1½ cups sifted flour
1 cup butter	2 egg whites
2 egg yolks	Granulated sugar

Combine cream cheese and butter, creaming well. Add egg yolks. Blend in flour and mix well. Chill in refrigerator overnight. Roll out on lightly floured surface as thin as possible and cut with cookie cutter (or shape chilled dough into rolls and slice thin). Spread with stiffly beaten egg whites; sprinkle with sugar. Place on ungreased baking sheets. Bake at 425° for 20 minutes. Makes 5 dozen. *Irene Silberman*

KICHEL BUTTERFLIES

2 eggs	1 teaspoon salt
3 tablespoons milk	2 tablespoons melted butter
2 tablespoons granulated sugar	1 teaspoon vanilla
Pinch salt	1 teaspoon lemon juice
2½ cups sifted flour	

Beat eggs well; add milk, sugar and pinch salt; continue beating. Gradually add flour, 1 teaspoon salt, butter, vanilla and lemon juice, using only enough flour to make a soft dough that will roll easily. Mix well. Roll out dough as thin as possible. Cut into rectangles, squares, diamonds, etc., with a knife. Crimp, or twist with fingers into various shapes. Deep fry in melted shortening at 360° to 370° for about 60 seconds, turning as soon as browned on one side. Fry only 5 or 6 at a time for even browning. Drain on absorbent paper. Makes about 6 dozen.   *Jenny Frost*

THREE-LAYER COOKIE BARS

½ cup butter	½ cup chopped nuts
¼ cup granulated sugar	½ cup soft butter
⅓ cup cocoa	3 tablespoons milk
1 teaspoon vanilla	2 tablespoons vanilla pudding mix
1 egg, slightly beaten	2 cups sifted confectioners' sugar
2 cups graham cracker crumbs	⅔ cup semi-sweet chocolate pieces
1 cup grated coconut	1 tablespoon butter

Combine ½ cup butter, granulated sugar, cocoa and vanilla in top of double boiler. Cook until blended. Add egg and continue cooking for 5 minutes longer, stirring constantly. Add crumbs, coconut and nuts. Press into 9x9x2-inch pan. Let stand for 15 minutes. Meanwhile, cream soft butter until light and fluffy. Combine milk and pudding mix. Add to butter and mix thoroughly. Add confectioners' sugar gradually and beat until smooth. Spread over first layer in pan. Let stand for 15 minutes or until firm. Melt chocolate pieces and 1 tablespoon butter in top of double boiler over hot, *not boiling,* water; cool. Spread over second layer. Cut into bars. Makes about 3 dozen.   *Alice B. Weitzenfeld*

CANDIES
AND
CONFECTIONS

KRISPY DELIGHTS

2 6-oz. packages semi-sweet chocolate pieces

2 cups honey

1 teaspoon vanilla

1 package crisp rice cereal

1 cup ground or chopped nuts

Melt chocolate pieces and honey in top of double boiler over hot, *not boiling,* water. Add vanilla; mix well. Place rice cereal in large bowl; add chocolate mixture and toss until all is absorbed. Press mixture into greased 15½x10½x 1-inch (jelly roll) pan. Sprinkle ground nuts over top. Allow to set before cutting into squares. Makes about 6 dozen.   *Rose Kahn*

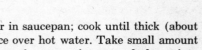

GINGER CANDY

1 cup granulated sugar

½ cup honey

½ cup water

1 tablespoon ground ginger

1½ cups matzo meal

Combine sugar, honey, water and ginger in saucepan; cook until thick (about 3 minutes). Remove from heat and place over hot water. Take small amount of matzo meal in hands; pull off pieces of sugar mixture and shape into rolls, coating well with meal.   *Stella Ellyne*

Make candy on a cool, dry day for best results.

COCONUT CREAM CHEESE BONBONS

1 3-oz. package cream cheese

¼ teaspoon vanilla

Pinch salt

2½ cups sifted confectioners' sugar

Shredded coconut

Combine cream cheese, vanilla and salt; blend until smooth. Gradually add sugar, creaming well after each addition. Shape into small balls, using 1 teaspoonful of mixture for each. Roll in coconut; chill in refrigerator until firm. Makes about 2½ dozen.   *Poppy Brooks*

BOURBON BALLS

2½ cups fine vanilla wafer crumbs

1 cup sifted confectioners' sugar

2 tablespoons cocoa

1 cup chopped nuts

¼ cup bourbon, rum or brandy

3 tablespoons light corn syrup

Combine all ingredients in order listed, mixing well. Shape into small balls. Dip in confectioners' sugar. Makes about 3 dozen.   *Mollie Appelman*

EASY ENGLISH TOFFEE

1 cup granulated sugar

1 cup butter

3 tablespoons water

1 teaspoon vanilla

5 small sweet chocolate bars

¾ cup chopped pecans

Combine sugar, butter and water in saucepan; cook over medium heat for 10 minutes, or until brown, stirring constantly. Remove from heat; add vanilla. Pour in thin layer into greased 13x9x2-inch pan. Place chocolate bars on hot mixture; spread evenly. While still warm, sprinkle nuts over top. Chill in refrigerator until firm. Break into pieces.   *Elnora Weissbuch*

CANDIED ORANGE PEEL

Peel of 4 oranges, cut into lengthwise
   pieces

Cold water

1 cup granulated sugar

½ cup water

2 tablespoons light corn syrup

Granulated sugar (or dipping chocolate)

Place peel in saucepan with enough cold water to cover. Bring quickly to boiling; reduce heat. Simmer until peel is soft. Drain; scrape off white part of peel with spoon (this comes off very easily). Cut peel into thin strips with scissors. Combine sugar, water and corn syrup in saucepan; add peel and cook slowly until peel is clear. Drain; place peel on greased platter to cool. Roll in granulated sugar, or dip in melted chocolate and place on waxed paper.

SHORT-CUT FUDGE

1 12-oz. package semi-sweet chocolate pieces	1 tablespoon water
	1 teaspoon vanilla
⅔ cup sweetened condensed milk	1 cup chopped nuts

Melt chocolate pieces in top of double boiler over hot, *not boiling,* water Remove from heat; stir in milk, water, vanilla and nuts, mixing until smooth. Turn into lightly greased 10x5x3-inch pan. Cool until firm. Makes about 1¼ pounds.   *Lois Payne*

CHOCOLATE CLUSTERS

1 6-oz. package semi-sweet chocolate pieces	1 cup raisins
	1 cup peanuts or other nuts
¼ cup light corn syrup	
1 tablespoon water	

Combine chocolate pieces, corn syrup and water. Melt in top of double boiler over hot, *not boiling,* water. Remove from heat; divide mixture into 2 parts. Stir raisins in one part, nuts into remainder. Drop by teaspoonfuls onto lightly greased baking sheet. Cool until firm. Makes 3 dozen.
                                                          Lois Payne

FUDGED NUTS

1 package quick fudge mix	1¼ cups nut halves (walnuts or pecans)

Prepare fudge according to directions on package. When mixture is glossy, pour a little into a cup; keep remainder hot over *hot* water. Dip nuts, a few at a time, into fudge mix in cup. If mixture in cup hardens during dipping process, return to hot mixture and start again. Place nuts on waxed paper or greased baking sheet until hardened.   *Beverly Fine*

CANDIED BRAZIL NUTS

½ cup firmly packed brown sugar

¼ cup granulated sugar

¼ cup light cream

1 teaspoon vanilla

½ teaspoon almond extract

2 cups whole Brazil nuts

Combine sugars and cream; cook over low heat to soft-ball stage (240° on candy thermometer). Remove mixture from heat; add vanilla and almond extract. Add nuts; stir until nuts are completely coated with mixture. Turn out on greased baking sheet. Separate nuts with 2 forks while still warm.

Ethel Feigon

GLACÉ NUTS

2 cups granulated sugar

1 cup water

½ teaspoon cream of tartar

1 to 1½ cups whole pecans or Brazil nuts

Combine sugar, water and cream of tartar; cook until syrup becomes yellow (310° on candy thermometer). Remove from heat and place in pan of hot water. Using wooden pick, dip each nut into syrup, coating thoroughly. Work quickly. Place nuts on waxed paper or greased platter to cool. Remove picks before serving.

Ellen Sigal

SPICED NUTS

1 cup granulated sugar

¼ cup boiling water

¼ teaspoon nutmeg

¼ teaspoon cream of tartar

1 teaspoon vanilla

1½ cups nut halves (walnuts or pecans)

Combine sugar, water, nutmeg and cream of tartar; cook to firm-ball stage (246° on candy thermometer). Remove from heat; add vanilla. Add nut halves, stirring until nuts are well coated with mixture. Turn out on greased baking sheet. Using 2 forks, quickly separate any nuts that are stuck together. ·

Ethel Feigon

Use your candy thermometer—it is an accurate guide to the correct cooking stage in candy-making.

BEVERAGES

Cocktail is a
stimulating liquor,
composed of spirits
of any kind, sugar,
water and bitters.

In the *New York Balance*
May 13; 1806

COFFEE AND TEA

PARTY ICED COFFEE

3 cups coffee

3 cups double-strength coffee

Confectioners' sugar

Light cream

Whipped cream

Pour 3 cups coffee into ice-cube tray; freeze. Place 4 or 5 coffee ice cubes in each 10-oz. glass. Fill glass with double-strength coffee. Season as desired with sugar and cream. Stir. Top with dab of whipped cream. Makes 4 servings.

ICED FRUIT TEA

4 tablespoons tea

8 cups boiling water

1 cup granulated sugar

Juice of 2 lemons

Juice of 1 orange

Juice of 1 lime

Steep tea in boiling water for 5 minutes. Strain and chill in refrigerator. Dissolve sugar in combined juices; chill. Mix tea and juices together. Place ice cubes in tall 10-oz. glasses; pour chilled tea over ice. Makes about 8 servings. *Alice B. Weitzenfeld*

TALL DRINKS

ORANGE COOLER

2 cups fresh or frozen orange juice

1 pint orange sherbet

2 bottles lemon-lime carbonated
beverage

3 ounces vodka or gin

Maraschino cherries

Beat orange juice and sherbet together with 1 cup cracked ice. Pour into
tall 10-oz. glasses. Add lemon-lime beverage and vodka. Stir. Garnish with
cherries. Makes 4 servings. *Robin Crystal*

ORANGE GROVE

1½ ounces fresh or frozen orange juice

1½ ounces dry gin

Quinine water, chilled

Sprig of mint

1 orange slice

Nutmeg

Place 4 to 6 ice cubes in tall 10 or 12-oz. glass. Add orange juice and gin.
Fill with quinine water; stir. Garnish with mint, orange slice and nutmeg.
Makes 1 serving. *Roslyn Flegel*

HAWAIIAN JOY

1 No. 2 can pineapple juice

1 egg white, beaten

2 tablespoons confectioners' sugar

1½ ounces dry gin

1 teaspoon maraschino cherry juice

1 dozen ice cubes

Mix all ingredients; stir until ice cubes begin to melt. Shake until frothy.
Serve at once in 6-oz. glasses. Makes 4 servings. *Elaine Goldberg*

*Remember—a jigger usually equals 1½ ounces, but since some
jiggers are more (or less), all liquor measurements in this section
have been given in ounces.*

ORANGE MINT FREEZE

1 cup granulated sugar	½ cup grated orange rind
2½ cups water	1 cup orange juice
1 cup light corn syrup	1 cup mint leaves, well washed
1½ cups lemon or lime juice	Sparkling or iced water

Dissolve sugar in water; add corn syrup and boil for 10 minutes. Pour hot syrup over combined lemon juice, orange rind and juice and mint leaves. Cover and let stand 1 hour. Strain. Fill tall 10-oz. glasses with crushed ice. Pour ⅓ cup juice mixture in each glass; fill with sparkling water. Stir. Makes 10 to 12 servings.   *Cele Malvin*

FRUIT FIZZ

3 medium oranges	¾ cup granulated sugar
3 medium lemons	1 pint ginger ale, chilled

Squeeze oranges and lemons; remove seeds, but do not strain juice. Add sugar and stir until dissolved. Add ginger ale. Place 4 ice cubes in tall 8 or 10-oz. glasses. Pour mixture over ice and serve immediately. Makes 4 servings.   *Jean Russell*

CARUMBUS

2 ounces rum	2 drops vanilla
4½ ounces pineapple juice	Sparkling water, chilled

Pour rum over ice cubes in tall 10-oz. glass. Add pineapple juice and vanilla. Stir; fill glass with sparkling water. Makes 1 serving.

GIN COOLER

1½ ounces dry gin	1 cup pineapple juice
1 heaping tablespoon lime sherbet	Sprig of mint

Blend gin, sherbet and pineapple juice in blender. Place 4 to 6 ice cubes in tall 10 or 12-oz. glass. Pour mixture over cubes. Garnish with mint. Makes 1 serving.

POLYNESIAN PUNCH

1½ cups pineapple juice

½ cup orange juice

Juice of 4 lemons

5 ounces cognac

Grenadine to taste

Combine all ingredients and shake with 1½ cupfuls finely crushed ice. Pour into tall 10-oz. glasses. Makes 4 servings.

RASPBERRY MINT COOLER

½ cup fresh mint leaves

¼ cup granulated sugar

1 cup boiling water

1 10-oz. package frozen raspberries

1 6-oz. can frozen pink lemonade concentrate

2 cups iced water

Combine mint, sugar and boiling water. Let stand for 5 minutes. Add raspberries and lemonade; stir until melted. Strain into pitcher half full with crushed ice or ice cubes. Add iced water. Stir. Serve in tall glasses; garnish with mint leaves and raspberries. Makes about 4 servings. *Sandy Ornstein*

COCKTAILS

ORANGE SHERBET COCKTAIL

½ cup dry white wine

½ cup bourbon

1 pint orange sherbet

1 pint ginger ale, chilled

Combine all ingredients. Beat until sherbet has melted. Pour into cocktail glasses. Serve immediately. Makes about 10 servings. *Norma Kramer*

SCARLETT O'HARA

1½ ounces Southern Comfort

½ ounce fresh lime juice

1 ounce cranberry juice (or ½ ounce grenadine)

Shake well with finely crushed ice; pour into cocktail glass and serve. Makes 1 serving.

BRANDY ALEXANDER

3 ounces cream

1½ ounces creme de cocoa

3 ounces brandy

Nutmeg

Combine all ingredients with about 1 cupful crushed ice. Shake well. Pour into cocktail glasses. Sprinkle nutmeg over top. Makes 2 servings.

Mrs. Julius Lackner

❖❖❖❖❖❖❖❖❖❖❖❖❖❖❖❖❖❖❖❖❖❖❖❖❖❖❖❖❖❖❖❖❖❖❖❖❖

To frost cocktail glasses, dip rims ¼ inch into lemon juice or slightly beaten egg whites, then into granulated sugar. Set aside to dry until serving time.

❖❖❖❖❖❖❖❖❖❖❖❖❖❖❖❖❖❖❖❖❖❖❖❖❖❖❖❖❖❖❖❖❖❖❖❖❖

FROSTED ALEXANDER

1½ ounces dry gin

2 heaping tablespoons vanilla ice cream

½ teaspoon vanilla

Combine gin, vanilla and ice cream with ½ cup cracked ice. Mix on blender. Serve in cocktail glass. Makes 1 serving.

OMAR'S DELIGHT

1½ ounces Southern Comfort

Dash curacao (or 1½ teaspoons orange juice)

Juice of ½ lime

½ teaspoon granulated sugar

1½ teaspoons lemon juice

Combine all ingredients and shake well with crushed ice. Pour into cocktail glass and serve. Makes 1 serving.

ORANGE BLOSSOM

3¾ ounces orange juice

1 tablespoon granulated sugar

½ ounce lime juice

6¾ ounces dry gin

Shake with cracked ice. Strain into cocktail glasses. Garnish with ½ orange slice, if desired. Makes 4 servings.

SAMOAN FOG CUTTER

2 ounces lemon juice	½ ounce dry gin
1 ounce orange juice	½ ounce brandy
1½ ounces Puerto Rico rum	½ ounce simple syrup

Combine all ingredients and shake with 1 cupful crushed ice. Pour into large brandy snifter; float dry sherry on top. Place 2 short straws in snifter. Makes 2 servings.

HAWAIIAN DAIQUIRI

2 canned pineapple slices	Juice of 1 lime
3 ounces pineapple juice	4½ ounces rum

Measure into blender container 2 champagne glassfuls crushed ice. Add all ingredients. Blend for 2 minutes. Pour into champagne glasses and serve at once. Makes 3 to 4 servings.

RASPBERRY SHRUB

1 10-oz. package frozen raspberries	½ cup lemon juice
1 cup granulated sugar	2 cups iced water
1 cup water	½ pint raspberry sherbet

Place raspberries, sugar and water in saucepan; stir and simmer for 8 to 10 minutes. Put through fine sieve, rubbing through all pulp. Cover and chill in refrigerator. Just before serving, add lemon juice and iced water. Pour into slender stemmed glasses. Float small scoop raspberry sherbet in each glass. Makes 6 to 8 servings.   *Alma E. Perlish*

BLACKBERRY FRAPPÉ

1½ ounces blackberry liqueur	1 pint vanilla ice cream, slightly softened
1½ ounces bourbon	1 quart ginger ale, chilled

Combine all ingredients in blender container; blend. Serve immediately in champagne glasses. Makes 12 to 16 servings.

AMERICAN BEAUTY PUNCH

3 cups fresh orange juice

1 cup grenadine

1 fifth sauterne, rhine or other white table wine, chilled

1 quart ginger ale, chilled

Place block of ice or ice cubes in punch bowl. Pour in all ingredients; stir to combine. Makes about 24 4-oz. servings.

BRIDE'S BOWL

½ fresh pineapple, cut in chunks

2 cups pineapple juice

1 cup lemon juice

½ cup simple syrup

1½ fifths golden Puerto Rico rum

2 quarts sparkling water, chilled

1 pint hulled, washed strawberries, sliced

Place pineapple in large pitcher with pineapple juice, lemon juice, simple syrup and rum. Chill in refrigerator for at least 2 hours. Pour over block of ice in punch bowl. Add sparkling water and strawberries. Makes about 40 4-oz. servings.

HAWAIIAN PUNCH

3 cups granulated sugar

5 cups orange juice, chilled

2½ cups cold water

2¼ cups pineapple juice, chilled

2 cups lemon juice, chilled

1 quart champagne or ginger ale, chilled

Fresh berries, or lemon or orange slices

Combine ingredients in punch bowl with block of ice or ice cubes. Stir. Garnish with berries. Makes 40 to 50 4-oz. servings.   *Sylvia J. Rosenstein*

For simple syrup to sweeten punch or mixed drinks, combine 1 part water with 2 parts granulated sugar and boil for 5 minutes. Store in bottle in refrigerator.

SPICED TEA PUNCH

½ cup granulated sugar

½ cup water

1 teaspoon lemon juice or rind

2 teaspoons orange rind

2 sticks cinnamon

¼ cup orange juice

¼ cup pineapple juice

2 tablespoons lemon juice

3 tablespoons tea

3 cups boiling water

Combine sugar, water, 1 teaspoon lemon juice, orange rind and cinnamon sticks. Boil for 5 minutes; remove and discard cinnamon sticks. Add orange juice, pineapple juice, 2 tablespoons lemon juice. Keep mixture hot, but do not boil. Steep tea in boiling water for 5 minutes. Add to juice mixture. Serve hot in demitasse or punch cups. Makes 8 to 10 servings.

Louise Merkin

SURE-BET PUNCH

1 quart orange sherbet

1 pint raspberry sherbet

1 No. 3 can pineapple juice, chilled

4 quarts ginger ale, chilled

Mix all ingredients together in punch bowl. Ladle into punch cups. Makes about 50 4-oz. servings.

Edith Lirtzman

FESTIVE PARTY PUNCH

1 quart vanilla ice cream, slightly softened

1 quart Malaga or Concord grape wine, chilled

Beat ice cream on electric mixer until creamy. Gradually add wine. Ladle at once into punch cups. Or chill in refrigerator until ready to serve. If mixture thickens upon standing, beat again. Makes about 16 4-oz. servings.

Mrs. Maurice Klotz

JAMAICA PUNCH

2 quarts coffee, chilled

½ cup Jamaica rum

2 quarts vanilla ice cream

Combine coffee, rum and vanilla ice cream in chilled punch bowl. Stir until most of ice cream is blended in. Ladle into punch cups while bits of ice cream are still floating. Makes about 16 4-oz. servings.

EGGNOG

6 egg yolks	2 cups milk
¾ cup granulated sugar	2 cups bourbon
6 egg whites	1 ounce Jamaica rum
2 cups cream	Nutmeg

Beat egg yolks, adding ½ cup sugar gradually, until frothy. Beat egg whites until stiff, adding remaining sugar gradually. Fold egg whites into egg yolk mixture. Stir in cream and milk. Add bourbon and rum. Stir. Chill in refrigerator until ready to serve. Ladle into punch cups. Sprinkle nutmeg on top. Makes about 24 servings.

EGGNOG DE LUXE

6 egg yolks	3 egg whites
1 cup sifted confectioners' sugar	Pinch salt
2 cups dark rum (or part rum, part brandy)	2 cups heavy cream, whipped
2 cups milk	Nutmeg

Beat egg yolks until light and fluffy; add sugar gradually, beating constantly. Slowly stir in rum and milk. Beat egg whites with salt until stiff. Fold into egg yolk mixture. Fold in whipped cream. Serve in punch cups with sprinkle of nutmeg on top. Makes about 24 servings.   *Marian Peterman*

HOT BUTTERED RUM

7 ounces apple cider	1 teaspoon butter
2¼ ounces dark rum	Cinnamon stick

Heat apple cider. Pour into mug; add rum and butter. Stir with cinnamon stick. Makes 1 serving.

MENUS
FOR EVERYDAY
AND
SPECIAL OCCASIONS

My wife had got ready a very fine dinner—viz., a dish
of marrow-bones; a leg of mutton; a loin of veal; a
dish of fowl; three pullets and two dozen of larks all in
a dish; a great tart, a neat's tongue, a dish of anchovies, a dish of prawns, and cheese.   Samuel Pepys (1660)

*Mrs. Pepys menu is not recommended for everyday living, but careful
planning will produce results of equal magnitude for you. Planning a meal—
whether it be for family or friends, for special occasion or everyday—
demands attention to detail. The menu need not be composed of complicated
or expensive dishes to be successful. By following some time-tested pointers,
every cook can create menus that will be sure to delight: 1. Vary textures
and shapes (crisp and creamy; round and small). 2. Choose harmonizing
colors; add gay garnishes. 3. Select products in season for nutrition, flavor
and economy. 4. Avoid repetition of a food or flavor in more than one dish
or course of a meal. 5. Feature only one dish with a distinctive flavor. And
when you entertain . . . plan all steps ahead; choose a simple menu and
avoid dishes that require last minute fussing to leave you free for hostess
duties; concentrate your efforts on a background that will dramatize the
menu—tablecloth, dishes and centerpiece should combine to enhance, not
overpower, the menu and create a festive mood.*

** * *. BETTER BRUNCHES * * * **

BROILED HALVES OF GRAPEFRUIT AU KIRSCH
POACHED EGGS ON TOAST ROUNDS
MIXED VEGETABLES MORNAY, *page 156*
CHERRY-CRANBERRY RELISH, *page 198*
COFFEE PUFFS, *page 50*
BEVERAGE

•

SHERRIED CHICKEN LIVERS, *page 96*
WILD RICE RING, *page 141*

RHUBARB ICE   POPOVERS, *page 43*
COFFEE

RASPBERRY SHRUB, *page 300*

FISH BAKED IN PAPER, *page 112*   AMANDINE SAUCE

POTATOES DELICIOUS, *page 158*

RELISH PLATE   SYLVIA'S NUT BREAD, *page 46*

BEVERAGE

•

SUGARED STRAWBERRIES AND FRESH PINEAPPLE SPEARS

CRAB PUFFS, *page 122*

BUTTERED ASPARAGUS TIPS   CARROT CURLS AND RADISH ROSES

SCHNECKEN, *page 52*

BEVERAGE

`.·.·.*'SPECIALLY FOR THE GIRLS `.·.·.

CHICKEN KIEV, *page 86*

SPINACH SUPREME, *page 163*

FRESH FRUIT SALAD   HONEY FRENCH DRESSING, *page 193*

CRESCENTS, *page 51*

RAINBOW SNOWBALL CAKE, *page 249*

COFFEE

•

ARTICHOKE AND SEA-FOOD CASSEROLE, *page 118*

LEMON-BUTTERED CARROTS   CHERRY WINE MOLD, *page 179*

BAKING POWDER BISCUITS, *page 45*

RUM CHIFFON PIE, *page 228*

BEVERAGE

•

ASPARAGUS OMELET, *page 144*

GRILLED TOMATO HALVES   CRISP VEGETABLE RELISHES

MELBA TOAST ROUNDS

FRUIT COMPOTE SUPREME, *page 235*

BEVERAGE

•

FROZEN FRUIT SALAD, *page 176*, ON CURLY ENDIVE

COFFEE OR TEA

CANDIED ORANGE PEEL, *page 292*   EASY ENGLISH TOFFEE, *page 292*

•

SPICED TEA PUNCH, *page 302*, OR PARTY ICED COFFEE, *page 295*

MACAROONS, *page 280*   SOUR CREAM HORNS, *page 286*

FUDGE BALLS, *page 285*

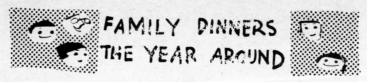

FAMILY DINNERS THE YEAR AROUND

FALL

CHICKEN CONTINENTAL, *page 90*
CHOW-MEIN NOODLES
ORANGE FROTH MOLD, *page 180* • DINNER ROLLS
CARAMEL WALNUT UPSIDE-DOWN CAKE, *page 215*
BEVERAGE

•

STUFFED FLANK STEAK
GREEN BEANS À LA DILL, *page 151*
BAKED ACORN SQUASH, *page 166*
FESTIVE CRANBERRY MOLD, *page 178* BRAN MUFFINS
APRICOT STRUDEL, *page 263*
BEVERAGE

•

VEAL BIRDS
BROCCOLI NEW ORLEANS, *page 151* SWEET POTATO BALLS, *page 161*
WALDORF SALAD CLOVERLEAF ROLLS
MOCHA LOG, *page 209*
BEVERAGE

•

ROUND STEAK ROLL-UPS, *page 58*
LIMA BEAN CASSEROLE, *page 149*
GRAPEFRUIT AND ORANGE SECTIONS FRENCH DRESSING, *page 194*
HARD ROLLS
MELT-IN-YOUR-MOUTH POUND CAKE, *page 216*
BEVERAGE

WINTER

VIENNESE POT ROAST, *page 63*
POTATO KUGEL, *page 158*
GRAPEFRUIT AND AVOCADO SALAD ON CRISP GREENS
SESAME SEED ROLLS
FILBERT TORTE, *page 258*
BEVERAGE

GLAZED DUCKLING HAWAIIAN, *page 101*
BRUSSELS SPROUTS   BUTTERED RICE
LETTUCE WEDGES WITH THOUSAND ISLAND DRESSING
ORANGE MUFFINS, *page 44*
BRANDIED APRICOT PIE, *page 222*
BEVERAGE

•

SOUP GARNI À LA NEW ORLEANS, *page 33*
CHOW-LOONG-HAR, *page 134*
TOMATO ASPIC RING, *page 186*   ASSORTED HARD ROLLS
HEAVENLY BANANAS, *page 235*
HOT TEA

•

CHICKEN JUBILEE, *page 90*
BUTTERED GREEN BEANS   CARROT RING, *page 153*
CUCUMBER-COTTAGE CHEESE MOLD, *page 187*
PARKER HOUSE ROLLS
DRIED APPLE PIE, *page 221*
BEVERAGE

SPRING

LEG OF LAMB, *page 80*
FRESH ASPARAGUS WITH HOLLANDAISE SAUCE
BROWNED NEW POTATOES
GARDEN SALAD MOLD, *page 189*   ORANGE MUFFINS, *page 44*
STRAWBERRIES ROMANOFF, *page 237*
COFFEE

•

LOX SOUFFLE, *page 112*
BUTTERED PEAS AND CARROTS   WATERMELON PICKLES
PINEAPPLE-CUCUMBER RING, *page 180*
COFFEE CRUNCHIES, *page 278*
BEVERAGE

•

COLD SLICED ROAST BEEF
CREAMED NEW POTATOES
TOSSED VEGETABLE SALAD   SPICED PEACHES, *page 198*
POPPY SEED ROLLS
BLUEBERRY TARTS, *page 232*
BEVERAGE

MINUTE STEAKS
ASPARAGUS AU GRATIN, *page 149*   BROILED TOMATOES
PINEAPPLE-VEGETABLE MOLD, *page 180*
ORANGE SPONGECAKE, *page 206*
BEVERAGE

SUMMER

SCRAMBLED EGGS DE LUXE, *page 143*
BEEF SAUSAGE LINKS   FRUIT CHILI SAUCE, *page 196*
POTATO BALLS, *page 159*   MUFFINS
LEMON SHERBET, *page 252*
ICED BEVERAGE

•

SPICED CHICKEN, *page 86*
RELISH PLATE   CORN-ON-THE-COB
BROWN 'N' SERVE ROLLS
HONEYDEW PARFAIT, *page 234*
BEVERAGE

•

FISH DINNER, *page 110*
PERFECTION SALAD   SLICED TOMATOES
HOT ROLLS
FRESH PEACH KUCHEN, *page 45*
BEVERAGE

•

JELLIED CONSOMME
LONDON BROIL, *page 58*
SOUR CREAM POTATO SALAD, *page 168*
FRESH PEAS   WHOLE WHEAT ROLLS
BANANA FREEZE, *page 250*
CHOCOLATE CINNAMON BARS, *page, 275*
BEVERAGE

THE BOUNTIFUL BUFFET

REAL LASAGNA, *page 138*
TOSSED GREEN SALAD   ITALIAN DRESSING, *page 194*
SALT STICKS
BISCUIT TORTONI, *page 238*
CAFFÉ EXPRESSO

SUPREME MEAT BALLS, *page 70*
ROAST TURKEY
GREEN BEANS FAR EAST, *page 150*
BRANDIED SWEET POTATOES, *page 162*
BEET RING, *page 188*, FILLED WITH VEGETABLE STICKS
ASSORTED ROLLS   BUTTER BALLS
FRUITY TOOT, *page 237*
COFFEE

•

BEEF STROGANOFF, *page 59*, WITH RICE
SPINACH SURPRISE SALAD, *page 167*
REFRIGERATOR ROLLS, *page 48*
PINEAPPLE AND GRAPES IN KIRSCH, *page 236*
BEVERAGE

•

ROAST BEEF
NOODLES ROMANOFF, *page 136*
FRESH FRUIT PLATTER   INDIVIDUAL TOMATO ASPICS
CRESCENTS, *page 51*
CONTINENTAL CREAM PUFFS, *page 250*
COFFEE

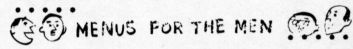

MENUS FOR THE MEN

ORANGE SHERBET COCKTAIL, *page 298*
BROILED STUFFED LAMB CHOPS, *page 80*
ASPARAGUS WITH LEMON-BUTTER SAUCE
TWICE-BAKED POTATOES
TOMATO SALAD   CREAMY ROQUEFORT DRESSING, *page 192*
CREAMY ROQUEFORT DRESSING, *page 192*
PARKER HOUSE ROLLS
MYSTERY PIE, *page 229*
BEVERAGE

•

GOLDEN ROCK CORNISH HENS WITH HERB BUTTER, *page 102*
BROCCOLI SPEARS   WILD RICE-MUSHROOM STUFFING, *page 106*
TOSSED GREEN SALAD WITH LEMON-BASE FRENCH DRESSING
DINNER ROLLS
GRAPEFRUIT BAKED ALASKA, *page 252*
BEVERAGE

COCKTAILS

OATMEAL PUFFS, *page 24*   PETITE CABBAGE ROLLS, *page 23*
BROILED BEEF TENDERLOIN WITH MUSHROOM SAUCE, *page 57*
FRENCH-STYLE GREEN BEANS   POTATO PUDDING, *page 158*
GINGER ALE FRUIT SALAD, *page 178*
DINNER ROLLS
MOCHA TORTE, *page 257*
COFFEE

•

ST. CLAIR ROQUEFORT SALAD, *page 168*
BREAD-WITH-A-FLAVOR, *page 56*
FRESH FRUIT   PUDDIN' COOKIES, *page 281*
ICED TEA

 PASSOVER MENUS

BREAKFASTS

STEWED PRUNES OR APRICOTS   BANANAS OR STRAWBERRIES IN CREAM
POPOVERS, *page 43*   FLUFFY BREAKFAST PANCAKES, *page 146*
HONEY AND COTTAGE CHEESE   PRESERVES
BEVERAGE   BEVERAGE

LUNCHEONS

FRUIT CUP   CHICKEN SALAD
BAKED, BROILED OR FRIED FISH   LETTUCE AND TOMATOES
TOSSED GREEN SALAD   POTATO KUGELACH
WINE CAKE, *page 207*   LEMON MERINGUE PIE, *page 226*
BEVERAGE   BEVERAGE

DINNERS

VEGETABLE SOUP   BORSHT WITH BOILED POTATOES
STUFFED LAMB OR VEAL BREAST   BROILED OR ROAST CHICKEN
MATZO STUFFING   CRANBERRY AND ORANGE SALAD
CANDIED BEETS, *page 197*   POPOVERS, *page 43*
SPICED APPLESAUCE   SPONGECAKE SUPREME, *page 206*
BEVERAGE   BEVERAGE

INDEX

INDEX **315**